TRANSLATION AND THE ARTS IN MODERN FRANCE

TRANSLATION AND THE ARTS IN MODERN FRANCE

Edited by Sonya Stephens

INDIANA UNIVERSITY PRESS

This book is a publication of

INDIANA UNIVERSITY PRESS
Office of Scholarly Publishing
Herman B Wells Library 350
1320 East 10th Street
Bloomington, Indiana 47405 USA

iupress.indiana.edu

The paper used in this publication
meets the minimum requirements of
the American National Standard for
Information Sciences—Permanence
of Paper for Printed Library
Materials, ANSI Z39.48-1992.

Manufactured in the
United States of America

Cataloging information is available
from the Library of Congress.

ISBN 978-0-253-02563-0 (cloth)
ISBN 978-0-253-02614-9 (paperback)
ISBN 978-0-253-02654-5 (ebook)

1 2 3 4 5   22 21 20 19 18 17

FOR ROSEMARY LLOYD

CONTENTS

FOREWORD

IN ONE OF HER FIRST PUBLICATIONS, ROSEMARY LLOYD IN-
cluded as an epigraph a quotation from a letter written by Baudelaire.
The correspondence in question charges Julien Lemer with selling *Les
paradis artificiels* (Artificial Paradises) and some other works of criticism,
and is dated February 23, 1865. Her citation of Baudelaire in 1981 was a
reflexive gesture, evoking a shared critical motivation: "J'ai une assez
vive envie de montrer ce que j'ai su faire en matière de critique" (I have
a very keen desire to show you what I have done as a critic).[1] In 2007, the
year in which the same handwritten letter was sold for twice its estimated
price by Christie's, Rosemary retired from Indiana University, having
more than demonstrated her own worth to the critical enterprise, and in
a career spanning three continents, three decades, and more disciplines.[2]
Central to Rosemary's identity as a scholar has been her commitment
to translation and to the question of intermediality. She has translated
Baudelaire's letters and prose poems, as well as Mallarmé's correspondence and George Sand's *Master Pipers,* and continues her work in this
area. She has worked on still life, women writers, jealousy, and childhood, rooted in nineteenth-century France, but almost always with a
comparative and intermedial perspective.

The essays in this volume were written with a desire to honor Rosemary Lloyd's critical legacy and interests. Some of the scholars were
former students, all were colleagues, and all learned from their work and
interactions with Rosemary. This volume is dedicated to her, as was the
conference that crystallized these ideas, because collectively we had the

desire to show her what she had given, and what we could do "en matière de critique" to honor her.

Sonya Stephens

NOTES

1. Lloyd, *Baudelaire's Literary Criticism.*
2. Christie's, sale 5481, lot 77, November 20, 2007. The letter sold for €30,250 ($44,617). Baudelaire, *Correspondance,* 2:441–443.

ACKNOWLEDGMENTS

I WOULD LIKE TO EXPRESS MY GRATITUDE TO ALL OF THE contributors for their participation, patience, and cooperation during the preparation of this volume. I also extend my thanks to Fitzwilliam and Murray Edwards Colleges at the University of Cambridge, for enabling the original encounter among these scholars; to the College of Arts and Sciences, the Department of French and Italian, and many other colleagues at Indiana University, Bloomington for their consistent support; to Raina Polivka, Janice Frisch, and Darja Malcolm-Clarke at Indiana University Press for their advice and forbearance; to the museums, libraries, and other copyright holders for their assistance with the images; and to Mount Holyoke College for helping to bring this to fruition.

TRANSLATION AND THE
ARTS IN MODERN FRANCE

Introduction

SONYA STEPHENS

IN THE OPENING PAGES OF *IS THAT A FISH IN YOUR EAR: TRANS-lation and the Meaning of Everything,* David Bellos argues that the value of translation lies in the fact that it is "a process with no determinate results," and that "the variability of translations is incontrovertible evidence of the limitless flexibility of human minds."[1] What translation and transposition describe is both difference of expression in a (somewhat) shared endeavor, and the fact of each work as an object in its own right, a "new reality."[2] Translation is an effort of creative minds to convey meaning from one language in another. Most often, this posits a binary structure, and usually an opposition, resulting in the valorization of one over the other. In translation, the original is normally upheld as superior—the source text is valorized and its translation often cast as secondary, or an approximation. In the case of transposition, which describes the transfer of meaning or effect to another form, the representational differences are such that, while the creative reworking is less likely to be seen as secondary ("it is a deliberate *mis*reading that emphasizes difference rather than similarity"[3]), it may still be seen as oppositional. Indeed, intermedial creativity has long been shown to be paragonal, that is, a struggle for dominance between competing forms.[4]

Paul St.-Pierre has argued, however, that "the relations between the original text and its translation must always be defined in terms of a third element," or a "third term, at least in part extrinsic to the texts themselves." This third term, he contends, leads to an uncertainty that raises questions about authority.[5] "Ekphrasis" (the verbal representation of a visual representation), or the "transposition d'art," similarly provokes

questions of authority—in the sense of interart competition and the su-
premacy of one form over the other—while, at the same time, promoting
all high art as exceptional, as having universal value, hence the existence
of shared artistic circles—and perhaps the notion of great art.

This notion of authority (or artistic elitism) is, one law—the third of
five—in what Peter Dayan has called a "nexus" of principles underpin-
ning the "interart aesthetic." These principles are useful in describing
what we mean by transposition, as well as for explaining the nature of
artistic exchange in a particular moment that has defined cultural production since the 1830s. The first, as we have already seen, is that each
work of art is an object in its own right (a "new reality") whose value "is
not in what it says, but in what it is." The second law of the interart aesthetic is the incalculability of any equivalence between artistic expressions in different media (translation is never direct, and collaborations
are never unproblematic). The third principle, as stated above, asserts
the universal value of art (its "timeless and international validity") while
insisting, in the most authoritarian and often elitist terms, that this cannot be defined. The fourth law states, however, that, while the properties
of art are indefinable, it is the uniqueness of each new work that defines
its status as art, so that some common value intrinsic to each work connects it to a whole through this quality. Fifth and finally, Dayan posits
that the only way to convey the "incalculable relations" of the interart
aesthetic is "to describe work in one medium as if it were operating in
another"—something akin to Charles Baudelaire's assertion that "ainsi
le meilleur compte rendu d'un tableau pourra être un sonnet ou une élé-
gie" [the best rendering of a painting may be a sonnet or an elegy.][6] It is
this phenomenon, Dayan argues, that is "the interart analogy."[7]

These are loose principles, to be sure, but they have the virtue of
offering some shape to an aesthetic and defining in quite performative
ways the essential features of works that explore and expose their own
procedures more than they (re)work similar subjects. Stephen Bann has
underscored this problem, asking whether ekphrasis could not draw attention to "the modern conviction (deeply rooted at least since the time
of Baudelaire) that a good proportion of what is experienced in looking
at a work of art simply cannot be expressed in verbal terms?"[8] It is this
"incompleteness," whether experienced as a lack or a plenitude, or irre-

solvable differences in the correspondence, which invites creative reinvention, re-presentation, and similarly provokes critical exploration of both translation and transposition and process and cultural production.[9]

Much has been written about the relationship (or correspondence) among the arts, and the particular importance of time and place—Paris in the nineteenth century—for the development of patterns of production that constitute an aesthetic practice. Drawing on this work, and on the general acceptance that there are no agreed terms of reference for this phenomenon, nor a stable critical platform,[10] this set of principles common to all arts reasserts the importance of nineteenth-century Paris as the place and moment in which this interart aesthetic came to be, positing both that it developed in the French capital from the1830s onward,[11] and that "Paris retains a unique place in its history because of the way in which it was felt to be the home of universal values. For the interart aesthetic is international as well as intermedial. It refuses absolutely to consider the quality of art as bounded by national borders."[12]

Indeed, this is not only the case for intermediality. Translation studies, a field that has also undergone enormous change over the last twenty-five years, has questioned how patterns in translation "indicate a tendency towards denationalizing literary production in the world market of translation" at the same time that such translations internationalize literary relations (of a particular geopolitical order) and can offer an opportunity for partisanism or even activism. In his most recent work, Lawrence Venuti talks about his own trajectory as a theorist and practitioner, discussing the ways in which he "began to develop a more rigorously conceived hermeneutic model that views translation as an interpretive act, as the inscription of one interpretive possibility among others."[13] Venuti notes, "The different model I began to imagine opens up the interpretive possibilities of translation, allowing them to vary with the nature of the interpretants applied by the translator but enabling the interpretations to be described and evaluated with clarity and precision in the conditions—linguistic and cultural, social and political—under which the translation is produced and circulated." This initiates "new ways of thinking inspired by an interpretation of the source text."[14]

Rethinking translation in this way, and bringing to the fore theoretical frameworks from both sociology and literature, enables us to understand more clearly the relationship between interlingual renderings and those that are intermedial; the connections between translation and transposition. The most important of these, the one that links translation to transposition most powerfully, is surely that equivalence (or even similarity) in form and meaning (or indeed in reception) is elusive, so that irreducible differences are not resolved but rather exacerbated, problematizing the process and creating generative new artifacts whose difference from one another is as significant as their correspondences.

This volume of essays sets out to explore these processes, differences, and interconnections, and further elaborates the many ways in which modern France has provided fertile creative and intellectual ground for the exploration of translations of different kinds, exposing in each of the four sections, and in each chapter, the ways in which cultural production in France and beyond has participated in translation and/or in this intermedial aesthetic. The volume brings together international scholars in a project of shared inquiry relating to both translation and transposition—terms that include but are not limited to the interlingual, the intercultural, the intermedial, the intertextual, and, necessarily, the interdisciplinary. It situates its concerns within the domain of translation studies, as well as the fields of ekphrasis and visual culture, literary criticism and history, postcolonialism and exile, autobiography, cultural studies, film studies, musicology, and art history. And it ranges freely across these, because the cultural production at the heart of each piece strains consciously at the boundaries of disciplinarity and convention, precisely with the purpose of demonstrating not only the limitless flexibility but also the limitless creativity and invention of the human mind, as it engages with forms of representation in their reception as well as their production.

The nineteenth-century Parisian cultural moment of the interarts aesthetic is also a contemporary critical moment, an expression of the different approaches and objects that we can bring to the same conversation. About fifteen years ago, Stephen Greenblatt commented on this very phenomenon. He saw an innovative conversation going on behind the traditional disciplines, forming a new alignment from "an extravagant range of concerns, a heterogeneous collection of cultural objects being scrutinized, a jumble of films, poems, paintings, novels, operas, performance pieces, and plays from different times, places and countries, [and] a cacophony of methods." In 1997, he wrote, "It is too early to give this alignment a formal name, let alone a formal structure. The term 'Interart' has a deliberate air of the temporary, the hybrid, the betwixt-and-between that is exactly right for this fluid moment."[15] In the time since then, work done across those boundaries, and in the fields of translation, visual culture, and cultural studies, have, much like the universal value of art in nineteenth-century Paris, solidified these precepts, enabled us to identify some principles, and established translation and the interart aesthetic as fundamental to an understanding of cultural production since 1830 in ways that do not make the heterogeneous concerns of these essays seem like a jumble at all.

So, while there have been studies focused on transposition and ekphrasis, and on translation, this volume presents a wide-ranging set of examples involving intersections of the disciplines and critical approaches listed above, focusing on cultural production from 1830 to the present and privileging French culture, but in its interactions with other cultures, countries, and continents, often explicitly equating intercultural permeability with representational (ex)change. These essays resonate with each other across periods and forms, across boundaries and borders of every kind, including the sections of this volume. Questions of colonization, slavery, subjugation, memory, migration, and exile connect Hispaniola to Brittany, and political philosophy to the sentimental novel and film. Autobiographical writings are explored from critical practice to creative endeavor, in the effort of translating life and letters. And other questions of performance are pursued with respect to musical renditions of the *Song of Hiawatha*, art criticism, Auguste Rodin's sculptural stagings and re-appropriations, Colette's stage show at the Moulin Rouge, the vocality of poetic expression, and high-speed video still-life.

In the first section, the chapters are focused on cross-cultural translations, exploring the ways in which different forms of expression, and the act of translating otherness, apply as much to cultural difference as to that of each medium. In the opening essay, which also marks, chronologically speaking, the beginning of the period under consideration, Marshall C. Olds considers the changes to the French novel in the 1820s, as a result of both the abolitionist movement and the literary production of women. Focusing on Gabrielle de Paban's novel *Eulalie* (1825), published as a response to Madame de Duras's *Ourika* (1823), Olds describes the ways in which the second novel represents a kind of reverse image of the first, and imaginatively translates the different subgenres of the sentimental novel. Specifically, this essay examines the way in which the sentimental novel, in the form of *Ourika*, broke new ground by "directly engaging contemporary material that placed individual lives within a specific social and historical context," as well as developing into an "effective vehicle for ideas." Situating his analyses within the context of French writings on European expansion, colonial activity, and the slave trade, Olds demonstrates how the narrative and critical apparatus of *Eulalie* serves a purpose well beyond the putative truth of the account, and effectively enables Gabrielle de Paban to translate one culture for the benefit of another, in a form and language accessible to a contemporary public. Arguing that the conventional narrative structure of the sentimental novel—based on hope, impossibility of union, and despair—enables reinvention, Olds demonstrates that the transposition of this hitherto "noncommittal genre" created a new form, one that was politically motivated as well as well-adapted to promote racial understanding and harmony.

In a similar analysis of growing cultural awareness and its translation, Heather Williams looks at representations of Bretonness, beginning in the 1830s. Widely viewed as a turning point in the positive representation of Breton culture, the 1830s and its legacy are better understood, she argues, as "an exercise in translation." Unpacking this idea, Williams proposes that a range of fields are now looking at translation in order better to understand the ways in which culture is constructed and society is manipulated. As she demonstrates, this is especially true in borderland or postcolonial cultural contexts, and in bi- or multilingual situations, where translation is both "an essential and unstoppable part of any creative thought" and a significant part of intercultural transfer, as well as a driver of cultural change. Contextualizing her analysis of Brittany with reference to other Celtic countries and cultures, Williams explores the besetting problems of those writing in French and Breton in the nineteenth century, and demonstrates the importance of translation in establishing Brittany's history and place in France, as well as "making of the Breton language a repository of cultural truths." Translation and the critical field that has developed from it, she argues, have enabled us to approach critically the literary production of Brittany as a category. By apprehending Bretonness and Frenchness through the lens both of nineteenth-century translations and of translation studies, Williams raises important questions about Breton culture and the history of translation in France, as well as about authenticity in a postcolonial context.

L. Cassandra Hamrick explores a similar problem of translation across linguistic and cultural boundaries, here further complicated by the interart aesthetic, to offer an exceptional example—the story of Henry Wadsworth Longfellow's *Song of Hiawatha* (1855), Robert Stoepel's musical transpositions of it (1859–1863), and the request he made of Baudelaire to translate it for a French version of his *Romantic Symphony*. While it is well known that Baudelaire translated the works of Edgar Allan Poe, his interest in the (at that time) better-known American writer Longfellow has received less attention, though some critics have examined Baudelaire's self-avowed "plagiarism" and considered the influence of *Voices of the Night* (1839) on the poet of *Les Fleurs du Mal*. In her detailed account of Baudelaire's *Hiawatha: Légende indienne*, Hamrick raises questions about whether the constraints of time, form, and money were responsible for the failure of the enterprise, and demonstrates that the poet's task was not to translate Longfellow's work as such but to develop from it, according to Stoepel's requirements and Mathilda Heron's instructions, "a composite narrative organized into fourteen scenes that follow a sometimes complex scheme of intertwining passages." As Hamrick's comparative analysis of documents shows, Baudelaire sometimes ignored instructions, adding to the poem's text to communicate mood or other effect. In so doing, she shows, he created not a standalone, or in any sense direct, translation of the *Song of Hiawatha;* rather, he participates in what can only be described as "a piece of a multidimensional work whose different, but interconnected, parts are designed to be experienced as a living whole at the moment of performance."

Questions of colonial and postcolonial heritage in the nineteenth century, and complex issues about projection and exchange between two cultures, lead us to a more contemporary perspective in Emma Wilson's piece about migration in recent French cinema. Wilson's chapter focuses on Julie Bertuccelli's 2003 movie *Depuis qu'Otar est parti,* and more particularly on the notion of nostalgia—the tension between home and longing—and the ways in which the missing or missed home is represented. Wilson discusses the material organization of homes and houses through a series of still lifes and installations on different film sets—from Tbilisi to Paris. Wilson exposes the way in which Bertuccelli chooses to actualize France, and Paris, in a culturally rich, souvenir-filled home in Georgia, as a dreamed-for homeland, while the reality of immigrant existence in the 18th Arrondissement represents the dereliction not only of Otar's existence there but of his mother's state in her increasing apprehension of his absence. Wilson also shows how the screenplay and movie diverge, so that in the movie, the disavowal of Otar's death enables the three women to reassert their dreams in a touristic vision of Paris represented by Bertuccelli's collage of the city's sights. These images of places, and their material referents, are, Wilson argues, structured in ways that recall each other "through internal rhymes of the images and returning tactics of framing," so that neither place seems preferred in this thoughtful representation of "longing for an elsewhere."

Michael Tilby's essay, which begins the next section focused on cross-textual transpositions, also considers representations of Paris, exploring the way in which Honoré de Balzac self-consciously translated the capital in his novels of the mid-1830s. While contextualizing this in historical and literary terms, Tilby argues, much as Emma Wilson does, that the fictionalization of the city goes beyond the way it is represented as "an imaginary or textual entity" to offer a reinvention of the adventure story in a modern city, and a self-conscious reflection on fictionalization and the role of the reader. Like the fiction itself, then, Paris is "an oscillation between what is seen and what cannot be seen," "a verifiable topography [and] an artificial construct." Through his analysis of novels such as *Le père Goriot, Ferragus, Histoire des treize, La fille aux yeux d'or,* and *Gambara,* Tilby also unpacks the notion of the "armchair traveler" as simultaneously an opportunity for fantasy, for the gendering of the reader, and for the complex work of that (often inadequate) reading.

It is in this section that in many ways we see just how the interart aesthetic took hold in nineteenth-century Paris, demonstrating the contact, affinities, and exchanges among writers and artists, the systems of interpretation proposed by them, the institutions within and against which they had to operate, and the forms of expression that emerged from this intermediality. The growth of the *salon* as a form of criticism in the eighteenth century, and especially Denis Diderot's engagement with it, provided a form and context for increasing innovation in the nineteenth century.[16] So, despite a reigning theory in the nineteenth century that devalued landscape, despite the disintegration of landscape painting into genre painting, and despite the art administration's robust measures to curb naturalism, landscape became a major focus of change in nineteenth-century art. Tracing the friendship between Eugène Fromentin and Gustave Moreau, Barbara Wright develops an account of the artistic relations that are most evident in their shared interest in landscape painting and writing, explaining the significance of the painters' common understanding of aesthetics, their shared neoclassicism, and their increasing concern with "the domination of color and paint over any concern with direct representation." At the same time that she highlights Moreau's influence, she also explores the ways in which Fromentin's Orientalism was essentially incompatible with that neoclassicism, and provides a new understanding of the ways in which his literary descriptions are often better able to exemplify his aesthetics than his history painting. Indeed, as Wright so engagingly demonstrates, the combination of word and image, so central to the achievement of both Moreau and Fromentin, is most prevalent in landscape painting. It is, she argues, in their approach to transposition, that is, in the "ongoing potential for recreation in either medium—by the reader/spectator or by the artist himself," that we see most clearly a shared aesthetic and approach.

In a similar vein, Wendelin Guentner examines the journalistic writings of the female art critic Marie-Emilie Chartroule de Montifaud, writing in *L'Artiste* under the pseudonym Marc de Montifaud, between 1865 and 1877. Montifaud, she argues, "conceptualized both the production and reception of artworks as translation," and transposed in her own work both the paintings under scrutiny and her own aesthetic impressions. For Montifaud, this conception of art and art criticism as translation is most apparent in the implied dialogical nature of communication.

What is more, Montifaud demonstrates that she fully understood the influence of art criticism on the artist and the reading/viewing public, and her transpositional efforts were directed at this very question of reception. Guentner shows us just how she did this, contextualizing Montifaud's stylistic techniques in the broader debates about the pen and the paintbrush, and through recourse to synaesthesia and particularly to aural metaphor, thereby also linking the visual to music in ways that echo Hamrick's arguments and demonstrate that the interart aesthetic enables us to talk about such works as if they were operating in the same way. Guentner argues, too, that landscape painting is where Montifaud was most expressive, because the interest of landscape "resid[es] in its potential to communicate a subjective state." Here, then, we see the full impact of Montifaud's translation of the work, producing for the reader through an autonomous creative work, "an aesthetic experience analogous to the one [Montifaud] herself had received when she initially viewed the painting."

Robert Lethbridge's essay takes up the challenge of briefly reviewing thirty years of critical understanding of transpositional practice in the nineteenth century (and beyond), before turning his attention to the way in which Émile Zola's work exemplifies and extends such practice, informing us about the writer's position in relation to various artists of his time, as well as about the "pictorial fabric of his own writing." Pivoting on the much discussed example of Édouard Manet's *Nana* (1876–1877), and passages from Zola's serialized novel of the same title (1878–1879), Lethbridge argues that Zola's own art criticism is instructive in terms of the way that it represents a "translation of a pictorial *reality* filtered through the originality of his own individual talent and marked by . . . 'improvisations.'" Lethbridge extends this argument to other fictional and artistic examples, arguing that we must understand Zola's practice in the context of his concerns with "the discursive capacities of painting," uncovering the ways in which correspondences are marked, rather, by "calculated difference at odds with the generality of reference"—difference that reframes the point of departure.

Similarly focused on ekphrasis and the *transposition d'art,* my own chapter examines Rodin's sculpture and its relationship with poetic texts that explore female beauty and eroticism, arguing that Rodin's visual poetics is dependent on intermediality, and that the literary texts to which he often turns are themselves texts that depend on images. On more than one occasion, Rodin reached for a poetic analogy, but such texts are usually marked by their references to sculpture. Furthermore, through a comparative consideration of Rodin's sculptures, illustrations, photographs, drawings, collages, and "assemblages," as well as through his conversations with contemporaries, I reveal the improvisation—or re-appropriation and reinvention—at work in Rodin's various artistic enterprises. Rodin is seen to use his own works as a repertory from which he can create new compositions, sometimes photographed, sometimes reconstituted as works of sculpture or on paper. These imaginative unions, and his creation of new conjunctions or performances within his own work, demonstrate the extent of his transpositional impulse and promote a more general understanding of the ways in which the *making* of these transpositional compositions is as significant as the new reality that emerges from them.

The staging or performance of such improvisations, which foreground the conditions of production and implicate the reader-spectator, find an erotic parallel in the nineteenth-century fascination with Egyptian mummies, the unveiling of their secrets, and, at the fin de siècle and in the early twentieth century, in the exotic, veiled figures of female sexuality. Taking this parallel as her starting point, Juliana Starr compares the performances of three women in adaptations of Théophile Gautier's work, in order to demonstrate the ways in which these were used to "resist regulatory norms of feminine behavior" and "subversively lay bare sexual differences." The first of these performances, *Rêve d'Égypte,* was performed at the Moulin Rouge in 1907. Based on the prologue of Gautier's *Roman de la momie* (1857), the sketch featured Colette as a mummy brought back to life by an Egyptologist, played by her female lover, Missy de Belbeuf, and would become known simply as "The Scandal of the Moulin Rouge." The second, this time based on Gautier's short story *Une nuit de Cleopâtre* (1838), was a ballet performed in 1909 at the Théâtre du Châtelet featuring Ida Rubinstein in the title role. Starr's consideration and comparison of the two emphasize the innovation of these performances, and draw attention to the ways in which these staged transpositions of Gautier's works, featuring provocative, sexualized women from the worlds of both high and low art, underscore the author's representation of "creative, powerful women" with "revolutionary notions of gender identity."

Such self-representation, or self-translation, is a significant new direction for interart relations, and yet it informs almost every essay in this volume, in some way or other. As the field of life-writing has developed, there has been increased attention to the question of the self as a construct, the challenge of self-scrutiny, the relation to the reader or spectator, the role of memory and its relationship to objects, and the influence of other texts, images, and people.[17] This is a problem that sits squarely within that of translation and that of the interart aesthetic. Not surprisingly, then, a significant feature of translation and transposition would seem to be the questioning of the artistic self in relation to an artistic other, sometimes as embodied by the work but often, especially in the case of interart relations, in lived collaboration and increasingly in terms of a representation of "the mind observing the flickering formations of its inner vision."[18]

So it is that taking up the matter of Colette's identity in a very different way from Juliana Starr, and self-consciously critiquing her own strategies, Janet Beizer lays bare the risks and challenges of reading Colette's three mother-centered novels as in any way related to the author's own life story. Beizer does this to demonstrate the difficulty—a difficulty already exposed in Starr's essay—of keeping Colette's life and art separate and to "call attention to the questions of legitimacy and authenticity posed by letting auto/biography intrude . . . into fiction's text." In her reading of *La Naissance du jour*, Beizer elaborates on the broad problem of critical distance, as well as that of a "*constructed* autobiography" in which, she argues, "Colette is combating not only cultural assumptions about women and writing but also a philosophical tradition that equates sex with truth." Through a series of examples and critical moves that mirror each other at every turn, Beizer deftly demonstrates the relationship between literature's responsibility to life and criticism's responsibility to literature, concluding that "life and art are two corresponding media for

Colette," and that "she transposes freely in both directions, challenging the reader to decipher and recode and make sense."

Much of what these essays discuss points toward artistic process and practice as revealing of the translational or interart aesthetic and its implied subjectivities, suggesting that it is often in looking to the performance (or production) of art that we can better understand those incalculable relations. In the final section of this volume, the chapters explore questions of praxis—the *testing* of translation, in both senses of the word. Mary Ann Caws brings together the challenges of autobiography and translation, from a critical perspective different from that of Beizer but related in a number of ways. In Caws's essay, she recounts the experience of translating the poetry of René Char, of being in contact with Char throughout that process, and of the conflation of him, a mountain of a man and poet, with the Mont Ventoux. In sharing both successful and less felicitous translations, so connected with a cherished being, Caws relates the problems of both spiritual and linguistic translation, even as she explores the transpositions of voice, auto/biography, and fidelity. In her final example, related to the translation of sexual climax, Mary Ann Caws asserts that "we have to read that 'plaisir' and that poem in full voice . . . in the full voice that fidelity can be." In this exhortation, she connects critical authenticity with fidelity in translation, as well as in life, and posits the problem of poetry as voice, which Clive Scott pursues in the essay that follows.

His piece begins, then, with two critical propositions relating to translation. The first is that literary translation should not be governed by the notion that it is intended for readers ignorant of the source language. The second is that it should not be based on the objective of a single-version translation, which implies a single correct interpretation. Rather, he argues, the role of translation should be "to diversify the text's perceptibility." He goes on, indeed, to diversify his own arguments, resisting the implied knowns of translation and promoting an approach, and a system, driven by the unknown, the futuristic, and the experimental. He conceives of this as a tabular, rather than linear, process, and attempts to explore how voice might be dramatized performatively and then textually. Scott's argument for tabularization is that "the linear page is the page we pass through," whereas the "tabular page is the page we spend time in." Tabularization introduces a new temporality into the experience of reading and allows, Scott contends, for new images, new energies, and new acoustic events. In an example, his own translation of Apollinaire's "La porte," he demonstrates this tabular approach, introducing hand-written elements to lend voice ("supposing that handwriting guarantees a unique vocality in the writing"); different fonts, which are suggestive of sculptural or architectural styles; and marginal notations that retain, on the left-hand side, versificatory information, and, on the right, a dramatization of the differences, the "noncoincidence" of source text and target text. Through this, and in ways that echo the self-reflexivity inherent in each of these essays, he emphasizes the speculative possibilities of translation as a literary act, and makes that act "a value, not by virtue of its ability to communicate a text in another language but by virtue of its capacity to foster an autobiography of reading and . . . an ongoing meditation about writing the activity of another text."

As each of these essays demonstrates, artistic production, whatever form it takes, often defines itself in relation to an "other." This engagement might be oppositional or inclusive, it might be interlingual or intermedial, it is both inclusive of the past and forward-looking, and it is always inventive. In the concluding chapter of this volume, Catherine Bernard explores the ways in which modern art has insisted on breaking with past conventions and, in so doing, "turned all appropriations or transpositions of past references into a purposeful gesture." Indeed, Bernard argues that transposition has "acquired greater critical acumen in contemporary art," and that the renewal implied by reenactment emphasizes our relationship with aesthetic experience. Exploring modern re-appropriations of works from Vermeer to Manet, Bernard exposes the degree to which the contemporary can locate and dislocate in meaningful ways. This, she shows, is even possible in that genre that would not seem to lend itself to such antagonistic praxis—still-life. And yet, as Bernard demonstrates, "still-life, with its preordained form and range of subjects, its allegorical depth and pragmatic agenda, is there to be reworked, translated, and reinvented." With reference to Sam Taylor-Johnson's sped-up video *Still Life* (2001), which shows fruit rotting in a bowl, Bernard underscores the ways in which the longevity of genre meets fragile transience, stasis is challenged by movement, and transposed aesthetic experience invites renewed contemplation.

Through these original and thought-provoking essays, the authors demonstrate the extent to which translation and transposition describe intellectual and creative processes that foster continuous engagement with a cultural, linguistic, or aesthetic other, inventing and performing narratives of continuity and disruption, and inviting speculative activity that does indeed diversify perceptibility. In so doing, the authors expose the extent to which moving between media and codes—the very process of translation and transposition—is a defining aspect of creativity and interpretation, across time, space, and disciplines.

SONYA STEPHENS is professor of French and acting president at Mount Holyoke College, having taught previously at Indiana University, Bloomington, and Royal Holloway, University of London. She has published widely on nineteenth-century French poetry and its relation to visual culture, and is currently working on questions of process and iconicity in modern France, as well as on a study of illustrated editions of *Les Fleurs du Mal*. She is author of *Baudelaire's Prose Poetry: The Practice and Politics of Irony* and editor of *A History of Women's Writing in France, Ebauches/ Esquisses: Projects and Pre-Texts in Nineteenth-Century France,* and coeditor of *Birth and Death in Nineteenth-Century French Culture.*

NOTES

1. Bellos, *Is That a Fish in Your Ear,* 9.
2. This is Peter Dayan's "first law of the interart aesthetic," an aesthetic to which we shall return in due course. He is quoting Igor Stravinsky: "A new piece of music *is* a new reality." See Dayan, *Art as Music,* 2.
3. Peter Collier and Robert Lethbridge, introduction, in Collier and Lethbridge, eds., *Artistic Relations,* 12.
4. See Mitchell, *Iconology.* See also Heffernan, *Museum of Words,* 1.
5. St.-Pierre, "Translation and Writing," 224.
6. Charles Baudelaire, "Salon de 1846," in Baudelaire, *Œuvres complètes,* 2:418.
7. Dayan, *Art as Music,* 2–3.

8. Bann, *The True Vine,* 29.

9. Alastair Fowler asserts that "the notion of a universally valid systematic corre-spondence between the arts must be regarded as a chimera." See Fowler, "Periodization and Interart Analogies," 99.

10. These are the problems to which Peter Collier and Robert Lethbridge point in *Artistic Relations,* 5.

11. This is the subject of Dayan's book *Music Writing Literature.* Others have made this case, too, including Henry F. Majewski in *Transposing Art into Texts,* and Peter Collier, Robert Lethbridge, and others in *Artistic Relations.*

12. Dayan, *Art as Music,* 5.

13. Gisèle Sapiro, "French Literature in the World System of Translation," trans. J. Gladding, in Macdonald and Suleiman, eds., *French Global,* 316.

14. Lawrence Venuti talks about his own trajectory, and identifies these shifts toward "recovering history, textuality, and agency," in his introduction to *Translation Changes Everything,* 4, 5–6.

15. Greenblatt, "The Interart Moment," 15.

16. See Valazza, *Crise de plume et souveraineté du pinceau,* especially "Diderot et l'émergence de la critique," 23–64.

17. See Sheringham, *French Autobiography,* and *Everyday Life.*

18. Collier and Lethbridge, introduction, in Collier and Lethbridge, eds., *Artistic Re-lations,* 12.

PART ONE
CROSS-CULTURAL TRANSLATION

ONE

Transposing Genre, Translating Culture

MARSHALL C. OLDS

CHANGES BROUGHT TO A LITERARY GENRE—IN THIS IN-
stance, the sentimental novel circa 1820—may result from any number
of factors, including the need to accommodate and make accessible a
new subject matter (slavery and racial equality). As I hope to show, this
change was effected by the transposition, or overlay, onto the frame of
the sentimental novel that of the historical novel, a sister-form in France
that allowed for substantial documentation of the novel's veracity. The
resulting form could effectively translate for the French reader of 1825
much that was foreign and new using the different cultural discourses
of scientific observation and sentimental persuasion.

The focus of this opening chapter, then, is on literary history,
prompted by the fact that the long overlooked narrative literature of the
Restoration (1815–1830) is beginning to receive new attention. This is occurring primarily from the perspectives of feminist inquiry, since much
of the production of the period was by women novelists, and of race and
the ongoing abolitionist movement in France during the first half of the
nineteenth century. Also requiring more study, it seems to me, are the
effects that this radically new subject matter was having on traditional
literary forms and, more especially, the changes that were occurring to
the novel in the 1820s. For the purposes of illustrating this new literary
history, I focus on only one genre, the sentimental novel, and present
only one example of that genre, hoping that I can show, with a kind of
Mallarméan logic, *que le reste peut exister* [that the rest can exist].

That example is the 1825 novel by Gabrielle de Paban, *Le nègre et
la créole; ou, Mémoires d'Eulalie D**** [*The Negro and the Creole; or, The*

Memoirs of Eulalie D], referred to hereafter simply as *Eulalie*.[1] Little is
known of the putative author—Gabrielle Paban, not the aristocratic de
Paban—beyond the fact that she was the sister-in-law of Jacques Collin
(who often signed as Jacques Collin de Plancy), one of the most prolific
littérateurs [writers in all genres] of the Restoration. He published scores
of books under his own (slightly embellished) name and used more than
a dozen pen names, some of them feminine. Collin de Plancy seems to
have maintained a veritable *atelier* of writers, which included his wife,
churning out books on all manner of subjects, and so it is entirely possible that he had a hand in the composition of this six-hundred-page
opus, which was Gabrielle's one and only novel, or at least the only novel
to have appeared under her name.

Eulalie is of interest to us today, as it certainly was in 1825, because
it was published in response to Madame de Duras's widely discussed
novella *Ourika*, which appeared in print two years earlier:

> C'est la publication de la touchante histoire d'Ourika qui me décide à mettre au
> jour les aventures d'Eulalie D***: le sort de cette jeune créole semble fait pour
> contraster avec celui de l'intéressante négresse; et pourtant leurs malheurs ont
> entre eux un point de ressemblance bien frappant, puisqu'ils sont dus à la même
> cause, c'est-à-dire à leur déplacement dans l'ordre social.
>
> [It is the publication of Ourika's touching story that compels me to make public
> the tale of Eulalie D***. The fate of this young Creole seems to contrast perfectly
> with that of the interesting Negress, and yet their misfortunes have a striking
> similarity because, due to the same cause, each lost her place in the social
> order.][2]

The second novel is, in many respects, the reverse image of the first. The
créole of the title, Eulalie, is the five-year-old child of a plantation and
slave owner on Saint-Domingue at the moment of the slave uprising
of August 22, 1791. Separated from her family during the violence, she
is hidden and saved by her slave nanny, Maky. A captured ship allows
those of the newly liberated population who wish to return to the Guinea
Coast to do so. Having been separated from her husband while pregnant
nine years previously, Maky decides to return to the Kingdom of Benin
with her young son, Zambo, and her now adoptive "daughter," Eulalie.
Renamed Lily by her new community, Eulalie will grow up in the city of
Benin as a member of Maky's family. In a variant of Ourika's conflicted
feelings for her childhood companion, Eulalie will come to have a similar

relation with her adoptive brother. Although among the Béni there is no taboo with respect to racial miscegenation, she cannot bring herself to think of Zambo as anything other than her brother, and because she cannot bear the thought of being separated from him and from Maky, she resolves in her heart that she will never marry.

Eulalie catches the eye of the young king, who determines to marry her, and so she, Zambo, and Maky flee Benin in an attempt to make their way to Sierra Leone, of which Zambo has some vague knowledge from his hunting and warring expeditions. Far beyond Benin and dangerously near the coast, they are captured by black profiteers and sold to English slavers. After adventures too numerous to relate but that include a failed revolt onboard, led by Zambo, the ship reaches San Juan, where Eulalie and Maky are put in the care of a priest and Zambo is sold to a plantation owner from Martinique. It is 1805. With the tireless help of the priest, Eulalie makes her way to Paris where she will be rejected as an adventuress by all surviving members of her family except her youngest brother, who, having left the imperial army—it is now 1813—recognizes her as his sister. Eulalie's health is poor and in 1815, the two go to live with an aging uncle on Martinique, recently recaptured from the English, where, meanwhile, Zambo has been busy. Having escaped from his master, he leads a community of runaways in the mountain region of the island. He is captured by the authorities and sentenced to hang. Eulalie recognizes the identity of the rebel leader and, with grief added to her weakened condition, will herself expire directly after Zambo's death. After the novel's close, in 1815, there follow some twenty-five pages of notes containing historical, philosophical, and literary material.

Eulalie's memoir is clearly in the tradition of sentimental literature. It presents an impossible obstacle to personal happiness and fulfillment. The main character is a young woman, which was true for many of these novels, though appreciably less frequently than is sometimes claimed. Her health will be eroded by moral conflict—again mostly true—and she will die an early death, which is just about always the case in this genre. The novel's form shares traits of the two principal subgenres, bringing them together in a fruitful way.

By about 1815, the two forms of the sentimental novel were the historical and what might be best called the ahistorical novels. The historical variety presents conflicts between virtue and interest where the exemplary lives of famous historical figures could be dramatized. The genre's main practitioner was Madame de Genlis, who, in novels such as *Les chevaliers du cygne* (1795), about Charlemagne, and *Pétrarque et Laure* (1825), admittedly and unabashedly wrote to illustrate moral principles. In her critical writings, she forcefully defended the historical accuracy of her accounts. They were researched, and her novels concluded with many pages of notes documenting her sources and discussing their value. The notes were central to her conception of the historical novel and separated such works from legendary tales. Following Stendhal and Balzac, the post-1830 novel would find other means of documentation, but for the historical novel of Madame de Genlis, the notes were an integral part of the work's meaning and also of its form.

The second mode of the sentimental novel is the "ahistorical" variety where no dates are given, and no major social events are referenced. Deborah Jenson has helped us to recognize these works as marked by the collective trauma of the Revolution and regicide, but quietly and indirectly, where the characters are orphaned or otherwise cut off from their past.[3] *René* (1802), *Corinne* (1807), and *Adolphe* (1816) are prime examples of this genre as it came to the Restoration. Where *Ourika* and *Eulalie* differ from their immediate predecessors is in their treatment of historical and contemporary subject matter. Those earlier works are so intently focused on the drama of the characters that little else that may be going on in the world is brought into play. If they are historically marked, it is only indirectly through what might be characterized as a modern consciousness or sensibility. What in 1823 made the publication of *Ourika* such a broad topic for praise, deprecation, and imitation was not only its author's prominence and her presentation of a main character who was black, but the fact that *Ourika*'s private story coincided exactly and explicitly both in time and place with the public story of the French Revolution and, in that coincidence, engaged a very new understanding of the Revolution, especially with respect to narrative. The sentimental novel was, then, breaking new ground: it was directly engaging contemporary material that placed individual lives within a specific social and historicized context. *Ourika* was not alone: as Doris Kadish has shown, there had been, since the turn of the century, other works of narrative fiction—some of them sentimental—and of the theater that were tied to the abolitionist movement, an ongoing part of the unfinished agenda of the Revolution.[4] Sentimental literature brought the heroine in touch with *anti-esclavagisme* [abolitionism] and so encouraged the tie between these two oppressed groups: black slaves and women. The practice was broader, however. Other populations provided subject matter during this period, notably Jews, suggesting a literary program that was larger than abolitionism and feminism. If in the 1820s the Revolution was largely viewed as a failed social experiment, the disappointment registered by some suggested that important Enlightenment ideals persisted.

Along with the historicizing of the sentimental novel, the second important development of the 1820s was that such books became, in their own way, an effective vehicle for ideas. I do not wish to exaggerate this claim; it would take some time—perhaps until the early work of Émile Zola in the 1860s—for the discourse of sentimental persuasion to be replaced fully by a discourse of ideologies. In its new militancy, however, the sentimental novel was becoming informed by social philosophies and other branches of science.

The thinkers whose writings lie behind the narrative and the argument deployed in the notes to *Eulalie* are the two militant abbots, Guillaume-Thomas Raynal and Henri Grégoire. As is well known, both had an immense influence on abolitionist thought, in France and abroad. Raynal's opus magnum was the eight-volume *Histoire philosophique et politique des établissements et du commerce des Européens dans les deux Indes* [The Philosophical and Political History of European Trade in the Two Indias], published in 1770. The work was an encyclopedic and scientific view of European expansion and colonial activity. Widely read until the time of the Revolution, though far less so in France after the Terror, the section that held the interest of abolitionist sympathizers were the chapters documenting the Guinean slave trade. These pages were frequently excerpted as a standalone volume and were doubtless the book evoked in the short history of the liberation of Saint-Domingue given in Paban's notes: "Toussaint-Louverture marchait à la tête des insurgés, ... tenant à la main le livre de Raynal" [Toussaint led the insurgent army, ... holding Raynal's book in his hand].[5]

Raynal strives to give as complete a portrait as was possible at the time from original sources of the geography, flora, and fauna of the coastal regions of Guinea. An exact understanding of climate and local physical conditions, for example, was seen as necessary to a scientific accounting for differences of temperament. Raynal also discusses the different theories explaining skin color: theological, anatomical, chemical, and climatological, which he espouses, based on the preponderance of observed evidence. He is equally balanced on all topics, from Guinean topography to the economics of slavery ("Méthodes pratiquées dans l'acquisition, dans le traitement et dans la vente des esclaves" [Methods practiced in the acquisition, treatment and sale of slaves]). The discussions are detailed and descriptive. All of this is to make as sharp a distinction as possible between fact and opinion, the clearest example of which is the chapter entitled, "Origine et progrès de l'esclavage. Arguments imaginés pour le justifier. Réponses à ces arguments" [The origin and development of slavery. The various arguments justifying slavery. Responses to these arguments].[6] The first half of this crucial chapter is an economic and social history of Western civilization from earliest antiquity to the present, as studied from the point of view of forced servitude. Raynal follows the different ameliorations and relapses in the conditions of slaves according to cultures and events, outlining a very modern sense, for the times, of historical dynamism.[7]

This historicist view situates the present and discusses, and refutes, the justifications put forward for the then-current practice of slavery. Not surprisingly, these justifications reflect the mentality of nascent colonialism, appealing to the right of the strongest and to the view that Africans were born for slavery, that slavery was the surest way to convert a heathen population to Christianity, and that slavery was necessary to economic development.[8]

There are numerous references in *Eulalie* to the ideas and precepts enunciated by Raynal. The kingdom of Benin into which Eulalie arrives is neither a place without characteristics nor a European fantasy. On the contrary, it is as replete as contemporary knowledge allowed, down to its vegetation and wild animals, its architecture, cultivation and what people ate, domestication of horses and cattle, marriage customs, how warfare was conducted, and how war was propagated by the slave trade. And, unlike her adoptive family, Lily is constantly having to protect herself from the sun, not out of some sense of the delicacy of European women of a certain class but simply because she's white. Continued pressure from the American slave trade for sellable captives results in frequent wars. Using Raynal's historicist's lens, Gabrielle de Paban presents the kingdom of Benin as a feudal society having recognizable parallels with medieval France. The survival of a small but perseverant Christian church, which had been introduced by the Portuguese a century earlier to compete with fetish worship, offers a further suggestion of possibility for social change.

The second prominent cleric-philosopher, the Abbé Grégoire is often quoted in the notes to *Eulalie* as well as being referenced throughout the narrative. His principal work on the subject of slavery is the 1808 *De la littérature des nègres; ou, Recherches sur leur facultés intellectuelles, leurs qualités morales et leur littérature* [On the Literature of Negroes; or, An Inquiry into Their Intellectual Faculties, Their Moral Qualities and Their Literature]. He continues Raynal's universalist and historicized view of humanity, providing responses to newer, putatively scientific arguments about racial difference based on relative cranial size.[9] His work is also an updated compendium of European and North American published materials. More accounts of travel to Guinea had been written, in Dutch, English, and French, sometimes by ship's surgeons, who described coastal and now interior life in some detail: dress, agriculture and diet, more on religion, marriage and warfare, funerary customs, relations among peoples, and also unpleasant truths of slavery and human sacrifice, and the equally painful details of the European slave trade. All of these observations are incorporated into the novel.

As proof of his arguments for universal humanity, Grégoire provides published or otherwise documented examples of prominent social, intellectual, and literary achievements of slaves or former slaves. Although Grégoire's literary examples come from Europe and the New World, to make this point, Gabrielle de Paban supplies in her novel a purported sample of African poetry, almost certainly of her own invention, the "Romance des négresses," "un chant répandu sur toute la côte de Guinée" [a song commonly heard along the Guinea Coast] for which she provides a "traduction presque littérale" [a nearly literal translation] in octosyllabic, cross-rhymed *huitains,* or eight-line stanzas.[10] This sort of awkward translation was not uncommon in the factual texts of the time;

in his travelogue from 1820, one John McLeod, a ship's surgeon, provided the musical transcription of a dance tune he had heard. It is in G Major and in dotted 2/4 time.[11]

Introducing the reader to the novel's *arrière boutique* of the notes, the author of *Eulalie* states, "Les mémoires d'Eulalie offrent au moins des détails de la plus grande vérité sur les mœurs et les coutumes des nègres" [At the very least, Eulalie's memoirs offer details of the greatest truth of the mores and customs of Negroes].[12] This declaration contains a full literary program, going well beyond the conventional insistence on the putative truth of the story, a claim already made in the introduction with the mention of the ten-year-old manuscript that an otherwise disinterested individual was now putting before the public—the sort of revelation that surprised no one and was clearly to be understood as part of the fictional compact. To be *d'une très grande vérité*, documentation about Africa and the contemporary world had no choice but to be informed by *les savoirs,* that is, grounded in a proto-anthropology, naturalism, economics, politics, and social law, and shaped by enlightened philosophical argument, which allowed the author of *Eulalie* to translate one culture for the benefit of another in a language that the public in 1825 could understand. That linguistic vehicle was the sentimental novel.

As mentioned above, what distinguishes this novel from the genre I have called the ahistorical variety is the incorporation of a referentiality that makes it fully contemporary: events are evoked and dates are given that frame the story of the principal character and give her life a meaning beyond that of a private drama. Moreover, the various milieus necessary to this contemporary aspect are evoked with specificity: the colonial islands and Paris, but above all West Africa. The fusion of the two principal subgenres of the sentimental novel has brought about something quite different from either. Whereas the aim of the one was to present a moral drama played out within a modern sensitivity, and the other to offer the didactic edification of seeing private moral conflict confronted by illustrious historical personages, *Eulalie* presents a private conflict that parallels social debate and so raises its significance above the case of individuals to that of universal humanity.

Beyond the truth provided by documentation was a necessary reworking of the discursive vocabulary of the sentimental novel. Sentimental truth now had to correspond with objective truth. As a general rule, the language of the sentimental novel is straightforward and dramatic: it relates what characters did and what they said. There are apostrophes, exclamations of happiness and grief, supplications to the divinity, tears and melancholy; a poetic language of ambiguity, metaphor, and allusion is absent. Meaning is meaning as stated, and expanded meaning arises from the exchange of views between characters. There is no extended meaning, primarily because there is no interplay between description and figurative language. In *Eulalie,* however, the extensive development of comparisons between the races provides the possibility for something approaching extended meaning. This occurs during moments of heightened pathos. There are many examples of sentimental conventions used to a new end: fervently clasped hands, one black and one white, *baignées de pleurs* [bathed in tears], where the benediction of the lovers is also that of two races. The supreme moment in sentimental literature, dramatically and semantically, is always the death of the heroine; this is when literal action takes an idealizing turn and the accrued suffering from the impossibility of union and happiness is transformed into longing or regret. The deaths of Amélie, Atala, Eléanore, Corinne, Ourika, and even Madame de Rênal serve this function. In *Eulalie,* the principals will die at the same moment, he from execution, she from grief. Usually an emblem for the story that precedes it, here the sentimental death metonymically survives the fiction and carries over as a call for social change. With the strength that only the sentimental heroine can muster, Eulalie is able to transcribe in a letter her last conscious moment:

> C'en est fait mon amie! Dieu m'appelle; il m'a annoncé sa volonté. Il a fait sortir du tombeau l'ami de mon enfance. Ce nègre qui marchait à la mort. . . . Je n'ai pu éviter sa rencontre fatale. Il avait ses traits, son regard. . . . Il m'a vue. . . . J'entends ce cri. . . . C'était lui. . . . C'était. . . . Dieu! ayez pitié de tous vos enfants!"

> [It is done, my friend! God calls me, He has made His will known. He has raised my childhood friend from the tomb. This Negro walking to his death. . . . I could not avoid a final encounter. He had his features, his eyes. . . . He saw me. . . . I hear that cry. . . . It was he. . . . It was. . . . God, have pity on all your children!][13]

As a form available to writers in the 1820s, the sentimental novel proved to be an effective medium for the militancy of the abolitionist movement. Its narrative structure based on hope, impossibility of union,

and despair was a good fit for the history of the movement in France, and
its thematic structure was a convenient means to convey the desired goal
of racial understanding and harmony. Transposing the annotated form
to what had been a rather noncommittal genre with respect to current
social issues created a new form. Were there to be any lingering doubts
in the reader's mind, in 1825, as to the novel's relevance, the notes at the
end of the book bring the text fully up to date with a clipping from *Le
Pilote,* dated August 24, 1824, or to within a year of the first readership. It
reviews a recent incident of the horrific practice of jettisoning slave cargo
in mid-ocean. Beyond grounding an important event from the novel, the
point is to show where the legal abolition of the slave trade remained un-
enforced. The choice of using Pierre-François Tissot's recently founded
liberal, antigovernment newspaper lends the novel a specific political
bent. Far from the fragile vessel that even recent criticism has characterized it as being, the sentimental novel of the Restoration underwent a
significant transformation, and, well prior to the mythical threshold of
1830, was already doing some of the heavy lifting as it became militant,
and scientifically and philosophically biased. In doing so, it provided its
own take on *le roman contemporain.*

MARSHALL C. OLDS is professor of French in the Department of
Romance and Classical Studies at Michigan State University. His
research interests center on poetics and narrative in nineteenth-
century French literature. He is the author of *Au pays des perroquets:
Féerie théâtrale et narration chez Flaubert* and *Desire Seeking Expression:
Mallarme's "Prose pour des Esseintes,"* and has published editions of
*Oxiane; ou, La Révolution de Saint-Domingue, Le nègre et la créole; ou,
Mémoires d'Eulalie D***,* and *The Temptation of Saint Anthony.* He was
editor of the journal *Nineteenth-Century French Studies* (1999–2014).

NOTES

1. Paban, *Le nègre et la créole; ou, Mémoires d'Eulalie D**** (Paris: Boulland, 1825).
This novel has recently been reedited by Marshall C. Olds (Paris: L'Harmattan, 2008).
References are to the new edition.

2. Ibid., 3.

3. See Jenson, *Trauma and Its Representations.*

4. Kadish and Massardier-Kenney, eds., *Translating Slavery.*

5. Paban, *Le nègre et la créole,* 227.

6. Raynal, *Histoire philosophique et politique,* 3:186–205.

7. History for Raynal is the new intellectual paradigm: "S'il m'était permis de hasarder une prédiction, j'annoncerais qu'incessamment les esprits se tourneront du côté de l'histoire, carrière immense où la philosophie n'a pas encore mis le pied" [If I might hazard a prediction, I would say that thought will unfailingly turn toward history, that immense domain where philosophy has yet to set foot]. Ibid., 3:128.

8. "Tout le monde profite de la traite: depuis le premier propriétaire, jusqu'à tous les intermédiaires, jusqu'à l'acheteur final" [Everyone profits from the slave trade, from the first owner, to all the middle men, to the final buyer]. Ibid., 3:146. His response to this last justification was to change the economic model, proposing economic colonies of free workers similar to Sierra Leone, founded some seventeen years later. Ibid., 3:204.

9. Grégoire, *De la littérature des nègres,* 10–11.

10. Paban, *Le nègre et la créole,* 109–111.

11. McLeod, *A Voyage to Africa,* 96–98.

12. Paban, *Le nègre et la créole,* 221.

13. Ibid., 219.

TWO

Translating Bretonness—
Colonizing Brittany

HEATHER WILLIAMS

AFTER THE REVOLUTION OF 1789 THE FRENCH STATE MAN-
aged to turn the culturally heterogeneous peasants of even the furthest
corners of the provinces into Frenchmen, creating the most centralized
administration in Europe, both politically and culturally.[1] In nineteenth-
century Europe the idea of a "national language" became a powerful
unifying symbol of the nation, and nowhere more so than in France,
where it became an instrument for developing a "cult of the nation."[2]
In tackling France's internal differences in the name of *égalité,* the new
republic's linguistic policy displayed something of an obsession with the
French language, to the point of willing the eradication of all regional
languages and *patois* in favor of French.[3] It has been suggested that "more
than half the population of France may be asserted to have changed language, to French, since 1789."[4] Brittany, in northwest France, arguably
provides the starkest example of cultural difference within the *Hexagone,*
and a minority of people today still speak Breton, a Celtic language that
is closely related to Welsh and Cornish; send their children to Breton-
medium schools; and watch television and listen to the radio in Breton.
Statistics relating to Breton are notoriously difficult to establish as cen-
suses in France do not take account of linguistic data; however, it has
generally been accepted that Breton is still practiced by up to 500,000
people.[5] This chapter examines a crucial time in the history of France
when Brittany was home to a majority of monoglot Breton speakers. The
region had become a fashionable topic in literature as well as a popular
travel destination, thanks to a new enthusiasm for all things natural. This
trend can be traced to Jean-Jacques Rousseau and a post-Revolutionary

valorization of the (Celtic) Gauls, who were perceived as the ancestors of the *peuple* over the Franks, who were rejected as the ancestors of the aristocracy.[6] A close look at the role of translation in Breton culture at this time reveals some of the details of the process of homogenization that took place in France, and demonstrates how a postcolonial framework is just as relevant to the study of France's indigenous minorities as it is to its far-flung (former) colonies.

A revival in Breton cultural awareness is thought to have taken place in nineteenth-century Brittany. While historians analyze Breton nationalism proper as a twentieth-century phenomenon, it is widely acknowledged that this particular national movement, which grew out of late nineteenth- and early twentieth-century regionalism, has its origins in a much earlier rise in Breton feeling that was largely confined to the literary cultural sphere and that gathered pace in the first half of the nineteenth century.[7] Historians of Brittany's nineteenth-century "revival" have identified the 1830s as a key decade, as that period saw an intensification of cultural activity and a crystallization of images and representations of Bretonness.[8] Opening with the highly successful *Marie* (sentimental patriotic poems by Auguste Brizeux, 1831), which were followed by Émile Souvestre's most lasting legacy, *Les derniers Bretons* (The Last Bretons, published in book form in 1836),[9] the decade closed with La Villemarqué's *Barzaz Breiz,* Breton ballads translated into French with elaborate introduction and commentaries (1839). These three works were crucial in the development of the Breton movement, or "le bretonisme," and had a profound effect on subsequent representations of Brittany and Bretonness in literature. In a seminal discussion of images of Bretonness, Catherine Bertho dwells on the 1830s as the point when the dominant images went from negative to positive, from male to female, from dark to light.[10] A convenient illustration of the pivotal character of this decade, as far as representations of Brittany are concerned, is provided by Honoré de Balzac, who offers a primitive, savage, danger-filled Brittany in *Les chouans,* his first "Breton" novel of 1828, only to produce an idealized version ten years later in *Béatrix* (1838).[11]

However, a more rounded view of Breton culture might not see this period of intense cultural activity as a revival. For if Brittany is considered in its entirety—as a rich amalgam of traditions and cultures expressed through different languages (mainly Breton and French, but also Gallo and Latin)—then it seems odd to label this episode a revival. That accolade might better be reserved for the growth of the "Diwan" Breton-medium schools, or for twentieth-century Breton-language broadcasting and publishing, all of which was made possible by the energy and vision of the Gwalarn movement. Under the leadership of Roparz Hemon, this movement produced a modern literature for Brittany that eschewed the local to embrace universal themes. This literature was Breton simply by virtue of its medium, in stark contrast to the literary activity of the 1830s, which used French as its medium but concerned itself almost exclusively with portraying and defining Brittany and Bretonness. The work that characterized the 1830s, together with its long legacy, might better be considered as an exercise in translation. It is as such that I consider the sum of French-language representations of Brittany produced in the nineteenth century, focusing on selected examples.

Privileging translation is not new; indeed, seeing it as "a primary shaping force within literary history," rather than as a fringe activity, is becoming commonplace.[12] Literary and cultural studies are now looking to discussion of translation for what it can teach us of how culture is "constructed" and society "manipulated." This is largely thanks to the pioneering work of Susan Bassnett and André Lefevere, whose book *Translation, History, and Culture* (1990) is credited with bringing about the "cultural turn" in translation studies, making possible a reciprocal turn toward the issue of translation within literary criticism.[13] Focus on translation is especially pertinent to the study of borderland or postcolonial cultural contexts, as in such bi- or multilingual situations, translating from one language to another becomes particularly urgent. Here more than anywhere it is widely accepted that translation, as "part of an ongoing process of intercultural transfer," can be a driver of cultural change.[14] Translation is also more pervasive than something that takes place when one work in one language is transformed into a new version in a different language; for instance, in the case of a bilingual writer, translating is an essential and unstoppable part of any creative thought. Although the precise linguistic balance is different in each of the Celtic regions, literary production in all of these cultures is arguably inseparable from the issue of translation, because of the sociolinguistic situation they have in common: two main, coexisting, if politically unequal, languages. Thus work on Ireland can show the way to other Celtic countries.

The beginnings of Anglo-Irish literature, sometimes referred to as the "Irish Renaissance," have been seen as an "exercise in translation" in Declan Kiberd's analysis in *Inventing Ireland*.[15] In a similar vein, Michael Cronin has tracked the representations of Ireland and Irishness in English and mapped the delicate relationship between Gaelic and English from the Middle Ages onward, under the title *Translating Ireland*.[16] Wynn Thomas bemoans the lack of similar work on Wales, himself providing an excellent starting point for the field in a chapter on translation in his *Corresponding Cultures: The Two Literatures of Wales*.[17] According to Thomas, work by Cronin and Seamus Heaney "unearth[s] comments that cry out for application in the Welsh context."[18] I would add Brittany to this picture, as it is in this respect poorer still: despite its tradition of bilingual "en regard" editions, and the self-translation habits of key figures such as Pierre-Jakez Hélias, translation from Breton into French has received very little critical attention.[19] The relationship between the two literatures of Brittany has not been the object of a sustained study either.[20] This is because, on one hand, Breton specialists tend to be purists, refusing to acknowledge that material written in French is anything other than a contribution to French literature.[21] On the other hand, French studies has dismissed this material as of relevance only to Brittany. Indeed, until recently, the existence of a Francophone Breton literature was barely acknowledged, inside or outside of Brittany. Using translation as a lens through which to view the mediation of Breton culture to the French-speaking world, I now turn to the golden age of "bretonism" in the second quarter of the nineteenth century.

At this crucial time in the development of a French-language literature of Brittany, when Breton-born writers set out for the first time to describe and explain their *pays* to a Francophone readership, an important role was played by translation proper. The story of the interpretation of Brittany for French readers is dominated by the translation work of Hersart de La Villemarqué, whose *Barzaz Breiz* (1839) is a collection of native Breton songs with translations into French prose. Although Jacques Cambry had included some translations in his *Voyage dans le Finistère* (1798), and Émile Souvestre had published "La poésie populaire

de la Bretagne" in the *Revue des deux mondes* (1834), neither of these
bears any comparison to the impact of La Villemarqué's translations.
Any subsequent attempts at putting native Breton material into French
were written in his shadow. La Villemarqué understood the Zeitgeist like
no other Breton has done since, and was unsurpassed even by Hélias,
whose phenomenally successful *Cheval d'Orgueil* (1975) benefited from
the vogue for "returning to nature" in the 1970s. In the first decades
of post-Revolutionary France, when French national identity had yet
to be forged, when the ancient Gauls had been revalorized as the true
ancestors of the French, and the collecting of folk songs in progress in
Germany and Britain was unmatched in France, La Villemarqué set out
to fill this gap. His aim was to prove the ancientness of Breton culture
while also offering France a past richness that would enable it to rival its
European neighbors. All this was to be achieved through translation.
Native songs that he collected directly from the mouths of peasants were
to be translated so faithfully and carefully that the evidence would speak
for itself: "Une traduction soigneusement revue et qui serre le texte de
très près" [A painstaking translation that stays very close to the text].
The manner of the translation was to be "aussi littérale que possible"
[as literal as possible], and the fact that the material was put into prose,
rather than into the artifice of verse, was a guarantee of authenticity.[22]
For La Villemarqué, translation was a way to open up an authentic past
and to prove Brittany's place in France and the world, making of the
Breton language a repository of cultural truths.

Producing an original piece in French, with the aim of interpreting
Brittany for a Francophone audience, is at first sight a totally different
project. Breton-born writers are keen to mark out their distance from
visitors to the region such as Balzac, and stress their privileged status
as insiders. Brizeux in particular used his linguistic competence ("avoir
parlé leur langue" [to have spoken their language]) as a guarantee of
authenticity.[23] Despite the lack of a Breton source, the importance of the
language to the credibility of Francophone Breton writing in the period
makes it a kind of sourceless translation. Before condemning the likes
of Brizeux for exploiting the language opportunistically, the precise role
played by the Breton language in "actual" translation can be questioned.
In La Villemarqué's case, the space occupied by the Breton on the page

changes and shrinks as the *Barzaz Breiz* went through its editions. In the first two editions (1839 and 1846), the Breton was printed as parallel text, but by the definitive 1867 edition, the French was given prominence on the main part of the page, in a larger font, with the Breton ultimately playing no more than the symbolic role it was assigned in Brizeux's project. Today there are editions that omit the Breton altogether, as well as those that omit the French translations.[24]

A paradoxical attitude emerged toward the Breton language, as it was both privileged—a reliable route to truth—and brushed over. But equally ambiguous is the attitude to the translation process itself, which was seen as unproblematic and smooth, despite the claim that it was necessary to be a native speaker in order to get it right. La Villemarqué has provided a wonderful illustration of this, in writing about the deep impression that reading Brizeux's work had on him. He was an admirer of Brizeux and attempted to protect him from charges that his *Marie* had been invented to please a Parisian audience, by telling of a pilgrimage that he made to Moustier, the village where *Marie* is set. According to his account, La Villemarqué spoke in Breton to a number of locals before tracking down a young girl named Fantik, who turned out to be Marie's cousin. He then translated some of Brizeux's poetry into the girl's own language, for her to be able to exclaim, "C'est pure vérité" [It's pure truth].[25] The fact that the Breton experience of these monoglot peasants had first been translated into French by Brizeux, and then back into Breton by La Villemarqué, is not deemed worthy of comment. So despite being uniquely capable of revealing the authentic Brittany, the language is relegated to the status of useful research tool, mere facilitator of communication with peasants. Mary-Ann Constantine, who has analyzed the ballads in depth while warning us against attempting to extrapolate a line on translation from his dense and sometimes contradictory prefatory material, concludes that La Villemarqué's verbal surface is basically a reassuringly smooth one, but one that undoubtedly benefits from the excitement provided by the presence of the "exotic" other language on the page.[26] In a sense Brizeux's use of the language is the same as collectors of ballads and songs who relegate it to the foot of the page, and claim authenticity by stressing they have received them directly (i.e., not yet translated), making themselves the reliable intermediary and translator:

"Tels que je les tiens des *bardes* et des *sonneurs*" [Just as I received them from the bards and singers], claims Narcisse Quellien in his preface to *Chansons et danses des Bretons.*[27] Or, "Textes bretons donnés tels absolument que je les ai recueillis de la bouche des chanteurs" [Breton texts presented exactly as they were when I collected them from the singers' lips], proposed François-Marie Luzel in his *Gwerziou Breiz-Izel.*[28]

But in his day it was not so much his exploitation of the language that got La Villemarqué into trouble; the accusations against La Villemarqué were of a different nature. In 1867, the year in which the definitive edition of the *Barzaz Breiz* was published, La Villemarqué's reputation was taken apart at the Celtic Congress, for some feared that he might be nothing more than a Breton Macpherson. The work of James Macpherson (1736–1796) in mediating Scottish Gaelic culture for the English in a cycle of poems centering on the character of Ossian[29] was so notorious that it is responsible for the coining of the term "pseudo-translation."[30] We cannot fully understand Luzel's choice of emphasis without realizing the importance of this controversy. Luzel, whose translations of Breton ballads, *Gwerziou Breiz-Izel,* appeared in 1867–1868, has to situate himself in relation to *Barzaz Breiz,* describing his aim as "tout opposé" [altogether different], and marking out his difference in a Celtic Congress in 1872.[31] He carefully protected himself from accusations of being another Breton Macpherson, and though he did not attack La Villemarqué, the way in which Luzel's comments in the preface stress the scientific reliability of his translations, right down to the emphasis on the type of language used, betray his fears. Luzel's comments on the nature of his translations in *Gwerziou Breiz-Izel* are mainly attempts to mark out his distance from La Villemarqué and from Macpherson. Luzel offers us a "traduction aussi littérale que possible" [translation that is as literal as possible]. In order to stress his scientific concern with accuracy, he claims to be prepared to compromise on the quality of the French:

> Enfin dans la traduction, j'ai fait tous mes efforts pour serrer le texte Breton d'aussi près que j'ai pu, *sans chercher l'élégance de la phrase, tout en parlant français, autant que possible,* et en rendant chaque vers Breton par une ligne correspondante de français.

> [In short, in translating I have done my utmost to stay as close as I can to the Breton text. I have produced French, as far as possible, by giving each Breton line an equivalent in French, with scant regard for elegance of phrase.][32]

He seems to be rejecting the smooth verbal surface of La Villemarqué's translations when he claims his method will provide the nonspeaker of Breton with "une idée de quelques inversions et particularités propres à notre langue" [an idea of some of the inversions and particularities of our language].[33]

Despite appearances, Luzel was no early advocate of foreignizing translation. Although he was perceived as a foreignizer in the French capital, where fashions were changing, Luzel's attitude toward translation was basically the same as La Villemarqué's, a fact borne out, for instance, in that he makes no mention of translation issues at all in relation to his own poetry in *Bepred Breizad toujours Breton: Poésies bretonnes, avec traduction française en regard*. The reality that he must have self-translated in this volume, and the status of the French version in prose (rather than in verse), are not mentioned. The lack of discussion in prefaces and notes by other writers provides further evidence that translation was not problematized at the time. For instance, Souvestre does not discuss the issue of translation in his "psychological portrait," and Anatole Le Braz is apparently just as unconcerned, as he keeps no record of the original Breton texts that make up his *La légende de la mort*.[34] The attitude toward translation is summed up by La Villemarqué in a passage of praise for Brizeux's *Marie*: "Le Breton s'était fait discrètement français" [The Breton had discreetly made itself French].[35] The adverb "discrètement" conveys how, in Francophone writing, the Breton disappears into the French, less obviously but arguably more devastatingly than the way in which, in translation proper, the space that the language occupies on the page shrinks. We must ask why La Villemarqué is complimenting Brizeux on the way the Breton goes away discretely, without a trace, without so much as surprising the French.

Translation studies allow for a fresh perspective on the issues of smoothness and discreteness. The smooth tradition in translation, born of a desire to paper over any cracks between different cultural experiences, is, appropriately enough, known as the "French" type of translation. It would correspond to the first of the three models of translation proposed by Bassnett and Lefevere.[36] In their account, the first model, named Jerome after the translator of the Vulgate, seeks "equivalence," and is basically unproblematized translation. The second, the Horace model, "fidus interpres," satisfies both parties, with negotiation rather

than faithfulness to the original, at its core. And the third, the Schleier-
macher model, emphasizes the preservation of the alterity of the source
for the target reader. This was an idea that developed from German Romanticism. Germany lived through an "age of translation" at end of the
eighteenth century, when Johann Goethe traced a movement in translation toward "ever closer encounter with the texture of foreign works."
Indeed, German writers referred disparagingly to "the French method,"
which required the foreign text to don the garb of the country it was visiting.[37] Tastes in the French capital finally changed in the second half of
the nineteenth century.

The gradual rejection of the smooth translation in favor of foreignizing is seen in the reception of Luzel, who was compared favorably to
Brizeux by a more mature Sainte-Beuve, on account of his supposedly
strange French.[38] The younger Sainte-Beuve had, by contrast, championed Brizeux. Similarly, Paul Verlaine championed Tristan Corbière
as a "Breton bretonnant de la bonne manière" [a real Breton-speaking
Breton], a view echoed in Jean Floressas des Esseintes's exclamation,
"C'était à peine français, l'auteur parlait nègre" [It was hardly French, the
author was speaking Negro], in J.-K. Huysmans's *A rebours*.[39]

The "smoothness" that we have seen in the "translations" mentioned
tell us something of the attitude toward the Breton language, and they say
just as much about the relationship with French. As Bassnett and Lefevere write, "literatures written in languages that are less widely spoken,
will only gain access to something that could be called 'world literature,'
if they submit to the textual system, the discursive formation, or whatever else one wants to call it, underlying the concept of 'world literature'."
In other words, Bretons had to write to fulfill expectations. Bassnet and
Lefevere talk of a "pattern of expectations," or what they helpfully term a
"grid." A grid is "the collection of acceptable ways in which things can be
said," and preexists language; they are "man-made, historical, contingent
constructs."[40] For instance, a grid could be a certain "genre": this would
be the reason why *Ossian* was written as an epic. Indeed, Fiona Stafford
says there is strong evidence that Macpherson saw it as his task to fill in
gaps; because there was an assumption that the ancient Celts must have
written epics, he went ahead and produced some.[41] In the case of Fin-
land, the grid was another language altogether: Swedish, as this was the

only literary language that the Finns, who wanted to construct a national epic for recognition as a "nation," knew when the *Kalevala* was written.[42]

The particular relevance of the grid to a minority culture such as Brittany's is seen in the choices made by La Villemarqué and Brizeux. The *Barzaz Breiz* owes its success to La Villemarqué's careful targeting of his material: he packaged it as of French interest and wrote in elegant French.[43] Brizeux was so careful in calculating the degree of familiarity required by a cultured Parisian that he went as far as to Gallicize place-names in line with the preferences of the great critic Sainte-Beuve.[44] The type of "translation" produced by Brizeux is translation as mimicry of the dominant discourse, that of the colonizer. His text is calculated to satisfy curiosity and, above all, to soothe by confining Breton difference and individuality to the level of the picturesque. If Breton culture wants to be acknowledged by French, it has to be whatever France wants it to be. So the translation issue can show us something of the way the "petite patrie" pleases its master by being polite enough never to appear *un*-French.

The same desire to please can be seen behind the bilingual, "en re-gard" editions, as Camille Le Mercier d'Erm noted in his authoritative anthology, *Les bardes et poètes nationaux de la Bretagne armoricaine*:

> Nous n'avons pas voulu, au contraire de nos devanciers, faire prevue d'exclusi-visme en composant une anthologie hermétique, toute de vers Bretons ou toute de vers français. C'eût été pécher par excès dans un sens ou dans l'autre.
>
> [Unlike our predecessors, we did not want to court exclusivity by compiling a closed anthology of only Breton or only French poetry. That would have been too much of a good thing in one direction or the other.][45]

Brittany, he goes on to write, is already and naturally bilingual but united by *one* patriotism. In his anthology, poems in both languages show this "parfaite unité d'inspiration" [perfect unity of inspiration]. Similar em-phasis is found in praise of Brizeux's ability to reconcile cultural con-flicts, and his love of both "petite" [the local] and "grande patrie" [the fatherland]. A study by A. Lexandre discusses the tension in Brizeux between "le poète né celte et le poète français du XIXème siècle" [the poet born a Celt and the nineteenth-century French poet], but only in order to assert what a patriot he is: "Il ne faudrait pas croire cependant que dans cette portion du territoire national, l'attache à la petite patrie soit un signe qu'on ne tient pas des entrailles à la grande" [An attachment to the local, in this portion of the national territory, should not be taken as a sign of anything but the most deep-seated commitment to the fatherland].[46] Thus, oppressed, "colonized" behavior is evident in issues around translation. The fact that translation out of Celtic languages into the dominant language of the region has long been perceived as tainted is cited by Wynn Thomas as an explanation for the lack of work on translation in Wales: "Welsh-speakers could naturally see in it [Welsh-English translation] a strategy of colonial appropriation, a means of bankrupting the language of its assets prior to liquidating its entire culture."[47]

However, as Thomas goes on to show, such work can be helpful. For instance, translation studies have changed the way that we view *Ossian*. Similarly, La Villemarqué is now, gradually, being rehabilitated, thanks to major work by Donatien Laurent on the notebooks containing the raw material from which La Villemarqué worked. These notebooks, rediscovered in the 1960s, prove he had not "invented" from nothing. As in *Ossian* studies, the practice of either condemning a writer as an "inventor," or defending him as a pure practitioner of translation, has been abandoned in favor of a more holistic exploration of the nature of the translation practiced, and the implications of this for understanding cultural connections and tensions at the time. As Constantine has shown with her work on La Villemarqué and others, we must see the translator as a mediator.

Translation studies help us to see Francophone Breton literature as a category, and to approach it critically. It was in the 1830s that Bretons first began writing about themselves in French in a concerted fashion. I have argued elsewhere that the publishing event that marks the beginning of the decade—Brizeux's *Marie* of 1831—represents the birth of a Francophone Breton literature.[48] But Francophone Breton literature is a category more often than not dismissed by the French, angrily rejected by many Bretons, and largely ignored by French scholars. For Celtic and Breton specialists, it is simply in the wrong language: there can be no "Bretonness" through the medium of French, as any utterance in French has to do with France and Frenchness. For French studies, Brittany is usually little more than a footnote in histories of the rise of French. Its literary production is either too marginal to mainstream Parisian culture, or not "Francophone" enough, as the term "francophone" conjures up discussions of faraway cultures such as France's former colonies, indeed anywhere *but* metropolitan France.[49] Also, the political and cultural situation in Brittany has not been thought relevant enough to postcolonial studies. The notable exception to this is the work found in *Plurial,* the journal of the Centre d'Études des Littératures et Civilisations Francophones at the University of Rennes, most notably in two articles: Pascal Rannou's "Approche du concept de littérature bretonne de langue française,"[50] and Marc Gontard's "Pour une littérature bretonne de langue française,"[51] which provides a survey of primary texts. These same critics are responsible for important re-readings of key figures; see, for instance, Rannou's close analysis of Hélias's language, which discusses bilingualism and issues of translation, and his work on Corbière, which focuses on the *métissage,* or hybridity, of the text.[52]

Translation studies allow us to approach this forgotten chapter in the literature of France and Brittany. They show how we can abandon rigid categories and look between languages, raising a number of questions: Is it possible to be both Francophone and authentically Breton? Can French-language representations of Brittany be authentic? Or are they necessarily flawed because of the language in which they are written, the politically dominant language of the oppressor? Is the category "Francophone Breton literature" a valid one? Or does any work written in French, no matter how "Breton" the subject matter, simply form a part of French literature? Considering the "revival" in Breton identity at this time as an exercise in translation allows us to see the cultural interaction, cultural conflict, and culture shocks that Brittany provides, revealing Brittany as a rich foraging ground for French studies and beyond. The history of Francophone Breton literature, then, is a test case for the history of translation in France, offering a window onto the issue of authenticity in a postcolonial context.

HEATHER WILLIAMS is Pilcher Senior Fellow at the Centre for Advanced Welsh and Celtic Studies at the National Library of Wales where she works on cultural exchange and translation studies among French, Breton, English, and Welsh. She is the author of *Postcolonial Brittany: Literature between Languages* and *Mallarmé's Ideas in Language,* as well as numerous articles on French and Celtic literatures.

She has also produced a short work of literary criticism on Mallarmé
for the reader with a background in Welsh literature, a work that
includes some of her own translations of Mallarmé's verse into Welsh.

NOTES

1. On this question, see the landmark study by Eugen Weber, *Peasants into Frenchmen.*

2. Burke, Language and Communities, 160.

3. See Balibar and Laporte, *Le français national;* Certeau et al., Une politique de la langue; and Ager, *Identity, Insecurity and Image.*

4. Press, "Breton Speakers in Brittany, France and Europe," 215.

5. The most recent authoritative survey (1997) was carried out by Fañch Broudic, who found that 31% of respondents (370,000 individuals) claimed to "understand Breton." For a breakdown and full discussion of these results, see his *Qui parle Breton aujourd'hui?*

6. See Ehrard and Vialleneix, eds., *Nos ancêtres les Gaulois,* 195–201, and Dietler, "'Our Ancestors the Gauls'," 587.

7. Bernard Tanguy has traced this connection in detail in *Aux origines du nationalisme breton.* More flamboyantly, Morvan Lebesque draws together the literary activities of the first half of the nineteenth century and post-1968 Breton nationalism in his account of reading a collection of Breton ballads, La Villemarqué's *Barzaz Breiz;* see Lebesque, *Comment peut-on être breton?* 14, 28.

8. See Guiomar, *Le bretonisme,* and Tanguy, *Aux origines du nationalisme breton.*

9. Souvestre, *Les derniers Bretons,* 1:36.

10. Bertho, "L'invention de la Bretagne." According to Bertho this period saw "l'aimable supplanter le sauvage et le bucolique détrôner l'étrange" [the likeable supplant the savage and the bucolic dethrone the strange] (58), and "le personnage le plus typique devient alors féminin: c'est la jeune Bretonne en coiffe" [at this time the most typical character becomes female: the young Breton girl in traditional headdress] (49).

11. For discussion of the evolution in Balzac's representations of Brittany in his novels, see Williams, *Postcolonial Brittany,* 49ff.

12. Bassnett, *Translation Studies,* 142.

13. Bassnett and Lefevere, *Translation, History, and Culture.* For a stimulating account of the contribution of Bassnett and Lefevere to the field, see Bassnett and Lefevere, eds., *Constructing Cultures.* The foreword to this volume by Edwin Genteler sums this up: "Rather than being a secondary and derivative genre, [translations] were instead one of the *primary* literary tools that larger social institutions—educational systems, arts councils, publishing firms, and even governments—had at their disposal to 'manipulate' a given society in order to 'construct' the kind of 'culture' desired" (x).

14. Bassnett and Trivedi, eds., *Postcolonial Translation,* 2.

15. "The Irish Renaissance had been essentially an exercise in translation, in carrying over aspects of Gaelic culture into English, a language often thought alien to that culture." Kiberd, *Inventing Ireland,* 624.

16. Cronin, *Translating Ireland*.

17. "Next to nothing has so far been done to map translation at this location [modern Wales]. The difference in this regard, as in so many others, from the situation in neighbouring Ireland is painful to contemplate." Thomas, *Corresponding Cultures*, 112. "Just as there exists no bibliography, however basic, of Welsh-English translation, so has there been next to no substantial discussion of either the history or the cultural implications of this long-established practice." Ibid., 113. This has now been remedied by Thomas's more recent work, with Rhian S. Reylonds, *A Bibliography of Welsh Literature in English Translation*.

18. Thomas, *Corresponding Cultures*, 113.

19. But see my preliminary discussion: Williams, "Between French and Breton."

20. The closest we have come is an impressive survey work: Balcou and Le Gallo, eds., *Histoire littéraire et culturelle de la Bretagne*. While it discusses both literatures, it does not address the relationship between them. Such work has begun on La Villemarqué and other collectors in Mary-Ann Constantine, *Breton Ballads*. She uses translation as a perspective on the general cultural scene.

21. See, for instance, Gwennolé Le Menn on literature produced in French from any part of Brittany: "Si elles sont parfois inspirées par la Bretagne, [elles] font partie intégrante de la littérature française" [If these pieces are sometimes inspired by Brittany, they form an integral part of French literature]. "Langue et culture bretonnes," in Pelletier, ed., *Histoire générale de la Bretagne et des Bretons*, 2:465.

22. La Villemarqué, *Le Barzhaz Breiz*, 37; La Villemarqué, "Préambule de la première et de la seconde édition," ix. It should be noted that La Villemarqué printed his "essais de traductions en vers" as an appendix to the first edition, only to remove them subsequently.

23. Brizeux, *Œuvres de Auguste Brizeux*, 1:2.

24. See, for instance, *Le Barzhaz Breizh: Trésor de la littérature orale de la Bretagne* (1997), and Kervarker, *Barzhaz Breizh*.

25. "C'est pure vérité, s'écria la jeune paysanne." La Villemarqué, "La renaissance bretonne," 4.

26. Constantine, "Ballads Crossing Borders," 211–212.

27. Quellien, *Chansons et danses des Bretons*, iii.

28. Luzel, *Gwerziou Breiz-Izel*, 2:i.

29. The first was James Macpherson, *Fragments of Ancient Poetry*, and his works culminated in *The Works of Ossian*.

30. Coined by Gideon Toury in "Translation, Literary Translation, and Pseudotranslation," 6:xv.

31. Luzel, *Gwerziou Breiz-Izel*, 1:ii.

32. Ibid., 2:ii; 1:iv, emphasis added.

33. The comment occurs in a footnote, where Luzel expresses the hope that this type of translation will help learners of the language. Ibid., 1:525.

34. Le Braz, *La légende de la mort* (Rennes: Terre de Brume, 1994). Its first edition was published in Paris by Champion in 1893, after which it expanded until it became two volumes in a definitive edition of 1928.

35. La Villemarqué, "La Renaissance bretonne," 3.

36. For a fuller account, see Bassnett and Lefevere, eds., *Constructing Cultures*, 2–8.

37. Quoted in Louth, *Hölderlin and the Dynamics of Translation,* 7.

38. "Brizeux, que vous chantez si bien, était un Breton qui l'était en quelque sorte redevenu après coup. Il semble que vous l'êtes plus naturellement.... Vous y avez des accents qui nous atteignent même à travers la traduction et qui doivent mordre deux fois dans la langue natale" [Brizeux, whom you write about so well, was a Breton who became one, as it were, in retrospect. It seems that you are a more natural Breton.... In your writing there are accents that reach us even through the translation and which must have twice the bite in the native language]. Sainte-Beuve to Luzel, May 18, 1865, in Sainte-Beuve, *Correspondance générale,* 14:209–210.

39. Verlaine, *Les poètes maudits,* 22. Des Essintes is a fictional character, a quintessential aesthete living on the outskirts of Paris in Huysmans, *A rebours,* 212, first published in 1884.

40. Bassnett and Lefevere, eds., *Constructing Cultures,* 76, 5.

41. "Ossian, primitivism, celticism." Gillespie and Hopkins, *The Oxford History of Literary Translation in English,* 3:420.

42. For an overview, see Bassnett and Lefevere, eds., *Constructing Cultures,* 79.

43. "Il ne s'agit donc pas ici d'un intérêt purement local, mais bien d'un intérêt français; car l'histoire de la Bretagne a toujours été mêlée à celle de la France, et la France est aussi celtique par le cœur que l'Armorique est française aujourd'hui sous le drapeau commun" [So this is not a matter of purely local interest, but rather of French interest, because the history of Brittany has always been entwined with that of France, and France is just as Celtic at heart as Armorica is today French beneath a common flag]. La Villemarqué, *Le Barzazh Breizh,* 36.

44. This, and other ways in which Brizeux might be described as writing to Paris, are discussed in Williams, "Writing to Paris."

45. Le Mercier d'Erm, *Les bardes et poètes nationaux,* xxxi.

46. Lexandre, *Un pélerinage,* 70, 133–134.

47. Thomas, *Corresponding Cultures,* 114.

48. Williams, *Postcolonial Brittany.*

49. For a recent discussion of the word "francophone" and its "heavy baggage," see Forsdick and Murphy, "Introduction," 7, and Forsdick, "Between 'French' and 'Francophone'." An earlier discussion of terminology by Roger Little is essential reading: "World Literature in French." Little urges the adoption of the term "Francographic literature," as it "has the great merit of wiping the slate clean for a fresh start" (432).

50. In *Métissage du texte: Bretagne, Maghreb, Québec,* ed. Bernard Hue (Rennes: Presses Universitaires de Rennes, 1994), 75–86.

51. In *Écrire la Bretagne: 1960–1995* (Rennes: Presses Universitaires de Rennes, 1995), 17–31.

52. Rannou, *Inventaire d'un héritage;* Rannou, ed., *Visages de Tristan Corbière.*

THREE

Baudelaire and Hiawatha

L. CASSANDRA HAMRICK

CHARLES BAUDELAIRE'S TRANSFORMATION OF EDGAR ALLAN Poe's short stories into the ever popular and widely read *histoires extraordinaires* is generally considered to be without equal in terms of both its overall quality and the poetic sensitivity with which the original texts were transposed into French. Yet in Baudelaire's own time, it was not Poe but another American writer, Henry Wadsworth Longfellow, who commanded greater prestige both at home and abroad. In France, Longfellow, along with novelist James Fenimore Cooper, ranked among the best-known American authors of the period. Indeed, Longfellow's literary status, not just in France but in Western Europe in general, may account in part for the fact that he is the sole poet from America whose name appears in Baudelaire's list of persons designated to receive a copy of *Les Fleurs du Mal* in 1857.[1]

Baudelaire's ties with Longfellow's work are few but significant. A brief "Note sur les plagiats" (note on plagiarisms) containing the notation, "Longfellow (2 passages)," which Baudelaire added, as a reminder to himself, in one of his projected prefaces for *Les Fleurs du Mal,* has precipitated considerable discussion regarding the possible literary convergences between the two poets.[2] While critics agree on which poems contain the supposed "plagiats," exactly how Baudelaire may have "borrowed" the stanza beginning with the celebrated maxim "Art is long and Time is fleeting" from Longfellow's "A Psalm of Life,"[3] or whether the "trailing garments of the Night" found in the American poet's "Hymn to the Night" had an effect on the imagery in Baudelaire's poem "Recueillement," remain elusive.[4] What seems clear, however, is that Longfellow's immensely successful book of verse *Voices of the Night* (1839) contains visual as well as sonorous elements that struck the eyes and ears of a broad readership, including the author of *Les Fleurs du Mal.*[5]

Besides Baudelaire's self-avowed "plagiarisms" and their link with *Voices of the Night*, there is another Baudelaire-Longfellow connection involving a text the particulars of which have remained obscure.[6] It concerns Longfellow's most popular work of all, the *Song of Hiawatha.* Within a month of its publication in Boston in 1855, the 316-page poem consisting of 22 cantos was selling at the rate of 300 copies a day.[7] Numerous plays, parodies, and musical renditions, as well as an operatic extravaganza, soon followed.[8] In the twentieth century, *Hiawatha* continued to make cultural inroads in places as far away as Australia, where our own colleague Rosemary Lloyd sang, as a schoolgirl, Samuel Coleridge-Taylor's highly acclaimed *Hiawatha's Wedding-Feast,* the first part of the composer's *Hiawatha* trilogy (1898–1900), a cantata written for chorus, orchestra, and three soloists.[9] The simple song-like quality of the poem's octosyllabic trochaic verse form borrowed from the Finnish epic poem *Kalevala,*[10] the exoticism associated with the noble savage as prophet and teacher,[11] and the lyricism evoked by the vast tableaux of unspoiled prairies, rivers, and *coteaux,* offer an attractive combination for musical adaptations. As early as 1858 in St. Louis, an Alsatian immigrant and writer of vocal music, Emile Karst, in collaboration with French composer Jacques Ernest Miquel, performed *The Cantata of Hiawatha.*[12] The following year, first in Boston and then in New York, German-born Robert Stoepel performed his own musical rendition of Longfellow's poem under the title *Hiawatha: A Romantic Symphony,* later modified to *Hiawatha: Indian Symphony* (1863).[13] The score called for an orchestra, chorus, three soloists, two dances (a "Beggar Dance" and a "Magic Corn Field Dance"), and a narrator. The part of the narrator was initially performed by Stoepel's wife, Irish-born Matilda Heron, an actress known for her ability to sway the emotions of the audience.[14]

Stoepel's imaginative musical transposition of the *Hiawatha* poem met with considerable success.[15] Longfellow himself, who had a private box for the premiere performance at the Boston Theatre on January 8, 1859, noted in his journal: "The music is beautiful, and striking, particularly the wilder parts: the War Song and the Dance of Pau-Puk-Keewis."[16] When Stoepel arrived in Paris in November 1860, then, and asked Baudelaire to translate the passages from Longfellow's poem that would be needed for a French version of his *Symphonie romantique,* there was every reason to believe that the projected performance in the French capital could be a success as well. Memories of George Catlin's dazzling Indian picture gallery and of the Homeric grandeur of the Ojibwa and the Iowa Indians who performed at the Louvre and the Salle Valentino in 1845 were still alive, at least in the minds of writers like Baudelaire, as evidenced in his own *Salon de 1859,* where Catlin is evoked in three different contexts.[17] The same could be said for Chateaubriand's "l'épopée de l'homme de la nature" ["the epic of man in nature"], *Les Natchez,* which Baudelaire had recently reread with great satisfaction.[18] Simultaneously, on the musical front, Stoepel's compatriot Richard Wagner, whose concerts performed at the Théâtre Italien in early 1860 had made such a deep impression on Baudelaire's *psyche,* revolutionized the operatic genre by synthesizing music, drama, verse, legend, and spectacle.[19] Stoepel's own initiative, while of another register and more modest in objective and scope, nonetheless took as a point of departure the idea of bringing together multiple modes of performance. Baudelaire, who himself had contemplated writing an opera in 1853, might have oriented his poetic energy in quite a different direction in his later years had his career included involvement in a French *Hiawatha* production at the Théâtre Italien, the poet's proposed venue for the performance.[20]

However, what *might have been* was not to be—not because of any reticence on Baudelaire's part to involve himself with Longfellow's poem, but because of another crucial factor with which nearly all artists are doomed to struggle: money. Yet money did not seem to be uppermost in Stoepel's mind when he first spoke to Baudelaire about doing the *Hiawatha* translation. It was Baudelaire who was cautious, judging the seven thousand francs that Stoepel said he could advance for the first performance too little. At the same time, Baudelaire seemed intrigued by Stoepel's project, in spite of the fact that in the composer's search for someone to do a French translation of Longfellow's poem, Stoepel had looked to Baudelaire seemingly as a last resort. In a letter to Auguste Poulet-Malassis, to whom the poet apparently turned for help in negotiating the financial arrangements, Baudelaire expressed concern about the anticipated costs of the performance. He ended the letter to his editor on an ambiguous note: "Finalement, je désire que vous me trouviez le

plus possible, et en même temps que vous soyez charmant pour ce monsieur, qui d'ailleurs le mérite" [In the end, I would like for you to find me
as much as you can, and at the same time, to be charming to this man
who, moreover, deserves it].[21]

"TRISTE HISTOIRE"

Baudelaire's involvement with the translation of Longfellow's poem for
Stoepel has been considered a "triste histoire" [sad story] beyond redemption, a thankless job undertaken out of financial need.[22] After all, Stoepel
imposed multiple cuts in Longfellow's poem, rejected Baudelaire's initial
adaptations in verse form of *Hiawatha*,[23] and then in December 1860,
suddenly left Paris for London[24] without paying Baudelaire for his work,
thereby dooming all plans for a French *Hiawatha* production.[25] Moreover, Baudelaire's prose translation of *Hiawatha* has been judged to be
lacking in quality, especially in comparison with his translations of Poe's
tales or his adaptation of Thomas De Quincey's *Confessions of an English
Opium Eater.* "Jamais sans doute Baudelaire n'avait élaboré si rapidement
une matière aussi ingrate" [Doubtless Baudelaire had never worked so
quickly on such thankless material], observes Claude Pichois in com-
menting on the difficulties facing the poet. The disjuncture between the
naiveté "au bon sens" [in the good sense] inherent in the simple rhythm
and sounds of Longfellow's poem, and the stilted naiveté that marks the
French versions of *Hiawatha,* including Baudelaire's own rendition, is
sadly apparent.[26] Yet are we to dismiss Baudelaire's *Hiawatha* translation
simply as a thankless task executed under constraints of time, financial
exigency, and the need to fit a prescribed mold? Does this work show
nothing of Baudelaire's genius as a poet and translator?

Poe himself, in an essay entitled "Philosophy of Composition,"
which Baudelaire translated and published in the *Revue française* the
year before he met Stoepel, evokes the problem of constraint and the
effect it can have on composition:[27]

> Il m'a toujours paru qu'un espace étroit et resserré est absolument nécessaire
> pour l'effet d'un incident isolé; il lui donne l'énergie qu'un cadre ajoute à une
> peinture. Il a cet avantage moral incontestable de concentrer l'attention dans un
> petit espace.

[It has always appeared to me that a close *circumscription of space* is absolutely
necessary to the effect of insulated incident—it has the force of a frame to
a picture. It has an indisputable moral power in keeping concentrated the
attention.][28]

Poe's notion that constraint has the paradoxical effect of giving "force"
("energy" for Baudelaire) to a composition can also apply to the process
itself of composing, as Théophile Gautier notes when referring to contemporary artists' misconceptions about artistic freedom:

> C'est . . . un des préjugés familiers aux artistes, de croire qu'il faut au talent
> liberté pleine et entière, rien n'est plus faux. La gêne fait jaillir le talent plus haut,
> comme l'eau comprimée qui s'élance en gerbe brillante. La forme . . . incom-
> mode d'un caisson et d'un pendentif tracé par l'architecte, obligent à retourner
> une composition de cent manières, à essayer toutes les *postures* et tous les *rac-
> courcis* pour faire tenir beaucoup en peu d'espace; l'effet y gagne et l'ajustement
> des groupes est plus nourri et plus serré.—Un sujet commandé, chose qui effraie
> tant les artistes, a ceci de bon qu'il arrête le vagabondage de l'imagination et
> évite la perte de temps et l'hésitation, en concentrant tout de suite les facultés de
> l'artiste sur un seul point. Les gens qui ont vraiment du talent réussissent dans
> toutes sortes de sujet; tout leur est bon.

> [It is . . . commonplace among artists to believe that talent requires total and
> complete liberty; nothing is more false. Constraint makes talent shoot higher,
> like water under pressure that thrusts upward in a brilliant spray. The awkward
> form of a caisson and a pendent traced by the architect make it necessary to
> adjust the composition in a hundred ways, to try all kinds of *positions* and *size
> reductions* in order to make a lot fit in a small space; the effect is enhanced as a
> result and the arrangement of the groups is richer and denser.—A subject that
> is commissioned, something that frightens so many artists, has the advantage
> of keeping the imagination from wandering and of avoiding loss of time and
> hesitation by making the artist's mind concentrate on just one point. People who
> really have talent succeed in these types of subjects; everything comes out well
> for them.][29]

In the case of Baudelaire and *Hiawatha,* the monetary and temporal
difficulties connected with the Stoepel project are clear. Yet the textual
constraints faced by the poet in producing a French narrative for the
proposed musical rendition of *Hiawatha* have remained cloudy up until
now. What were the dimensions of literary space within which the poet
was asked to work? How did he wrestle with these limitations? What
literary "postures" and "raccourcis" (to use the words of Gautier) were
undertaken in order to preserve in Stoepel's libretto the "air poétique et

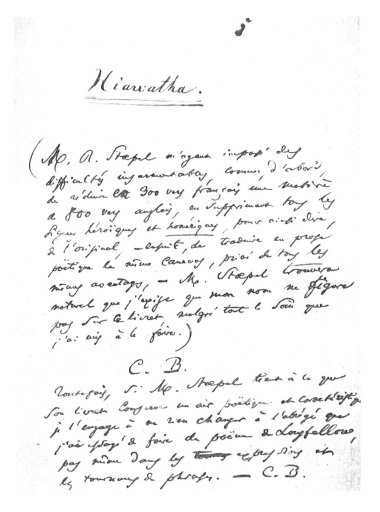

Figure 3.1. Manuscript note for Robert Stoepel, December 4 (?), 1860. Courtesy Special Collections Library, Pennsylvania State University Libraries, University Park, Penn.

caractéristique" [poetic and characteristic air] to which Baudelaire refers in a note for the composer that may have been prepared to accompany the prose translation of the *Hiawatha* manuscript (fig. 3.1)?[30]

Examination of two documents—the 1863 piano score of Robert Stoepel's *Hiawatha: Indian Symphony* and a copy of the original edition of the *Song of Hiawatha* that was annotated by Matilda Heron for Baudelaire's use in the preparation of the French translation of Longfel-

HIAWATHA.

PART I.

No. 1.—The Peace Pipe.
The Great Spirit's Allocution to the Tribes.
The stillness of Nature in the wilderness. The rising of the smoke, as a signal for the gathering of nations.
SONG OF THE GREAT SPIRIT.

No. 2.—The Stars; Hiawatha's Birth.
Remembering the promise of the Great Spirit, who has foretold the coming of a Prophet whose presence shall fill the land with blessings, the Tribes, as related in a reading, await his advent.
INTRODUCTION AND CHORUS,
Describing Nokomis' descent to Earth, the Birth of Wenonah, her betrayal by the West Wind, and the Birth of Hiawatha.

No. 3.—Cradle Song.
The reading describes the infancy of Hiawatha, and precedes the song of Nokomis, to her daughter's child.

No. 4.—Hiawatha's Sailing.
The story of Hiawatha's youthful sports is read, and is followed by the
CANOE BUILDING SONG,

No. 5.—The Fight with Mudjekeewis.
WAR SONG, . . . ORCHESTRA.
To avenge his mother's betrayal and death, Hiawatha seeks a conflict with Mudjekeewis, the West Wind. The reading relates the journey of Hiawatha to the kingdom of the West Wind. The orchestra gives the Indian War Song, which is gradually wrought into the movement describing the struggle.

No. 6.—Hiawatha's Wooing.
The reading tells of the return of Hiawatha, his visit to the Arrow-Maker, and his wooing of Minnehaha.
TRIO.

PART II.

No. 7.—Hiawatha's Wedding Feast.
PAU-PUK-KEEWIS' BEGGAR DANCE.
ORCHESTRA.

No. 8.—
CHIBIABO'S LOVE SONG.

No. 9.—Blessing the Corn Fields.
The Mystic Ceremony of Blessing the Corn-field is narrated. The Orchestra follows with the
MAGIC CORN FIELD DANCE.

No. 10.—The Ravens.
The plots of Kahgagee, the King of Ravens, are narrated. The reading is followed by the
RAVEN'S CHORUS.

No. 11.—The Harvest.
The reading describes the approach of Harvest Time, and introduces the
HARVEST CHORUS.

No. 12.—Winter.
The description of the approach of Winter is read, and musically illustrated. A second reading tells of the visit of the "Ghosts of the Departed," and leads to the
CHORUS OF GHOSTS, FAMINE, AND FEVER.

No. 13.—Minnehaha's Death.
The fatal sickness and death of Minnehaha, are related, and succeeded by the
DEATH SONG OF MINNEHAHA.
The reading tells of the burial of Minnehaha, and lamentation of Hiawatha. An Orchestral passage indicates the transitions of the seasons, the first budding forth of the early spring, the faint chirpings of birds, the rustling of the new-blown leaves, the murmurings of the streams:

No. 14.—Finale.
CHORUS OF SPRING AND SUMMER.

Figure 3.2. Robert Stoepel, *Hiawatha. Indian Symphony.* New York: William Hall and Son, 1863. List showing the division of the score into fourteen numbers. Courtesy W. T. Bandy Center for Baudelaire and Modern French Studies, Vanderbilt University, Nashville, Tenn.

low's poem—shed new light on this aspect of Baudelaire's work, which he himself entitled *Hiawatha: Légende indienne*.[31] First, the comparison of these two documents with Baudelaire's own *Hiawatha* text allows a better understanding of the parameters defining Baudelaire's translation task. Second, a careful reading of Baudelaire's text in light of the annotated edition shows that, beyond the obvious examples in which

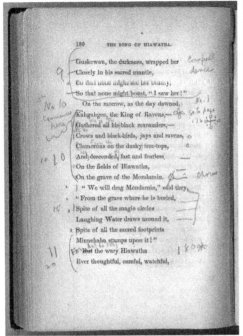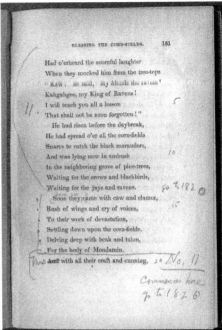

Figure 3.3. "Blessing of the Corn-Fields," pp. 180–181, in Longfellow's *Song of Hiawatha* (Boston: Ticknor and Fields, 1856), showing Matilda Heron's annotations as transcribed by W. T. Bandy. Courtesy W. T. Bandy Center for Baudelaire and Modern French Studies, Vanderbilt University. Reproduced with the kind permission of Carol Oberdorfer.

the original text has been deliberately altered in order to conform to Stoepel's textual requirements, there is evidence of Baudelaire's poetic genius at work.

BAUDELAIRE'S TASK

Concerning the parameters of Baudelaire's work, even a cursory look at the annotated edition reveals that the poet's task was not to translate the *Song of Hiawatha* exactly as the author had written it, but rather to create a composite narrative organized into fourteen scenes that follow a sometimes complex scheme of intertwining passages (fig. 3.2). In Stoepel's *Hiawatha* edition annotated by Matilda Heron, numerous passages have been crossed out, and at the beginning of some of the twenty-two original cantos, the word "out" has been inscribed, indicating that they

should be omitted in their entirety. Single lines to be omitted are indicated by the letter "o." Some of the fourteen scenes for which pieces of the
original cantos would be used are indicated in the annotated edition by
a clever system of cross-referencing devised by Matilda Heron and com-
posed of triangles, circles, dots, crosses, and even flowers! Examination
of the annotated edition reveals, for example, that Longfellow's canto 13,
"Blessing the Corn-Fields" (figs. 3.3a, 3.3b), is the source for parts of three
different scenes in the 1863 Stoepel musical score and, correspondingly,
in Baudelaire's translation:

· Scene 9 (Stoepel): "The Blessing of the Corn Fields" /
  Baudelaire's text: "Bénédiction des Champs de Maïs" (folios
  20–21;[32] OC, 1:259–260);
· Scene 10 (Stoepel): "The Ravens" / Baudelaire's text: "Les
  Corbeaux" (folios 22–23; OC, 1:260–261);
· Scene 11(Stoepel): "The Harvest" (piece no. 11) / Baudelaire's
  text: "La Moisson" (folio 24; OC, 1:261).

Table 3.1. Overview of the displacement and transposition of textual components in
Longfellow's original canto 13, "Blessing of the Cornfields," in the Song of Hiawatha as
seen in Baudelaire's adaptation and Stoepel's choral and orchestral score

Longfellow	Baudelaire	Stoepel
XIII. BLESSING THE CORN-FIELDS*	[Folios 20–21; OC, 1:259–260] BÉNÉDICTION DES CHAMPS DE MAÏS	Hiawatha, Part II **No. 9—Blessing the Corn Fields** The Mystic Ceremony of Blessing the Corn-field is
	ici la Danse magique Des Champs de Maïs	narrated. The Orchestra follows with the MAGIC CORN FIELD DANCE.
	[Folios 22–23; OC, 1:260–261] LES CORBEAUX	**No. 10—The Ravens** The plots of Kahgagee, the King of Ravens, are
*Note: Sections of this canto that were designated for translation in the annotated edition of the Song of Hiawatha are melded together to form the readings and musical composition as shown.	ici sans doute un morceau de musique instrumentale.	narrated. The reading is followed by the RAVENS' CHORUS.
	[Folios 24; OC, 1:261] LA MOISSON	**No. 11—The Harvest** The reading describes the approach of Harvest Time, and introduces the
	Chœur de la Moisson	HARVEST CHORUS.

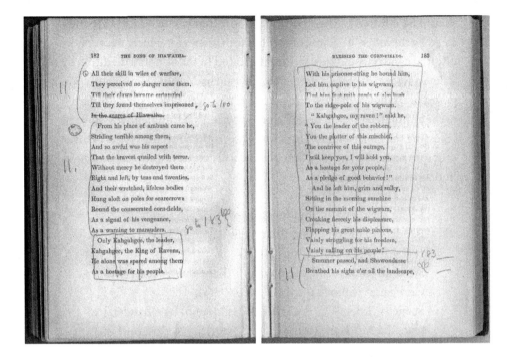

Figure 3.4. "Blessing of the Corn-Fields," pp. 182–183, showing Heron's directives, use of images for cross-referencing, and deletions. Courtesy W. T. Bandy Center for Baudelaire and Modern French Studies, Vanderbilt University. Reproduced with the kind permission of Carol Oberdorfer.

Table 3.1 shows the overall relationship of the different textual and musical components, from Longfellow's original canto—selections from which formed the basis of the narrative for which Baudelaire was charged with providing a French adaptation—through the choral and orchestral components of Stoepel's multifaceted initiative. The titles and other information are reproduced as found in the manuscript folios in the case of Baudelaire, and in the 1863 *Hiawatha* score in the case of Stoepel.

Parts of two other Longfellow cantos, "The Ghosts" (19; see fig. 3.5) and "The Famine" (20), serve to construct three parts of Baudelaire's text. Stoepel, probably in an effort to condense Longfellow's epic for his operatic score, combines material to form two scenes:

· "Winter" (Stoepel piece no. 12) corresponds to Baudelaire's "L'Hiver" (folios 26–30; *OC*, 1:262–265)

· "Minnehaha's Death" (Stoepel piece no. 13) contains thematic material found in Baudelaire's "Mort de Minnehaha" (folios 31–32; *OC*, 1:265–266) and the first part of "Lamentation d'Hiawatha" (folio 33; *OC*, 1:267)

These different components can be roughly organized as follows:

Table 3.2. Overview of textual transposition and evolution of Longfellow's original cantos 19, "The Ghosts," and 20, "The Famine," from the *Song of Hiawatha* as found in Baudelaire's adaptation and in Stoepel's musical score

Longfellow	Baudelaire	Stoepel
XIX. THE GHOSTS	[Folios 26–30; OC, 1:262–265]	**No. 12—Winter**
XX. THE FAMINE	L'HIVER	The description of the approach of Winter is read, and musically illustrated. A second reading tells of the visit of the "Ghosts of the Departed," and leads to the CHORUS OF GHOSTS, FAMINE, AND FEVER.
	Musique instrumentale	
	Chœur de fantômes	
	[Folios 31–32; OC, 1:265–266]	**No. 13—Minnehaha's Death**
Note: Designated sections from these two cantos are interwoven to produce the readings and musical score as shown.	MORT DE MINNEHAHA	The fatal sickness and death of Minnehaha are related, and succeeded by the DEATH SONG OF MINNEHAHA. The reading tells of the burial of Minnehaha, and lamentation of Hiawatha.
	Chant de Mort	
	[Folio 33; OC, 1:267] LAMENTATION D'HIAWATHA	

Two other Longfellow cantos (4, 20) are similarly dispersed to different scenes in Stoepel and in Baudelaire. Notations such as "Go to page 262 this mark" (see fig. 3.5b) are often accompanied by one of Heron's hand-drawn images for which a duplicate image is generally found on the designated page.

In spite of this elaborate system, however, Baudelaire did not always follow Heron's indications. It is not unusual to see lines of verse marked "o" in the annotated edition appear nonetheless in Baudelaire's translation, whereas entire passages designated by Heron for inclusion in the French narrative are missing in Baudelaire's manuscript (see fig. 3.6). In one instance, a section of Longfellow's canto 15 ("Hiawatha's Lamenta-

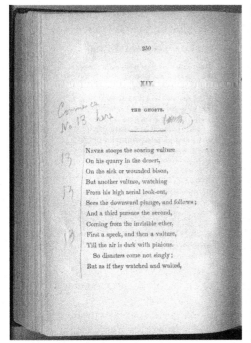
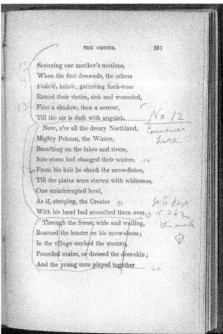

Figure 3.5. "The Ghosts," pp. 250–251. Baudelaire did not follow Heron's directive to begin No. 13 ("Mort de Minnehaha") as indicated. Courtesy W. T. Bandy Center for Baudelaire and Modern French Studies, Vanderbilt University. Reproduced with the kind permission of Carol Oberdorfer.

tions"), which was marked "out" in the annotated edition, appears as "Le Médecin" (folio 25; *OC*, 1:262) in Baudelaire's translation, which also includes the notation "un morceau de chant" near the middle of the translated passage. Yet the "morceau de chant" [sung piece] is not to be found in Stoepel's 1863 score. Even more crucially, the canto that constitutes the climax of Longfellow's poem, "Hiawatha's Departure" (22), and which appears in Baudelaire's translation (folio 34; *OC*, 1:268), is also absent from Stoepel's musical score. The composer, perhaps preferring to end the symphony on a note of renewal and hope, returned to Longfellow's idyllic description of spring located in the preceding canto (21, "The White Man's Foot"). In Stoepel's concluding section, entitled "Return of Spring," the "first budding forth of the early spring" is evoked instrumentally before the sweeping voices of the full chorus depict the

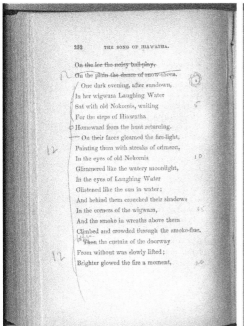
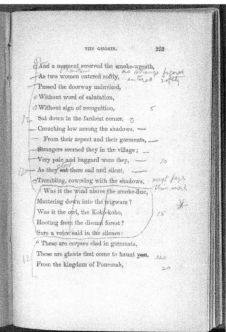

Figure 3.6. "The Ghosts," pp. 252–253. Lines marked "o" were to be omitted. The flower (p. 252) and the star (p. 251) indicate the order of the passages. Besides omitting the lines indicated, Baudelaire eliminated the entire paragraph beginning with "On their faces. . ." (p. 252). Courtesy W. T. Bandy Center for Baudelaire and Modern French Studies, Vanderbilt University. Reproduced with the kind permission of Carol Oberdorfer.

bursting forth of summer. Thirty-six measures after the beginning of the instrumental part, the word "Reading" appears, signaling the insertion of a narrative. In Baudelaire's translation, the "reading" would appear to correspond to the last paragraph of his manuscript (folio 36; *OC,* 1:268), which he dutifully added (with some alterations) in accordance with Heron's notation at the end of Longfellow's poem, "Go to page 277" (fig. 3.7), where the spring description could be found (fig. 3.8).

While Matilda Heron's notations in the *Hiawatha* edition confirm that the symphony would indeed conclude with the "Return of Spring" (fig. 3.8), it is also clear that "Hiawatha's Departure" was intended to be a part of the French libretto. In the left margin of the last page of "Hi-awatha's Departure," which is also the last page of Longfellow's poem,

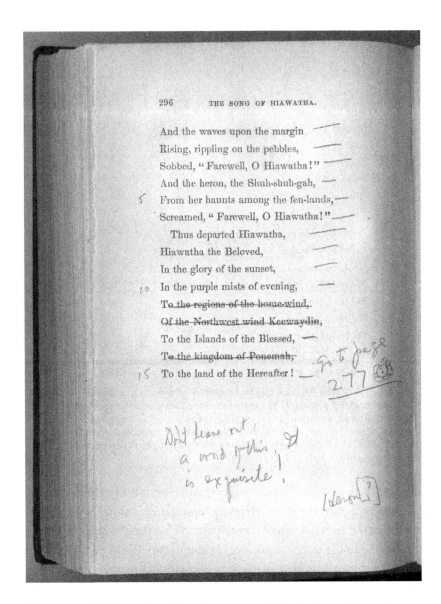

And the waves upon the margin

Rising, rippling on the pebbles,

Sobbed, " Farewell, O Hiawatha!"

And the heron, the Shuh-shuh-gah,

5   From her haunts among the fen-lands,

Screamed, " Farewell, O Hiawatha!"

Thus departed Hiawatha,

Hiawatha the Beloved,

In the glory of the sunset,

10   In the purple mists of evening,

To the regions of the home-wind,

Of the Northwest wind Keewaydin,

To the Islands of the Blessed,

To the kingdom of Ponemah,

15   To the land of the Hereafter!

Go to page 277

Don't leave out a word of this, & it is exquisite!

[Heron?]

Figure 3.7. The final lines of Longfellow's poem (p. 296) showing Heron's instructions, "Don't leave out a word of this. It is exquisite!" and the directive to return to the section depicting the arrival of spring. Courtesy W. T. Bandy Center for Baudelaire and Modern French Studies, Vanderbilt University. Reproduced with the kind permission of Carol Oberdorfer.

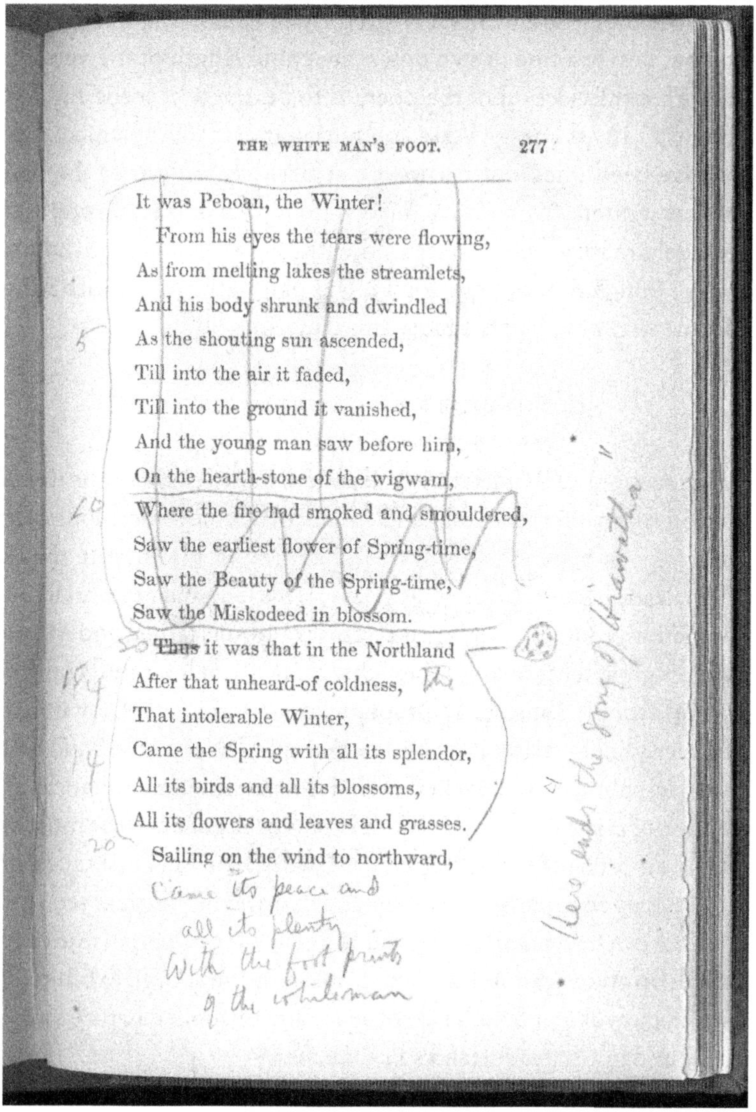

THE WHITE MAN'S FOOT. 277

It was Peboan, the Winter!
From his eyes the tears were flowing,
As from melting lakes the streamlets,
And his body shrunk and dwindled
As the shouting sun ascended,
Till into the air it faded,
Till into the ground it vanished,
And the young man saw before him,
On the hearth-stone of the wigwam,
Where the fire had smoked and smouldered,
Saw the earliest flower of Spring-time,
Saw the Beauty of the Spring-time,
Saw the Miskodeed in blossom.
~~Thus~~ So it was that in the Northland
After that unheard-of coldness,
That intolerable Winter,
Came the Spring with all its splendor,
All its birds and all its blossoms,
All its flowers and leaves and grasses.
Sailing on the wind to northward,
Came its peace and all its plenty
With the foot prints of the whiteman

"Here ends the Song of Hiawatha"

Figure 3.8. "The White Man's Foot," p. 277. The notation, "Here ends the Song of Hiawatha," shows Stoepel's symphony concluding with the arrival of spring rather than with the "Departure of Hiawatha." Courtesy W. T. Bandy Center for Baudelaire and Modern French Studies, Vanderbilt University. Reproduced with the kind permission of Carol Oberdorfer.

the number fourteen has been written three times. The numbers are spaced out beside a line drawn down the entire length of the verse, indicating that this section of the poem is to be a part of scene 14 of the symphony.[33] Three lines of verse containing Indian mythological references have been lined out. However, at the very bottom of the page, Heron has written, "Don't leave out a word of this. It is exquisite!" (fig. 3.7) Baudelaire may well have agreed with this assessment of the final stanzas of Longfellow's poem, for it is this part of the poem with which Baudelaire may have had the most empathy.

"UN AIR POÉTIQUE ET CARACTÉRISTIQUE"

In earlier sections of Baudelaire's translation, however, there are already indications of an effort to retain and enhance the epic dimensions of the original text. In Hiawatha's Odyssean-like travels, his "beauté majestueuse" [majestic beauty] (folio 7; *OC*, 1:252) ("his long and graceful figure" in Longfellow, canto 4), is admired by his traitorous father, and Minnehaha willingly assents to follow her "cher mari" [dear husband] (folio 14; *OC*, 1:256) (simply "husband" in Longfellow canto 10), thereby uniting two formerly enemy tribes. In another example, ("L'Hiver"), Baudelaire ignores Heron's instructions and includes a passage that enhances the perception of Hiawatha as "plus noble et plus beau encore" [the most noble and the most handsome] (folio 27; *OC*, 1:263). In other instances, images of vast, open expanses; of green prairies; and of the great red stone quarry that can be seen in Catlin's painting *Pipestone Quarry* (1836–1837; Smithsonian American Art Museum, Washington, D.C.), exhibited in Paris in 1845, evoke a poetic sense of space and unspoiled nature such as can be found in Chateaubriand's *Les Natchez*.[34]

Elsewhere, the poet exploits various dimensions of darkness to evoke different moods and give a sense of drama to scenes such as "L'enfance d'Hiawatha" [Hiawatha's Childhood], where "la vieille Nokomis" [the old Nokomis] tenderly nourishes the orphaned child in the safety of her wigwam, behind which looms "la noire et mélancolique forêt de pins" [the black and melancholic pine forest] (folio 4; *OC*, 1:249) (Longfellow's original text reads simply, "Dark behind it rose the forest, / Rose the black and gloomy pine-trees"; canto 3). Further on, in "L'Hiver," the whiteness of "cruel" winter paradoxically harbors dark signs announcing the imminent arrival of famine, fever, and death. This ominous feeling is evoked in the somber tones conveyed by words like "lugubre" (folio 26; *OC*, 1:262) ("dreary" in the original; canto 19) and "sinistre" (used for "dreary" but also for "ghastly"), which are used to describe winter and the vast *contrée* of the North. In "Mort de Minnehaha," Baudelaire adopts several lines of verse that had been lined out in the annotated edition to convey the unsettling feeling brought by two visitors of the night, "deux autres étrangers . . . silencieux et sinistres comme des ombres" (folio 31; *OC*, 1:266) (Longfellow writes, "two guests, as silent / As the ghosts were, and as gloomy"; canto 20), uncanny incarnations of death itself. At the other extreme, night can bring a sense of calm of the type found in the poem "Recueillement," in which the poet refers to "la douce Nuit qui marche" (*OC*, 1:140–141). At the conclusion of "Les noces d'Hiawatha," "les invités s'en allèrent, laissant Hiawatha à son bonheur, *à la douce nuit* et à Minnehaha" [Hiawatha's Wedding, the guests went away, leaving Hiawatha to his happiness, to the sweet night, and to Minnehaha] (folio 19; *OC*, 1:259, emphasis added).[35]

In all of these examples, it is important to realize that Baudelaire's translation is not a "stand-alone" text to be appreciated as a piece of literature in and of itself, but rather a piece of a multidimensional work whose different, but interconnected, parts are designed to be experienced as a living whole at the moment of performance. Unlike the translations Baudelaire undertook of Poe or the adaptation of the De Quincey text, the *Hiawatha* translation evoked for the poet little sense of identity with the author. Yet the poem offered other kinds of *correspondances* for the poetic mind. As a "doomed" figure, the Indian of North America is equated in Baudelaire's mind with dandyism, which, wrote the poet two years later, is "le dernier éclat d'héroïsme dans les décadences. . . . Le dandysme est un soleil couchant; comme l'astre qui décline, il est superbe, sans chaleur et plein de mélancolie" [the last burst of heroism in a time of decadence. . . . Dandyism is a setting sun; like the star that declines, it is superb, without heat and full of melancholy] (*OC*, 2:711–712).[36] In Longfellow's poem, the Indian-dandy analogy reaches the level of textual performance of operatic proportions in the last scene as Hiawatha bids farewell to his people and sails westward in his birch canoe to the "Land of the Hereafter," while the descending evening sun sets the clouds on "fire with redness":

> Westward, westward Hiawatha
> Sailed into the fiery sunset,
> Sailed into the purple vapors.
> Sailed into the dusk of evening. . . .
> Thus departed Hiawatha,
> Hiawatha, the Beloved,
> In the glory of the sunset
> In the purple mists of evening,
> To the regions of the home-wind
> To the Kingdom of Ponemah,
> To the Land of the Hereafter! (canto 22, "Hiawatha's Departure")

In translating, or rather *interpreting,* the final stanzas of the *Song of Hiawatha,* Baudelaire brings to the original text a melodic cadence that the singsong octosyllabic trochaic meter was incapable of rendering. The short, clipped rhythm of the last stanza of Longfellow's poem, "Thus departed Hiawatha . . .," becomes in Baudelaire's transposition:

> Ainsi s'en alla Hiawatha le Bien-aimé; ainsi il s'en alla vers la gloire du soleil couchant et les brouillards empourprés du soir, vers les régions du vent du Nord-Ouest; ainsi il s'en fut naviguant vers les Iles de la Béatitude, vers le pays d'outre-tombe!

> [Literally, Baudelaire's transposition reads as follows: . . . And so departed the Beloved Hiawatha; so he departed toward the glory of the setting sun and the purple-tinged fogs of evening, toward the regions of the Northwest wind; so he sailed off toward the Islands of the Beatitude, toward the country of the Hereafter!] (folio 35; *OC,* 1:268)

By creating ternary groupings where there were none in the original (through the addition of two "ainsi" clauses and the omission of the line "To the Kingdom of Ponemah"), and by enhancing the sense of movement through the repetition of "s'en alla" and the addition of a present participle ("s'en fut naviguant"), Baudelaire reached beyond establishing lexical equivalencies to evoke the final glorious moments of "recueillement" as the fading Indian hero begins his retreat with the coming of nightfall and the decay of advancing civilization. "L'irrésistible Nuit établit son empire" [The irresistible Night establishes its empire], writes Baudelaire in his poem, "Le coucher du soleil romantique" [The Romantic Sunset], published two years later.[37] Thus "Hiawatha's Departure"—the last canto in Longfellow's *Song of Hiawatha*—becomes in Baudelaire's "légende indienne" the last voyage of the Romantic poet-hero seeking to recover the irretrievable: the beauty and harmony of a premodern age.

In Baudelaire's adaptation of Longfellow's *Song of Hiawatha*, it is the farewell scene that reflects most closely the poet's effort to preserve in the *livret* "un air poétique et caractéristique." It is the scene that contains the best examples of the type of "expressions" and "tournures de phrase" [wording] that Baudelaire probably had in mind when he urged Stoepel "à ne rien changer à l'abrégé qu['il a] essayé de faire du poème de Longfellow" [to change nothing in the short version that he tried do of Longfellow's poem].[38] Today's readers, too, might do well to take note of Baudelaire's admonition. In attempting to understand Baudelaire's *Hiawatha* translation, it is important to keep in mind the unique combination of factors at play and not to make the text into something it is not, but rather to appreciate the poetic energy that this undertaking generated despite, or perhaps more importantly, *because of* the constraining effect of the "difficultés insurmontables" [insurmountable difficulties] imposed on Baudelaire as poet and translator.[39] More than in the case of his sensitive rendering of Poe's short stories, Baudelaire's *Hiawatha* shows the art of translation in its most challenging dimensions. The poet's struggle to transpose the majestic beauty and integrity of Longfellow's poem in the face of adverse forces can be likened to that of the artist whose study of beauty becomes "un duel où l'artiste crie de frayeur avant d'être vaincu" [a duel in which the artist screams with fear before being defeated],[40] in the prose poem "Le *confiteor* de l'artiste," which would appear just two years later.[41]

Many of Baudelaire's manuscripts that might have contributed to our understanding of the writer's genius have not survived the vicissitudes of fortune and time. Baudelaire's *Hiawatha* text offers a window on an important aspect of that genius by revealing the intimate and complex workings of poetic invention at play in the dynamic transposition process often referred to today simply as "translation."

L. CASSANDRA HAMRICK is professor of French at Saint Louis University. Her research interests include nineteenth-century French literature and the interrelationships between literature and the visual arts. She has published widely on Baudelaire and Gautier, and coedited (with Suzanne Nash) *Sculpture et Poétique. Sculpture and Literature in France, 1789–1859,* a special number of *Nineteenth-Century French Studies* (fall 2006). She is currently working on the new edition of Gautier's *Salons,* for the *Œuvres complètes.* Her critical edition of Gautier's *Salon de 1837* is a part of volume 1 in this series.

NOTES

1. The list, dated June 13, 1857, was addressed to Eugène de Broise, the associate of Baudelaire's publisher, Auguste Poulet-Malassis, in Baudelaire, *Correspondance,* 1:407 (hereafter *CPl*).
In the section of the list marked "Amérique," Longfellow's name appears just below that of journalist Nathaniel Parker Willis, who had defended Edgar Allan Poe. See also Baudelaire's *Carnet,* p. 3, in *Œuvres complètes,* 1:716 (hereafter *OC*).
In his essay "Edgar Allan Poe, sa vie et ses ouvrages" (first published in the *Revue de Paris* in March and April 1852), Baudelaire approvingly cited a letter in which the "pro-lixe auteur d'*Evangéline*"—despite having been the brunt of Poe's stinging criticism—expresses his high esteem for Poe's "puissance de prosateur et de poète." *OC,* 2:267; see also *OC,* 2:307.
2. *OC,* 1:184; see Pichois and Dupont, eds., *L'atelier de Baudelaire,* 4:3467, for an image of the manuscript page containing Baudelaire's note.
3. Longfellow himself borrowed from the original maxim of Hippocrates, "Vita brevis, ars longa," which Baudelaire reproduced in the margin of the 1851–1852 manuscript of "Le guignon." See *OC,* 1:861n1, and Pichois and Dupont, eds., *L'atelier de Baudelaire,* 3:1966. For a detailed discussion of the critical literature relating to the genesis of Baudelaire's "Le guignon" poem, see Pichois and Dupont, eds., *L'atelier de Baudelaire,* 1:167–175.
4. Alfred Engstorm is the first to point out that the source of the second "plagiarism" involving Longfellow may well be in the same book of verse as Baudelaire's "Le guignon." "Hymn to the Night," in which the "garments of the Night" sweeping through "marble halls" seem to parallel Baudelaire's own imagery in "Recueillement," immediately precedes "A Psalm of Life" in Longfellow's *Voices of the Night.* See Engstrom, "Baudelaire and Longfellow's *Hymn to the Night.*" Not mentioned by Engstorm are two of the "Crespuscule" texts (the verse poem "Le crépuscule du matin" and the prose poem "Le crépuscule du soir") in which similar textile imagery ("robes" and "draperies") can be found associated with the changing skies. James S. Patty offers another possible source for this imagery: Byron's poem "She walks in beauty, like the night." See Pichois and Dupont, eds., *L'atelier de Baudelaire,* 1:794.
5. By 1857, 43,500 copies of *Voices of the Night* had been sold, according to a notation in the poet's journal. See Cargo, "Baudelaire, Longfellow, and 'A Psalm of Night'," 198.

6. The presentation by W. T. Bandy and Claude Pichois of the documents and texts relating to Baudelaire's adaptation of *Hiawatha*—including Robert Stoepel's letters to Longfellow concerning his Hiawatha symphony—has sometimes eluded scholars; see Bandy and Pichois, "Un inédit." An abbreviated, but necessarily incomplete, account appears in *OC*, 1:1279–1282.

7. See Gartner, "New Study Examines the *Song of Hiawatha*," 1.

8. A reviewer from the *New York Times* characterized the opening performance at the Standard Theatre of a *Hiawatha* extravaganza (or "burlesque, as that once respectable word is now understood") by musician Edward Everett Rice and librettist Nathaniel Childs as an "incoherent mixture of weak trash, commonplace music, and silly horseplay." *New York Times,* February 22, 1880, 7.

9. Coleridge-Taylor's highly successful *Hiawatha* trilogy earned the composer the title "The Hiawatha Man." Known as *Scenes from the Song of Hiawatha,* the trilogy includes *Hiawatha's Wedding Feast* (1898), *The Death of Minnehaha* (1899), and *Hiawatha's Departure* (1900). See Self, *The Hiawatha Man.* It was a piano arrangement "for female or boys' voices" of *Hiawatha's Wedding Feast,* published by H. A. Chambers (London: Novello, 1934), that served as the score for Rosemary Lloyd's school production. The two-hundredth anniversary in 2007 of Longfellow's birth saw a renewal of interest and scholarship relating to the author of *Hiawatha,* including the publication of Indiana University professor of English Christoph Irmscher's *Longfellow Redux.*

10. The *Kalevala* was compiled by Elias Lönnrot from native Finnish and Karelian songs and poems. The completed version of the book was published in 1849.

11. In Longfellow's poem, Hiawatha is a mythical Indian figure inspired by Algonquin legends collected by the ethnographer Henry Rowe Schoolcraft. Longfellow. *Song of Hiawatha.*

12. While the musical score has not been found for the Karst-Miquel cantata, the program containing the libretto has survived: *Hiawatha: A Cantata,* with words by Henry W. Longfellow, vocal music by Emile Karst, and orchestral music by J. E. Miquel (St. Louis: R. P. Studley, 1858). See also Pisani, *Imagining Native America in Music,* 130.

13. The original orchestral score has not been found. In 1863, Robert Stoepel's *Hiawatha: Indian Symphony* was published as a piano score by William Hall and Son. The score was dedicated "to his friend," the virtuoso pianist Louis Moreau Gottschalk (born New Orleans, 1829; died Rio de Janeiro, 1869), whose background and interests converged to a certain extent with those of Stoepel (born Berlin, 1821; died New York, 1887). Both studied and performed in Paris, both performed before Longfellow, and both were inspired by aspects of the exotic dimension of American culture (the idyllic Native American in the case of Stoepel and the Louisiana Creole in the case of Gottschalk) in their musical endeavors. In dedicating the *Hiawatha* score to Gottschalk, Stoepel may have hoped to pique the interest of the highly acclaimed virtuoso, whose collaboration could bring him fame and fortune as a composer. On Gottschalk, see Starr, *Bamboula!* On Stoepel, see Pisani, *Imagining Native America in Music,* 126–157.

14. Matilda Heron (born Londonderry, 1830; died New York, 1877) prompted theatergoer Edmund Stedman to write in a letter dated January 30, 1857, to his mother: "'America's bright tragedienne' has at last appeared! Matilda Heron is the last wonder here. . . . She does not belong to the classic school . . . but is perfect in delineation of *common love* and *grief.* The crowded audiences are swayed, and sob like children—she is not clap-trappy—it is true, noble Art!" Stedman and Gould, *Life and Letters of Edmund Clarence Stedman,* 119.

15. "As a form of art quite novel and peculiar, to wit, the illustration of a poem, based on wild Indian life, by means of instruments and voices, with the aid of recitation, we found it deeply interesting to the end. There was a wild, romantic charm about it, entirely . . . in keeping with the poem." John Sullivan Dwight, journal dated January 15, 1859, cited in Pisani, *Imagining Native America in Music,* 134.

16. Entry for January 8, 1859, Houghton Library, Harvard University, Cambridge, Mass. Transcriptions of the passages relating to Stoepel's musical adaptation of *Hiawatha* are housed in the W. T. Bandy Center for Baudelaire and Modern French Studies, Vanderbilt University, Nashville, Tenn.

17. *OC,* 2:650, 668, 671.

18. Baudelaire to Auguste Poulais-Malassis, April 29, 1859, in *CPl,* 1:568. In his *Salon* of the same year, Baudelaire refers to Chateaubriand's *Les Natchez* to describe "l'ampleur de touche et de sentiments" of Delacroix's *Ovide en exil chez les Scythes. OC,* 2:635. The critic does not mention Delacroix's own interest in North American Indians, nor the painter's rendition of *Les Natchez,* exhibited in the *Salon de 1835.*

19. See *CPl,* 1:667, 672–674.

20. *CPl,* 1:212. Charles Asselineau notes that Baudelaire's plans for an opera in which Don Juan was to meet Catilina had long been a subject of conversation with Nector Roqueplan, director of the Paris Opera. Baudelaire was to seek the collaboration of musician Emile Douay, the same person who would have been responsible for the "traduction du chant" in Stoepel's *Hiawatha* symphony. *CPl,* 2:107. See Crépet and Crépet, *Ch. Baudelaire,* 294.

21. *CPl,* 2:107.

22. Pichois and Dupont, eds., *L'atelier de Baudelaire,* 1:859.

23. "Le Calumet de paix" and "L'Enfance d'Hiawatha," *OC,* 1:243–246. In an undated note, doubtlessly written around December 4, 1860, Baudelaire refers to the "difficultés insurmontables" caused by Stoepel's demands, which were twofold: "D'abord de réduire en trois cents vers français une matière de huit cents vers anglais, en supprimant tous les signes héroïques et *homériques,* pour ainsi dire, de l'original,—ensuite, de traduire en prose poétique le même canevas, privé de tous les mêmes avantages" [First, to reduce to three hundred lines of French verse material amounting to eight hundred lines of English verse, by eliminating all the heroic, or Homeric, elements found in the original—then translating into poetic prose the same basic structure, stripped of all the same advantages]. *CPl,* 2:109. See also note 30, below.

24. Ibid., 2:110. Stoepel's *Hiawatha* symphony would be performed at Covent Garden, London, on February 12, 1861.

25. For the relevant correspondence relating to these events, see ibid., 2:106–110, 116, 120, 149, 163, 170–171.

26. *OC,* 1:1280.

27. Baudelaire's translation of Poe's "Philosophy of Composition" ("Méthode de composition") and "The Raven" ("Le corbeau") appeared together under the title "La genèse d'un poème" in the *Revue française* (April 20, 1859) before becoming a part of *Histoires grotesques et sérieuses* (1865).

28. Poe, *Histoires grotesques et sérieuses,* 280. Just a few months later, Baudelaire observed with reference to the constraints of the sonnet as a poetic form: "Parce que la forme est contraignante, l'idée jaillit plus intense" [Because the form is so constrained, the idea springs from it more intensely]. Baudelaire to Armand Fraisse, February 18,

1860, in *CPl*, 1:676. In "Le Cadre," part 3 of Baudelaire's poem *Un fantôme,* the positive effect that a restricting framework can have on a work is again underscored. *OC*, 1:39, 902n3.

29. Gautier, "De l'application de l'art à la vie usuelle," emphasis added.

30. "Si M. Stoepel tient à ce que son livret conserve un air poétique et caractéristique, je l'engage à ne rien changer à l'abrégé que j'ai essayé de faire du poème de Longfellow, pas même dans les expressions et les tournures de phrases.—C.B." [If M. Steopel would like his libretto to retain a poetic and authentic feel, I urge him to change nothing in my abridged version of Longfellow's poem, not even the expressions and turns of phrase.—C.B.]. Undated note, *CPl*, 2:109. See also Bandy and Pichois, "Un inédit," 56–57.

31. Matilda Heron's annotations in the 1855 edition of the *Song of Hiawatha* were transcribed by Bandy in an 1856 edition containing the same page layout. The edition is housed in the W. T. Bandy Center for Baudelaire and Modern French Studies, Vanderbilt University. The present whereabouts of the original annotated edition, formerly a part of the Collection Jacques Marin, are not known. A microfilm of selected pages of the original edition annotated by Heron is also available in the Bandy Center. Due to the imperfect condition of the microfilm, the images in this article are reproductions from Bandy's transcription of Heron's original annotations. I wish to thank Yvonne Boyer, librarian, Jean and Alexander Heard Library, Vanderbilt University, and photographer Henry Shipman for their generous assistance in this undertaking. Special thanks are owed to Carol Oberdorfer, Bandy's daughter, for permission to reproduce images of the annotated edition of Hiawatha (fig. 3.3–3.8).

32. The folio numbers in Baudelaire's manuscript can be found in the text as reproduced in Bandy and Pichois, "Un inédit," 17–45.

33. The line drawn down the length of the poem and the repetition of the number 14 have been omitted on page 296 of Bandy's annotated edition (fig. 3.7).

34. The first stanza of Baudelaire's verse adaptation of "Le calumet de paix" is particularly revealing of a certain poetry of space.

35. The parallel with "la douce Nuit qui marche" in "Recueillement," dating from this same period, is noted by Bandy and Pichois, "Un inédit" 33.

36. In the "Vocabulary and Notes" appearing in an appendix at the end of Longfellow's *Song of Hiawatha*, "Yenadiz'ze" is indicated as the equivalent of an Indian dandy (316).

37. *OC*, 1:149.

38. *CPl*, 2:109; see figure 3.1 and note 30, above.

39. See note 23, above.

40. Charles Baudelaire, *The Prose Poems and La Fanfarlo,* trans. Rosemary Lloyd, 33.

41. "Le *confiteor* de l'artiste," *Le Spleen de Paris, OC*, 1:278–279. This poem appeared for the first time in *La Presse* on August 26, 1862, just two years after Stoepel abruptly left Paris.

FOUR

Migration and Nostalgia: Reflections from Contemporary Cinema

EMMA WILSON

I WANT TO BEGIN BY DRAWING ON A SHORT TEXT BY JEAN-LUC Nancy: *L'intrus* [*The Intruder*], published in 2000.[1] Nancy was commissioned to write a text about immigration, about the coming/arrival of the *étranger,* the stranger or outsider, for the review *Dédale.* He produced *L'intrus,* a text that is ostensibly an account of his experience of a heart transplant operation and ensuing illness. In Nancy's account, the physical trauma of being opened to receive what is other (and what is salutary) can be associated with a bid to open to what is other in society. For Nancy, the intruder's presence challenges us not to efface his or her strangeness: the intruder's coming is unceasing, he intrudes in his lack of familiarity, in his bringing of *dérangement,* of trouble.[2] Nancy conjures physical images—an opening of flesh—for reflecting on the sensation of opening to the other or intruder. There is in Nancy's text an intimation that this opening will be painful and that this pain brings with it a losing and a missing of the self, an exposure, a contingency, a becoming.

Nancy has written, too, about Nicolas Klotz's and Elisabeth Perceval's film *La blessure* [*The Wound*] (2004), an exploration of entry into France through the voices and perspectives of black African migrants. Blandine, one of the characters, is injured as she boards a bus, awaiting deportation at Roissy; her wound, the wound of the film's title, acquires pathos and meaning as it is tended patiently through the film. Nancy reflects on the ways in which the film operates ethically to encourage us to be attentive to a wound that remains open even as scar tissue is formed.[3] The image of opening, of the wound, recurs in his discussion of migration from the perspective of both insider and intruder. In both instances, matter, here human matter—Blandine's body, and Nancy's—is used to delay and rarefy our responses. Ian James argues that, for Nancy, "works of art, be they paintings, literary fictions, films, sculptures, musical compositions, or whatever, in their sensible materiality present to us a world or an experience that makes sense in ways not reducible to any fixed signification or order of the signified."[4] Here I argue that it is in a work's internal explorations of matter, animate and inanimate, that art can contend further with meaning complicated and rarefied by density and sensation.

My focus in this chapter is a film of 2003, *Depuis qu'Otar est parti* [*Since Otar Left*], made by Julie Bertuccelli. The director was a student of philosophy in Paris, worked as assistant director to Krzysztof Kieślowski on the *Three Colours* trilogy, and has made a number of documentaries. She speaks Russian and has worked at various times in Georgia with film director Otar Iosseliani. Although she is not an immigrant filmmaker herself, she is one of those who have brought the accents of a diasporic Europe into French cinema. *Depuis qu'Otar est parti* is her first feature film. With debts to Anton Chekhov, it is a film about three generations of women from Georgia: Eka, an elderly matriarch; her daughter Marina, who works in a flea market; and her granddaughter Ada, a student of French literature. Eka's son Otar, whose departure is named in the film's title, has left his position as a doctor in Georgia for Paris, staying in France as an illegal immigrant. He dies there in an accident on the building site where he works. Marina and Ada learn of his death but hide it from Eka, who must learn the truth later, belatedly, in Paris.

A film about migration from the former Soviet Union to Western Europe, *Depuis qu'Otar est parti* is at one remove from the questions about a colonial and postcolonial heritage conjured by a film such as *La blessure,* opening different but still complex issues about projection and exchange between two cultures. Key to thinking about these is the notion of nostalgia. In her volume *The Future of Nostalgia,* Svetlana Boym distinguishes two types of nostalgia: the restorative and the reflective. She writes, "Restorative nostalgia stresses *nostos* and attempts a transhistorical reconstruction of the lost home. Reflective nostalgia thrives in *algia,* the longing itself, and delays the homecoming—wistfully, ironically, desperately."[5] While her reminder of the etymology of the term, made up

of home and longing, is useful, through *Depuis qu'Otar est parti,* I want
to look at further gradations between restoration and reflection, further
investments in a missing or missed home. This involves discussion of the
material organization of homes and houses, as filmed by Bertuccelli, of
the installation and still lifes she creates on the various sets of the film.
From the heart and wound—material images for Nancy—I move to
different sites, the home and the ruin.

The major sections of the film take place in Georgia, filmed by the
foreigner Bertuccelli. In one of the extras on the DVD, she presents a
collection of her snapshots of Tbilisi. She has said that the plot of *Depuis
qu'Otar est parti* gave her a pretext to film in Georgia: "I wanted to make
a film a long way from home and use the distance to say something about
myself."[6] The home she films in Georgia, in turn, holds faded beauty
and eerie familiarity: it is a monument to a Georgian family's fantasies
of France. Eka speaks French at home to her granddaughter Ada; the
language becomes the conduit of their loving relationship. French volumes decorate the walls of the apartment, ordered from France by Ada's
great-grandfather. Bertuccelli explains in an interview: "Georgia is a land
which has a long tradition of links with France, though they are not well
known. Many French people have travelled there and many indeed have
settled there. There has been a constant process of exchange. Georgians
are fascinated by French culture." She continues, "I am not interested in
talking about France so much as in talking about how one comes to fall
in love with a foreign land one knows from one's imagination, with all
the potential for disillusionment that that contains."[7]

Rather than look at memories and constructions of Georgia from
an exile in France, Bertuccelli looks at the material props that actualize
fantasies of France in Tbilisi. Boym, writing about immigrant souvenirs,
has argued that "rooms filled with diasporic souvenirs are not altars to . . .
unhappiness, but rather places for communication and conversation."[8]
The same might be said of the fantasy props in the Georgian apartment,
which mediate interaction and communication in the family. Flea-mar-
ket images of Paris decorate Ada's corner in the apartment. There are
reproductions of paintings by Chardin and Renoir on the walls. Continuing this materialization of fantasy, the film shows close-ups of Ada

reading from Apollinaire's *Calligrammes* by candlelight. She is also heard reading aloud to her grandmother from Proust. In Bertuccelli's film, three women dream of Paris; they long for an elected homeland. They attempt to restore a place imagined but not yet lost. This is the place associated with their love for their missing relative, Otar.

Otar himself is entirely absent from the film; his presence is felt liminally in Georgia through telephone calls and the letters he sends from France. A large photograph of him is present in the family apartment in Tbilisi; since he is a traveler in France, his image is displayed among the French memorabilia of the set. But he lives and dies virtually unwitnessed, or witnessed only virtually in the film; the only access we have to the spaces and matter of his experience is in a journey to France by his elderly mother who travels in search of him, unwittingly confronting her fantasies of Paris with the city's immigrant actuality. In her search for him, she walks through the spaces he would have known, finding the imprint of his anterior presence and his state and mind in the material, the bricks and mortar, of the space where he has existed.

Writing on what he terms "accented cinema," Hamid Naficy offers a taxonomy of such cinema of exile and displacement. He lists narrative techniques—the multilingual, the epistolary, for example—yet more materially, he lists particular settings found in such films, speaking of "the important transitional and transnational places and spaces, such as borders, tunnels, seaports, airports, and hotels and vehicles of mobility, such as trains, buses, and suitcases."[9] I want to add to his list a different unhomely place: the apartment block, the house, housing estates, in states of dilapidation. I am interested in the meanings about migration and nostalgia that are collected together in these material images. Immigrant dwellings in France are notoriously precarious, offering a distressingly material form for the lack of care and value for this part of the community. I think of the fires in the multiple occupancy dwellings in Paris in the summer of 2005, of the displacements from the derelict university buildings to the Gymnase de Cachan in 2006. Recognition of this underlines the testimonial status of cinema treating this topic. Yet there seems more elaborate or indirect expressivity in the image too. The precarious homeplace offers a material image of an existence in exile, an embodiment of nostalgia (home and longing), homesickness, homelessness imprinted in desultory, dilapidated spaces. The home is emptied out, is empty and unhomely.

A further irony here is the frequent involvement of illegal immigrant workers, as illustrated, too, in *Depuis qu'Otar est parti*, in construction work: physical labor is devoted to building homeplaces away from home. Different precarious physical structures are literally and symbolically shown to dominate the waking and sleeping lives of the migrants represented. The transient spaces of immigrant Paris offer no safety or sanctuary. The unhomely home of the apartment building, its scratched and fragile fabric, through which we pass in an affective and sensory voyage through the film, gives no direct access to the pain of the films' protagonists and the disenfranchised groups they represent. Yet some delusion of reference or purchase is entertained for a time, some hint of sensory knowledge or recollection with the power to trigger fellow feeling, or response. In showing such material existences, filmmakers—Bertuccelli, the brothers Dardenne, Nicolas Klotz, Michael Haneke, and others[10]—offer, in the imagined contexts of their films, material that may bear some imprint of the psychical and physical pain of homelessness and displacement. Indeed, Laura Marks argues aptly that "intercultural cinema is in a position to sort through the rubble created by cultural dislocation."[11]

Eka takes a route into an immigrant Parisian space in her search for a live Otar. Bertuccelli roots the film in the 18th Arrondissement and its material signs: the fabric shop Reine and the clothing store Tati. Eka seeks here to enter the spaces that Otar has known, spaces for which his tourist commentaries on Paris have by no means prepared her. The Paris she visits here is not familiar to her. The camera imitates her surveillant gaze, disclosing what Otar has hidden in letters home. Within the corridors of the apartment building, you see her systematic moves from door to door, her repeated and frustrated attempts to gain access giving form, in nightmare fashion, to her growing awareness of the reality of Otar's absence. As she rises through the building, its state is gradually more derelict, the peeling paint and plaster of the stairway marking out the space as fissured and unhomely. These walls, the spiral of the staircase where Eka stands dwarfed, familiar settings from present-day Paris, inserted into the folds of her narrative, serve incrementally to intimate Eka's increasing despair and the move to dereliction in Otar's previous life in Paris. That he should be entirely absent from the film, and that Eka's own emotions remain opaque and enigmatic, enhances a sense that the knowledge we glean of their pain is found indirectly in the matter that surrounds them. The film's spaces are pregnant with their feelings. Otar's presence seems still to haunt his apartment block: his viewpoint remains as we catch a subjective high-angle shot of Eka in the courtyard below. When she learns of Otar's death, she refuses to enter the room of the man who makes her new dispossessed state apparent to her. She sits alone on the stairs. Later she is seen, again alone, in the disaffected, public spaces of the city, beneath and then beside the geometrical frames of the métro aérien, overhead and high-angle shots reminding us of our distance from her. In its filming of different netherworlds in contemporary Paris, despite its realism, *Depuis qu'Otar est parti* explores the ways in which places and settings may be made companion objects to unspoken and inexpressible feelings.

Eka's pain and her knowledge remain largely opaque; this is an advantage to the film that, while immersing us in her experience—and Otar's—still reminds us of our ignorance. After her lone excursion into a nightmare Paris, an underworld of vertiginous scale and perspective, and back into the bosom of her family, Eka, against all expectation, will invent a convenient fiction. This is a moment where the screenplay differs from the completed film: in the screenplay she finishes her fantasy of Otar's survival with the words, "and now I want to go home." The film, with more complexity, shows her using the fiction of Otar's survival to support her bid to discover the tourist Paris of her Francophile dreams—to discover the place for which she has always been homesick. Love of Paris here, in which the three women now indulge, depends on a disavowal of the brutal reality of Otar's death, on covering over the brutal matter of the city where Otar has lived and died. Buoyed by her lie about Otar, Eka can open a space of beauty and relief. Whether the lie is to comfort herself, to protect her relatives, or simply to delay knowledge of Otar's death, it is convenient in allowing pleasure as well as mourning and in keeping open not the wound, as in *La blessure,* but the longing that may impel migration.

Delaying Otar's death, the film presents a palliative collage of shots of the city. Bertuccelli stitches together locations: the Paris visited is a space of monuments, spectacle, culture, and luxury. By showing real locations and shop signs, Bertuccelli points to the fact that there are material referents for the dreams of these three women. Despite Otar's failure and death, the fantasy of Paris persists. At the end of the film, Ada, with Eka's help, chooses to remain in Paris. Eka's connivance raises the specter that the trip to France, for which Eka has had to sell all her French books, has never really been a trip to find Otar; it may always already have been a trip to set Ada free in the city of her fantasies. It seems puzzling that Ada should be delivered by Eka to the country that has removed Otar. Or maybe the film is more realistic and less clear-cut; with her language skills and culture, Ada may find a home in France. Through the film, shots of the cities in France and Georgia have recalled one another materially. This is achieved through the internal rhymes of the images and returning tactics of framing. Bertuccelli has let no clear hierarchy between France and Georgia emerge, yet in its sensitivity toward the longing for an elsewhere, for an elected home, the film does not discard the migrant fantasy that may impel us, Francophiles all.

Mieke Bal writes on nostalgia: "This sentiment has often been criticised as unproductive, escapist, and sentimental; it is considered regressive, romanticizing, the temporal equivalent of tourism and the search for the picturesque." But, she continues, "nostalgia can also promote combativity and bring comfort at the same time."[12] Bertuccelli risks sentimentality in her shots of Paris: the colored lights, the Christmas music Ada hears from the taxi. Yet, after the melancholy of Otar's loss and the film's painstaking attention to the cavity of his past dwelling, after our involvement in this, such a reprieve is doubly sweet. Where Nancy embraces the intruder who brings both pain and health, Bertuccelli shows nostalgia as a strategy of disavowal, as a means of pain management. Where the matter of the city may bear the imprint of migrant pain, its facades may also still be clothed in fantasy generated through distance and longing, and so reenchanted. In this sense, I see her approach as comforting, yet as combative too, as she involves herself and her viewer in the film's projections, as she imbricates fantasies of inside and intruder, as she makes any fixed sense of home recede.

EMMA WILSON is professor of French literature and the visual arts at the University of Cambridge. She is the author of *Love, Mortality and the Moving Image, Atom Egoyan, Alain Resnais, Cinema's Missing Children, Memory and Survival: The French Cinema of Krzysztof Kieslowski, French Cinema since 1950: Personal Histories,* and *Sexuality and the Reading Encounter.* She is currently working on a project on the reclining nude in the work of contemporary female visual artists.

NOTES

1. Nancy, *L'intrus.*

2. Ibid., 11–12.

3. Nancy, "La blessure—la cicatrice," 119.

4. James, *The Fragmentary Demand,* 205.

5. Boym, *The Future of Nostalgia,* xviii.

6. Zeitgeist Films, Pressbook for *Depuis qu'Otar est parti* (2003).

7. Ibid.

8. Boym, *The Future of Nostalgia,* 336.

9. Naficy, *An Accented Cinema,* 5.

10. See, for example, Luc and Jean-Pierre Dardenne, *La promesse* [*The Promise*] (1996), Michael Haneke, *Code inconnu* [*Code Unknown*] (2000) and *Caché* [*Hidden*] (2005), and Nicolas Klotz, *La blessure* (2004).

11. Marks, *The Skin of the Film,* 28.

12. Bal, *Quoting Caravaggio,* 71–72.

PART TWO
CROSS-TEXTUAL
TRANSPOSITIONS

FIVE

Parisian Decors: Balzac, the City, and the Armchair Traveler

MICHAEL TILBY

I

In this chapter our concern is with translating the city—to be specific, with Honoré de Balzac's translation of Paris into an overtly fictional entity; with the conscious and, indeed, self-conscious nature of that activity; and with its effects and implications. My principal focus is on certain texts from the mid-1830s in which Paris first established itself as the author's predominant concern, and which remain widely identified with their bravura descriptions of the French capital, namely *Le père Goriot, Melmoth réconcilié, Gambara,* and (especially) *Ferragus* and *La fille aux yeux d'or.* Interestingly, however, not all of these works were securely assigned by Balzac to his *Scènes de la vie parisienne.* Within this group of novels and stories, to which *Facino Cane* also clearly belongs, the primordial status of *Ferragus* was duly emphasized by Blaise Cendrars, who observed that the first of Balzac's *Histoire des Treize* narratives sketches "le plan psychologique, anatomique, physique, mécanique, économique de ce Paris moderne qui tiendra tant de place dans son œuvre" [the psychological, anatomical, physical, mechanical, and economic outline of a new, modern Paris that will become central to his writing], and may thus be regarded as "le prototype du récit balzacien et le premier en date de ses grands livres" [the prototype of the Balzacian narrative and the first of his major works].[1] Yet this was, equally, a period when Balzac added numerous passages on Paris to revised versions of his earlier fictions.[2]

To a certain extent, Paris imposed itself as a focus for the novelist's attention by virtue of the effects of the expansion of its population in the years following Waterloo. Georges Duby states that the city doubled in size between 1800 and 1850, by which time its population numbered more than a million, though Claude Pichois quotes figures suggesting that it had reached almost 900,000 by 1836.[3] This growth, coupled with the influx of visitors encouraged by improved modes of transport and by the administrators' concern to record the city's development in terms of unprecedentedly accurate and statistical detail, led not only to a vogue for guidebooks such as Jean-Baptiste-Augustin d'Aldéguier's *Le flâneur; ou, Mon voyage à Paris* of 1825 or Jean-Marie-Vincent Audin's *Le véritable conducteur parisien de Richard* of 1828,[4] but also to an obsessive concern with the city on the part of a new breed of *littérateurs* who fed the population with prolific examples of a "panoramic" literature (to use Walter Benjamin's influential term).[5] At the same time, Paris represented not merely a picturesque or specialist choice of subject for a reader who sought to be entertained or instructed, but a means by which the city-dweller could make existential sense of his relationship to an increasingly unfamiliar world. On the other hand, consciousness of the changing urban environment gave a new importance to the city's past and brought the need to inventory those streets and buildings that were beginning to disappear. As Balzac himself observes in "Ce qui disparaît de Paris," a piece he contributed to *Le diable de Paris* in 1845, "Encore quelques jours, et les Piliers des Halles auront disparu, le vieux Paris n'existera plus que dans les ouvrages des romanciers assez courageux pour décrire fidèlement les derniers vestiges de l'architecture de nos pères; car, de ces choses, l'historien grave tient peu de compte" [It will only be a few days before the "Piliers des Halles" disappear. The Paris of yore will exist solely in the works of those novelists who have the will to depict with accuracy the last vestiges of the architecture of our forefathers, since the serious-minded historian cares but little for such things].[6]

This historical representation of Paris is immediately recognizable as the context for the *Comédie humaine,* both in terms of what Balzac describes and in relation to his own prior participation in "panoramic" writing. His depictions of Paris in his fiction of the mid-1830s incontrovertibly provide the reader with an informative view of Parisian topography, one in which an individual character's *déplacements* possess, moreover, strong socioeconomic significance. It is sufficient to turn for illustration to Jeanine Guichardet's tracing of the Parisian itineraries undertaken by his various characters.[7] It is likewise from a socioeconomic perspective that Franco Moretti argues, "Instead of protecting the novel from the complications of Paris, he [Balzac] sees them as a fantastic *opportunity* for narrative structure: for the novel of complexity," the latter being defined in terms of "composite interactions."[8]

Yet, while it may look as if the reader of Balzac's Parisian novels is being guided, more or less straightforwardly, through the streets of the capital by the author and his narrator, to conclude that this is overridingly the case is to imply that the authorial/narratorial function is to provide indications in the manner of an authoritative *cicerone,* which is, in turn, to make a one-dimensional assumption about the status of observation in Balzac's fictions, when there is much within the compositions themselves to suggest a concern to highlight the problematical nature of such an activity.[9] When, for example, at the end of *Ferragus,* Desmarets and Jacquet come to the Père-Lachaise Cemetery (which, as Priscilla Ferguson points out, is in many ways Paris in microcosm[10]), they find, "comme à la porte des spectacles ou à l'entrée des musées, comme dans la cour des diligences, des *ciceroni* qui s'offrirent à les guider dans le dédale du Père-Lachaise" [as at the entrance to theaters and museums, or the stagecoach terminus, *ciceroni* clamoring to act as guides to the maze that is Père-Lachaise]. It is nonetheless emphasized that it was "impossible, à l'un comme à l'autre, de savoir où gisait Clémence" [impossible for either of them to discover where Clémence lay buried].[11] Jacquet eventually receives directions from the garrulous *portier,* but the latter is inclined to give priority to certain "novelistic" scenarios suggested by various anecdotal details that have caught his eye, rather than to the purely administrative information that he has been asked to supply. Visitors and porter alike are caught in a space where fact and fiction are seen as competing, and where neither element is able to give satisfaction, and where for the situation to be resolved, there is a need for cooperation between the two realms.[12] Given the visual image Balzac employs to depict the cemetery, it is also significant that the terms *dédale* and *labyrinthe* are frequently used in his writing with reference to cerebral complexities.[13] This serves to remind us that the *Études philosophiques* and the *Scènes de la vie parisienne* evolve together and, indeed, interact as categories. If stories such as *Sarrasine* and *Facino Cane* move between these categories, it is precisely because they do not belong exclusively within either. As for the reutilization in *La fille aux yeux d'or* of descriptive pieces originally published in the press, such a process provides an indication of the way the text is generically unstable and a further product of the oscillation between the fictional and nonfictional.[14]

On a general level, the Parisian tableaux in *Histoire des Treize* are more poetic than novelistic, to the point, arguably, of disturbing the aesthetic economy of the composition. Thus, instead of assuming the role of *cicerone* or *flâneur,* Balzac, as has already been intimated, can be seen to embark on a *fictionalization* of Paris, on what Italo Calvino has called, with specific reference to *Ferragus,* the author's endeavor to "far diventare romanzo una città" [transform the city into a novel].[15] The process consists of two parts. First, and more straightforwardly, there is the way the city is represented as an imaginary or textual entity. Second, there is the way its representation develops in relation to the reader, who is consciously inscribed in the text as a reader of fiction. I aim to demonstrate not only that Balzac's Paris is determined by the needs of the fiction but that the latter incorporates an implicit reflection on this fact, thereby intensifying both the fictionality itself and the reader's impression that "tout se tient" (to a remarkable degree, given the Balzacian passion for incidental detail).

II

The most obvious facet of Balzac's fictionalization of Paris in the early to mid-1830s is apparent in the way his new interest in the complex reality of the French capital is interwoven, in seemingly contradictory fashion, with a late flourishing of the adventure story format of his early, pseudonymous fiction. In *Ferragus,* the city is notably described as "la ville aux cent mille romans" [the city of a hundred thousand novels].[16] The invention of the Treize, with their background in crime and violence, and the related introduction of Vautrin in *Le père Goriot,* together present a continuation of Argow, the former pirate-convict whose story the young Balzac had told in *Le vicaire des Ardennes* and *Annette et le criminel.* As Paule Petitier has observed, "*Ferragus* est une sorte de roman gothique transposé dans le cadre de la ville moderne" [*Ferragus* is a kind of gothic novel transposed to a modern urban setting].[17] In the preface to *Histoire des Treize*, Balzac says of his secret society that it was "curieuse, autant que peut l'être le plus noir des romans de Mme Radcliffe" [as mysterious as the darkest of Mrs. Radcliffe's novels].[18] Maturin's Melmoth is highlighted in the same preface, and it is to this figure that the bereaved Ferragus is in due course compared. What is important from the present perspective is the fact that for Maulincour, whose "tête éminemment romanesque" [storybook hero's profile] looks forward to the character of the altogether more impressive figure of de Marsay in *La fille aux yeux d'or* (where he is specifically depicted as a connoisseur of the sensations procured by Radcliffe's fictions[19]), the Paris streets become dangerous locations,[20] whether he goes on foot or by carriage, since the *Chef des Dévorants* ensures from behind the scenes that building materials fall from the sky and carriage axles break at high speed.[21] Streets in this novel are not for nothing dubbed "meurtrières" [murderous] or "assassines" [treacherous].

In both *Ferragus* and *La fille aux yeux d'or*, as well as in *Le père Goriot* and, to a lesser extent, *Gambara* (where it is the exile Marcosini's political beliefs that arouse suspicion), the language of crime and its investigation is prominent, thereby revealing in embryo the intrinsic link between the city and the detective novel. At the same time, contact is established with historical reality through certain unmistakable echoes in these novels of the figure of Vidocq. If Maulincour's *flânerie* is reminiscent of the spy or detective (Ferragus indeed asks him outright whether he is a spy), his keenness to locate an appropriate *observatoire* recalls the practice associated with the evidence-gathering and arrests carried out by Vidocq. Maulincour is duly portrayed in terms of his attempts to resurrect the reality of the situation, the activity being compared to the wooden puzzle known as a "casse-tête chinois" [Chinese puzzle].[22] He is not unobservant, as the description of the apartment in the rue Soly implies, but the terms in which his inexperience is described nonetheless recall, through implicit comparison, the way in which Vidocq invariably proceeded with much greater success: "Novice en ce métier, il n'osait questionner ni le portier, ni le cordonnier de la maison dans laquelle venait Mme Jules" [Being a novice in this profession, he neglected to question either the porter or the cobbler in the building visited by Madame Jules].23 It is indeed as "Mme Jules" that Clémence Desmarets is mostly identified, which would seem an evident, if (in view of her high moral standards) ironic, reminder that Vidocq's nickname among "la pègre" [the criminal fraternity] was ... Monsieur Jules (as her stockbroker husband is himself designated, albeit to a lesser extent).24

It is, however, Ferragus himself who, in advance of Vautrin, most evidently recalls the example of Vidocq through, variously, his ambivalent position with regard to crime; his name Bourignard (in which it is just possible to see the word *bagnard* [convict]); his disguises; his use of pseudonyms; and, not least, his (un-Vautrin-like) skirt-chasing.25 He is more than a match for the police enquiries made at Maulincour's instigation,26 with regard to which Balzac, teasingly but in accordance with an "alibi-procedure" he uses elsewhere in the *Comédie humaine*, has the "sous-chef de police" claim that they will be conducted with the assistance of "Vidocq et ses limiers" [sleuths].27 Ferragus may well also be linked to Vidocq at another level, through the prominent reference to the rue Fromenteau in the tableau that constitutes the opening of the novel.28 The author of *Histoire de Vidocq écrite d'après lui-même* (1830) is one Froment, an "ex-chef de brigade du Cabinet particulier du Préfet," who in the same year published *La police dévoilée depuis la Restauration*. The connection is especially noteworthy because the author of a contemporary work that complained of the discretion displayed by Paris porters (*Le livre noir de MM Delavau et Franchet*, 1829) was one ... Desmarets.29 Also, later, when the author of *Les comédiens sans le savoir* needed an *état-civil* for a police spy, he chose the name Fromenteau.30

It is, however, also the case that Balzac's representation of Paris in the mid-1830s combines two opposing types of focus, a combination that can be seen to relate, in turn, to the fictionalization of the city. On one hand, there is a concern with the specific, the individual, the identifiable, the nameable, that is to say, with elements that purport to be the product of direct observation but which, in fact, associate seeing with a self-reflexive, interpretative activity. In contrast, the celebrated tableaux of Paris are concerned with Paris in its Protean entirety, a location that requires "une âme multiple" [a multiple soul], a capacity to embrace "mille passions ... mille sentiments" [a thousand passions or feelings].31

The city is, in other words, evoked in terms of an oscillation between what is seen and what cannot be seen. In this, it relates to the fiction itself, especially in respect of the unseen forces at work in *Histoire des Treize* and the elusive morality of the various members of the "secret society," who abide by a moral code in displaying loyalty to each other (and, in the case of Ferragus himself, paternal devotion) while not shrinking from murder, thereby representing a variation on the stock Romantic figure of the "noble bandit."[32] These figures, are, likewise, both seen and not seen; they are sometimes identifiable behind the simple reference to "l'inconnu," sometimes not. The opening description of the character of Ferragus is noteworthy for the fact that the extensive prose is devoted to what he does not resemble. The attempt to sum him up is made through the simple, negative definition: "Un type nouveau frappé en dehors de toutes les idées réveillées par le mot de mendiant" [A type wholly without precedent and whose cast incorporates not one of the familiar features evoked by the word "beggar"].[33]

Similarly, the Protean city entertains a reciprocal relationship with its various representatives: not only, for example, the *grisette* in *Ferragus* of whom it is said "elle personnifie trop bien Paris" [she personifies Paris only too well], but also the *mercier* in *La fille aux yeux d'or*. The latter, who doubles as a *basse-taille* in the Opéra chorus, is described as "le protée de la civilisation" [civilization's Proteus], and it is said of him, "cet homme résume tout" [this individual embodies the summary of everything]. De Marsay, a figure of significantly ambiguous sexuality, makes it clear to Paquita that he is bound to the city and cannot leave. The fiction requires an explanation in terms of an oath sworn by "Les Treize," but at another level, he is unable to leave because he and the city are one. Ferragus, for his part, is depicted as the Protean actor. As Justin conveys in his report to Maulincour, his grandmother and the vidame de Pamiers, "il . . . se déguise comme un acteur" [he employs an actor's disguises].[34] He possesses, in reality, a seemingly excessive number of "Christian" names with varying connotations, but is nonetheless merely the twenty-third of what one may suppose to be a still more Protean "dynasty."[35] If his disguises allow him to blend into strikingly diverse locations within the city, the fiction also requires both Maulincour and Madame Jules to seek recourse in disguise. This relates, more generally, to a recurrent emphasis in the novel on uncertain identity and illegitimacy. (Madame Jules is sired outside wedlock by Ferragus, while there is more than a hint to suggest that Ida Gruget is illegitimate and well-placed to continue the tradition up until the moment of her suicide.[36]) Characters are invariably shown to be both known and unknowable. Hypotheses in relation to them are encouraged yet never fully confirmed.

Attention is, moreover, drawn extensively to the fact that the city is, for all its precise references to verifiable topography, an artificial construct. Prominent is a cultivated sense of the mythical. The evocation of Paris in *La fille aux yeux d'or* in terms redolent of Dante's *Inferno* is too well known to require reproduction. The explicit emphasis in *Ferragus* on Paris as a monster, alongside a portrayal of the city, in accordance with contemporary convention, as "cette grande courtisane" [this great courtesan], is again familiar, but it leads Pierre Citron to remark that it is thus set to attract either a Hercules or a Don Quixote.[37] This immediately evokes a notion of narrative, not least when Balzac's emphasis on Paris as a labyrinth is recalled. Equally, the epithet "quixotic" might be considered to fit the behavior of a number of the smitten male characters in the texts under consideration: Maulincour, de Marsay, Montriveau in *La duchesse de Langeais*, and, above all, Marcosini in *Gambara*, who takes it upon himself to rescue Signora Gambara from her husband, though it is of Ferragus that it is said, "Il ressemblait tout à la fois à Voltaire et à don Quichotte" [He resembled at one and the same time Voltaire and Don Quixote].[38] It is striking that in all these cases, the Quixote figure inflicts acute distress or worse on the "damsel" he seeks to liberate. The extent to which Paris is a realm that invites a quixotic response is further confirmed when Vautrin, in *Le père Goriot*, announces, "Je suis comme don Quichotte, j'aime à prendre la défense du faible contre le fort" [I am like Don Quixote. I delight in defending the weak against the strong].[39] Needless to say, the Quixotic is not present here in a pure strain. One might, indeed, in shorthand talk of Cervantes meeting "le roman noir" in these fictions.[40]

Paris exists likewise in these texts as a theatrical decor of artificial confection. Following on seamlessly from his practice in *Ferragus*, Balzac's depiction of Marcosini in the first section of *Gambara* possesses an abundance of theatrical characteristics, not only with regard to costume and movement but also in terms of the way the setting is described.[41] In the case of *Ferragus*, the central role accorded to characters named "Auguste" and "Clémence" recalls, irresistibly, Corneille's *Cinna*, which, as Petitier has suggested, allows the novel to be read as "un anti-*Cinna*."[42] In the same novel, Justin is referred to as "un vieux Figaro retiré" [an ancient Figaro now in retirement] and "ce Scapin émérite" [this emeritus Scapin], just as his equivalent in *La fille aux yeux d'or*, Laurent, is both compared to Figaro and seen as a "garçon rusé comme un Frontin de l'ancienne comédie" [a cunning lad, like Frontin in one of the ancient comedies]. Desmarets, having noted the incriminating evidence of Clémence's rain-spotted hat, insists that he does not wish "faire ici le Bartholo" [to play the Bartholo here]. In *La fille aux yeux d'or*, de Marsay is depicted as "leste comme Chérubin" [sprightly as Cherubino]. Details in the description of the exterior of the Pension Vauquer reveal the extent to which the view from the street offers a scene conceived in terms of a reflexive painted decor: "Pendant le jour, une porte à claire-voie, armée d'une sonnette criarde, laisse apercevoir au bout du petit pavé, sur le mur opposé à la rue, une arcade peinte en marbre vert par un artiste du quartier. Sous le renfoncement que simule cette peinture, s'élève une statue représentant l'Amour" [During the day, a wicket gate with a shrill bell attached permitted the observer to glimpse, at the end of a little path, on a wall facing the street, a green marble arch painted by some local artist. In the painter's illusionary niche was set a Cupid in the form of a statue].[43]

The artifice also takes other forms. In *Ferragus*, Paris is seen, multifacetedly, in aquatic terms, starting with the evocation of the "île saint Louis" as a Parisian Venice.[44] The rue Montmartre, together with other streets of similar shape, is likened to a mermaid.[45] The associations continue with the reference to "le dernier frétillement des dernières voitures de bal" [the last wriggle of the last carriages returning from a ball] and the simile "comme les membranes d'un grand homard" [like the membranes of a giant lobster].[46]

There is a parallel emphasis in *Ferragus* on the "marécages parisiens" [Parisian marshlands] at the heart of the capital.[47] The Marais [Marsh] is a key location in the novel, with many of the principal figures being brought together, highly theatrically, in the shabby apartment-house that is home to the "widow" Gruget. As for the hapless Jules Desmarets, his name was originally spelt by Balzac "Des*marais*." The street highlighted in the opening tableau is the rue Froment*eau*. Water, which, as Bachelard has shown, possesses a strong function in Balzac's *imaginaire*, notably in *Séraphîta* and *L'enfant maudit*,[48] unites ground and sky in *Ferragus*, which could certainly lay claim to being "un roman pluvieux" [a rainy novel], even though the events take place in what would, in the Revolutionary calendar, have been the month of "ventôse." Maulincour and other pedestrians shelter, in the rue Coquillière, from a downpour that is compared to "les cascatelles de Saint-Cloud" [the Saint-Cloud cascades].[49] Foreshadowing the reference in *La fille aux yeux d'or* to the origin of Lutetia,[50] the street's surface becomes a stream of black, white, blue, and green water, as the *portière* sweeps all kinds of domestic detritus into its path.[51] Figuratively, the crowd in *Ferragus* is referred to as "[le] torrent de Paris" [the Parisian torrent].[52] As for the figure of the apparently landlocked *grisette*, who enjoys such a prominent evocation in *Ferragus*, she has been linked to the description of Paris with which the novel opens and been shown to be presented by Balzac in terms of an aqueous metaphor, as both "un produit filtré" [a filtered product] and "une nymphe ou une sirène insaisissable" [an elusive nymph or siren].[53] Significantly, the figures Balzac compares to his "Thirteen" are both pirates: Morgan and Trelawney, the alleged original of Byron's *Corsair* and the author of the recently translated *Mémoires d'un gentilhomme corsaire*.[54] When it is said of the former: "Morgan, l'Achille des pirates, se fit, de ravageur, colon tranquille" [Morgan, the Achilles of the pirate world, from being a marauder became a peace-loving settler], the motif of retirement from crime links the figure to both Argow the pirate (who becomes a banker) and Vautrin. Balzac duly picks up the pirate motif in *La maison Nucingen*, where the dining raconteurs are depicted as "quatre des plus hardis cormorans éclos dans l'écume qui couronne les flots incessamment renouvelés de la génération présente.... D'ailleurs braves à fumer, comme Jean Bart, leur cigare sur une tonne de poudre" [four of the most fearless cormorants ever hatched from the foam atop the relentless tidal waves of the present generation. . . . Moreover, ready, like Jean Bart, to smoke a cigar astride a powder keg].[55]

Most significant of all is the way in which the evocation of Paris in maritime terms in *Ferragus* constitutes a manifest translation of the city's coat of arms and motto: *Fluctuat nec mergitur* [though tossed by the waves, she does not sink]. In the tableau that sees the city as a vast building site, the narrator says of the scaffolding: "Il y a quelque chose de maritime dans ces mats, dans ces échelles, dans ces cordages, dans les cris des maçons" [There is something of the maritime about these masts, ladders, rigging, and building workers' cries]. It is significant that the figure whose identity Ferragus assumes is depicted as "le marin qu'ont mangé les poissons" [the sailor devoured by the fish], for it is clear that he has, to date, acquired considerable success in turning the tables on the ocean that is Paris. A related act of translation is responsible for the expansive and animated metaphor that forms part of the celebrated prologue to *La fille aux yeux d'or* and which incorporates the oft-quoted rhetorical question, "Paris n'est-il pas un sublime vaisseau chargé d'intelligence?" [Is not Paris a sublime vessel freighted with intelligence?][56]

Finally, the fictionalization of the city also proceeds in function of an explicit awareness of the reader in his armchair, the figure famously apostrophized in *Le père Goriot* as "vous qui tenez ce livre d'une main blanche, vous qui vous enfoncez dans un moelleux fauteuil en vous disant: 'Peut-être ceci va-t-il m'amuser'" [you who hold this book in your lily-white hand, you who are ensconced in the comfortable hollows of an armchair and confide to yourself: "Perhaps this will be an agreeable way of passing the time"].[57] The implicit inscription of a reflection on the reader's situation is manifest in the diversity that characterizes the representation of the armchair traveler in other of Balzac's Parisian compositions from this period. The figure's gender, for example, already uncertain in the apostrophe from *Le père Goriot,* has a clear capacity to vary. In *Ferragus,* the terms in which *flânerie* is introduced by way of a rhetorical question restrict it to being an appeal to the experience of the male reader: "À qui n'est-il pas arrivé de partir, le matin, de son logis pour aller aux extrémités de Paris, sans avoir pu en quitter le centre à l'heure du dîner?" [Who is there who has not set out from his residence in the morning intent on making for the extremities of Paris only to have not detached himself from the center by the hour of dinner?]. On the other hand, the reference

on the same page to "certaines maisons, inconnues pour la plupart aux
personnes du grand monde, dans lesquelles une femme appartenant à ce
monde ne saurait aller sans faire penser d'elle les choses les plus cruelle-
ment blessantes" [certain dwelling houses of which high society mostly
has no inkling and to which a lady who is of that society may not betake
herself without provoking the most cruel and offensive observations in
the minds of others] clearly has the needs of the female reader in mind,
implying that the street and its buildings are outside her experience.[58]
(One is reminded of the celebrated admonition "les dames n'entrent
pas ici" [ladies should proceed no further] of the *Physiologie du mariage*
and, more generally, of the extent to which it is, above all, in relation to
its *lectrices* that the Balzacian novel is keen to exert an illicit attraction.)
It is, thus, for the female armchair traveler that Madame Jules, suitably
disguised on her visits to the rue Soly, serves as a proxy. The perspective
of the social geographer is, in more than one sense of the phrase, only
half the story.

In other cases, the implied reader is less obviously gendered, though
the evocation of the city is nonetheless presented with the reader's specific status as a reader of fiction in mind. The central location in *Ferragus*
and *Gambara* is both central (the little streets around the Palais-Royal)
and at once peripheral, sordid and (fictionally) exotic. The emphasis
is on their inaccessibility (in some cases, there is, explicitly, no access
for *fiacres*,[59] thereby making the street in question still less penetrable
than the rue Neuve-Sainte-Geneviève in *Le Père Goriot*), but also on
their darkness and dampness. Rather than relying on the reader's prior
(first- or secondhand) experience of the city, the representation offers a
novel and forbidden experience, an opportunity for the reader to share,
vicariously, in the thrills of *déclassement*, in the manner of the equally
voluntary *déclassé*, Marcosini. As for the blindfolding of de Marsay in
La fille aux yeux d'or when he is conducted at full speed to Paquita's
residence, for all its being a requirement of the extravagant plot, it is
paralleled in the need for the armchair traveler also to be blindfolded
during a "journey" that, in respect of the precise locations traversed, has
no relevance. (The same might be said of the blindfolding of Antoinette
in *La duchesse de Langeais*.) On the first of the two occasions, the young
dandy is able, initially, to work out from various clues the itinerary being

followed, but ultimately, like the reader, he has to admit defeat. The activity doubtless requires from him too great an act of concentration, but there are deeper reasons. The anonymous destination lies just beyond the Parisian cobblestones and is a simulation of an oriental fantasy.[60] The lack of topographical precision is appropriate, because the location is a product of the imagination. The journey leading to it must, therefore, resemble a dream. The itinerary from the real to the fictional cannot be traced, though the interest of the Balzac novel comes from the fact that the distinction between the two is rarely, if ever, neat. Each invariably encroaches on the other.[61]

The centrality of the armchair is, moreover, confirmed by the role it plays within the diegesis in *Ferragus*. Both Maulincour and Desmarets at crucial moments flop into their armchairs as a prelude to an attempt to work out, in the manner of readers, the nature of the novelistic events in which they are caught up. The armchair represents a position outside the action, separated from the city that appears to control their destiny. To an important degree, the fiction is its reading.

If the relationship between individual and city in *Ferragus* and *La fille aux yeux d'or* is not rooted in the notion of *flânerie,* it nonetheless shares with it a concern with readability. Highlighted at the level of the fiction are examples of secrets and mysteries, and, as was noted with regard to the link with the detective story, the need for spying.[62] Reading is faced with the enigmatic, as exemplified by the Portuguese code that Jacquet has no difficulty cracking. Other forms of enigma presented by the Protean city are more troubling, there being a constant dialectic between the known ("qui n'a pas rencontré?" [who is it who will not have encountered?]) and the mysterious. The difficulty of the enigmas is enhanced by the emphasis placed on the knowledge of the city possessed by both Maulincour and de Marsay, in contrast to Marcosini in *Gambara,* who is obliged to ask a passerby for directions in the manner of a tourist. (It is precisely such local information that is said, in *Ferragus,* to be possessed by "les amants de Paris" [lovers of Paris]: "Ils disent à un ami dont la tabatière est vide: Prends par tel passage, il y a un débit de tabac, à gauche, près d'un pâtissier qui a une jolie femme" [They say to a friend whose snuff-box is depleted, take such and such a passage, there is a tobacconist's shop on the left-hand side, next to the premises of a pastry cook with a pretty wife].)[63] If the scorn heaped on the ability of the police to solve the enigma and protect Maulincour from Ferragus is to be explained at the level of the fiction by the hidden influence of the Thirteen, it is part of a reflection on a more generic interpretative challenge that ultimately always evades the complete solution. The examples of both characters and readers making a wrong assumption are legion, notably with regard to the identity of Paquita in *La fille aux yeux d'or,* with Balzac being ready to tease us with a number of red-herrings (followed by clues that correct them), in the manner of the already latent genre of the detective story.[64] This reaches comic proportions in the case of the orthographically challenged postman Moinot, who is convinced that there is no distinction in writing between himself and a sparrow ["un moineau"], while, as was noted earlier, there are other hints that might well be rooted in truth but which are never confirmed.

To conclude, Balzac in these various Parisian texts, beginning with *Ferragus,* draws the reader into a city that is both familiar and strange, with examples of behavior that are at once banal and extraordinary. Yet, by a familiar preemptive mechanism, this creates an impression of the real, and delivers parameters for its understanding, by the very fact of its self-conscious acknowledgment of the fictional components of the representation.[65] More specifically, the compositions in question can be seen to engage consciously with the reality of the activity in which we are engaged, namely the reading of fiction. Reading the city thus becomes an activity mediated through that of reading the *fiction* of the city. If Balzac shows that reading is never easy, the city nonetheless provides a splendid metaphor for a real that is always going to leave our interpretative performance inadequate, often comically so.

MICHAEL TILBY has been fellow in French at Selwyn College, Cambridge, since 1977. He has published on a range of nineteenth- and twentieth-century French authors, especially Balzac, and on the relationship between nineteenth-century French literature and the visual arts. Among his recent publications is the chapter on Balzac in the *Cambridge Companion to European Novelists.* He has completed a book-length study of the early Parisian *flâneur* and is currently writing a book provisionally entitled *Playing with Words: Language, Fiction, and Text in Balzac's "Comédie humaine."*

NOTES

1. Preface to *Ferragus* in Balzac, *L'œuvre de Balzac*, 2:379.

2. See Citron, *La poésie de Paris*, 2:200.

3. See Lotz, "L'image irréelle," 96, and Pichois, *Le romantisme*, 48. Pichois concludes that the population of Paris grew less rapidly in this period than might have been expected. See also Roger Caillois, "Balzac et le mythe de Paris," in Balzac, *L'œuvre de Balzac*, 4:i–xvii: "Ces diverses nouveautés aboutissent à une transformation totale du décor urbain et font de la grande ville moderne le lieu d'élection de toutes les aventures, de toutes les tragédies que les écrivains projetaient autrefois dans un passé stylisé ou dans des contrées mal connues" [these various innovations lead to a complete transformation of the urban decor and make the modern city the location of choice for those adventures and tragedies that earlier writers uniformly set in a stylized past or in regions of which they had little direct knowledge] (ii); and Harvey, *Paris, Capital of Modernity*, chap. 1.

4. On such guidebooks, see Ferguson, *Paris as Revolution*, and Thompson, "Telling 'Spatial Stories'."

5. The phenomenon, though rightly associated with the July Monarchy, began during the Restoration, as Pierre Barbéris has recalled: "Les innombrables articles de l'Hermite de la Chaussée-d'Antin (Jouy, Jay) et du Rôdeur français (Balisson de Rougemont), *Le Provincial à Paris* de Montigny (1825), *Le Voyage à Paris* de Lanfranchi [alias Étienne-Léon de Lamothe-Langon] (1830) avaient témoigné de l'existence d'une curiosité réelle pour les transformations de la ville, pour la population nouvelle qui s'y installait, pour les lieux publics, les métiers, les maisons, les salons, les problèmes nouveaux (misère, suicides), etc." [The innumerable articles by L'Hermite de la Chaussée-d'Antin (Jouy, Jal) and the French Prowler (Balisson de Rougemont), Montigny's *Le provincial à Paris* (1825) and Lanfranchi's *Le voyage à Paris* (1830) had highlighted the existence of genuine curiosity about the changes in the city's appearance, its new inhabitants, its public spaces, trades, housing, and salons, as well as its newly familiar problems (poverty and suicide), etc.]. Balzac, *Histoire des Treize*, 475. See for a selection of similar works published after 1830, ibid., 477.

6. Balzac, *La comédie humaine*, 12:575 (hereafter *Pl*). See also *Sur Catherine de Médicis*, in ibid., 11:209.

7. See Guichardet, *Balzac, archéologue de Paris*. See also Patrice Boussel, "Le Paris de Balzac," in Balzac, *L'œuvre de Balzac*, 16:5–272. Harvey observes, "his characters even change their personas as they move from one locale to another" (42).

8. Moretti, *Atlas of the European Novel*, 106.

9. This point is made from a different perspective by Citron, *La poésie de Paris*, 2:191. (The widespread belief that the Balzacian narrator operates in the manner of the contemporary *flâneur* is also open to question in some important respects, as I hope to demonstrate in a study of the pre-Baudelairian *flâneur* provisionally entitled *Reading the City*.) An important complementary perspective is adopted by Roger Caillois in "Balzac et le mythe de Paris," who insists on Balzac's Paris as a mythical entity: "Paris est une totalité. Il n'est fascinant qu'indivisible" [Paris exists as a totality. Its fascination is dependent on its being an indivisible whole] (xi). For a robust challenge to the tendency to see Balzac's representation of Paris straightforwardly in terms of a historical referent, see Vanoncini, "La disparition des espaces urbains."

10. Ferguson, *Paris as Revolution*, 68.

11. *Pl*, 5:894.

12. A related ambivalence is encountered in the reference in the *Physiologie du mar-iage* to the need for the *physiologiste* to have recourse to the *"arides et utiles* recherches de la statistique" [arid yet pertinent statistical investigations] as practiced by Benoiston de Châteauneuf. Ibid., 6:974, emphasis added. In *Ferragus*, the Balzacian narrator makes reference to the same *savant*'s calculation of Parisian mortality statistics. Ibid., 5:794. See also the references to Balzac in Hacking, *The Taming of Chance.*

13. On the labyrinth and "le fil d'Ariane" in the *Comédie humaine,* see Lotz, "L'image irréelle," 97. As Walter Benjamin observes, "le labyrinthe est la patrie de celui qui hésite" [the labyrinth is the habitat of the ditherer]. Quoted by Jean Lacoste in an editorial note appended to Benjamin, *Charles Baudelaire,* 261.

14. Andrew Oliver characterizes it as a "texte mobile" in "Opacité et transparence," 64. André Vanoncini notes, "La plupart des commentateurs de *La Fille aux yeux d'or* . . . ont été frappés par la fragilité des liens thématiques, temporels ou logiques entre les pages descriptives du tableau parisien et le début de la narration consacrée à l'histoire d'Henri de Marsay, Paquita Valdès et la marquise de San-Réal" [virtually all scholars who have discussed *La fille aux yeux d'or* have been struck by the fragility of the themat-ic, temporal, and logical links between the detailed portrait of Paris and the opening of the narrative recounting the story of Henri de Marsay, Paquita Valdès, and the marquise de San-Réal]. Vanoncini, "Les 'trompettes de 1789'," 224. See also Massol-Bedoin, "La charade et la chimère," and Massol, *Une poétique de l'énigme,* 90.

15. Calvino, "La città-romanzo in Balzac," 173. Calvino also quotes in full Cesare Pa-vese's 1936 diary entry on Balzac's representation of Paris (178).

16. *Pl,* 5:795.

17. Petitier, "La mélancolie de *Ferragus,*" 45. On the origins of *Ferragus* in the *roman noir,* see Massol-Bedoin, "L'énigme de *Ferragus.*"

18. *Pl,* 5:788. Later in the preface, he nonetheless maintains "un auteur doit dédaigner de convertir son récit, quand ce récit est véritable, en une espèce de joujou à surprise, et de promener, à la manière de quelques romanciers, le lecteur, pendant quatre volumes, de souterrains en souterrains, pour lui montrer un cadavre tout sec, et lui dire, en forme de conclusion, qu'il lui a constamment fait peur d'une porte cachée dans quelque tapis-serie, ou d'un mort laissé par mégarde sous des planchers" [in the instance of a narrative founded on reality, the writer must guard against transforming it into some kind of jack-in-the-box, obliging the reader, as is the wont of certain novelists, to accompany him in the course of four entire volumes from underground passage to underground passage, with the aim of introducing him to a desiccated corpse, and reiterating, by way of con-clusion, that he has consistently induced alarm in the reader through doors hidden in tapestries or cadavers improvidently concealed beneath floorboards]. Ibid., 5:789.

19. Ibid., 5:1078.

20. The Vicomte de Dampmartin described Paris in 1789 as a city divided into two classes: "celle des écrasans et celle des écrasés" [those who occasion accidents in the street and those who are their victims]. Dampmartin, *Un provincial à Paris,* 161. When Castanier is likened to a *flâneur* in *Melmoth réconcilié,* it is said, "Il . . . ne se fût pas dérangé pour éviter le coup d'une planche ou la roue d'une voiture" [he would not have stirred himself to avoid a falling plank or the wheel of a passing carriage]. *Pl,* 10:382. The anonymous author of "Le flâneur parisien" in *Le Figaro* (November 13, 1831) nonetheless observed, "Le flâneur . . . est prudent. Jamais cabriolet ne l'a écrasé, quoiqu'il ne se soit

jamais dérangé pour l'éviter" [The *flâneur* . . . is prudent. He has never been flattened by a carriage, yet has never taken steps to avoid the same].

21. Caillois, "Balzac et le mythe de Paris," observes, "Si la Cité apparaît désormais pleine de périls et de surprises, c'est parce qu'on a transposé dans son décor la *savane* et la *forêt* d'un Fenimore Cooper, où toute branche cassée signifie une inquiétude ou un espoir, où chaque tronc dissimule le fusil d'un ennemi ou l'arc d'un invisible et silencieux vengeur" [If the heart of the ancient city from now on is seen to present manifold dangers and surprises, it is because it has been made to take on the appearance of Fenimore Cooper's *savannah* and *forest,* where a broken branch is sufficient to indicate either cause for concern or reason for hope, where any tree trunk might conceal an enemy rifle or the bow of a silent and invisible individual intent on revenge] (iii).

22. *Pl,* 5:822.

23. Ibid., 5:813.

24. In the first edition, the opening chapter is entitled "Madame Jules." Ida Gruget, moreover, is made to observe: "Ce nom . . . est bien connu parmi les noms de guerre" [this name . . . is one of the most celebrated *noms de guerre*] (ibid., 5:853), a teasing comment that might tempt the unwary reader into seeing it as a reference to the pseudonyms adopted by courtesans. (The Madame Meynardie with whom Ida lodges is later revealed in *Splendeurs et misères des courtisanes* to be a brothel-keeper.) Balzac had made the acquaintance of Vidocq at the house of Monsieur de Berny, deemed by the police chief to be his closest friend. See Jean Savant, "Balzac et Vidocq," in Balzac, *L'œuvre de Balzac,* 13:viii. He subsequently dined with Vidocq at the philanthropist Appert's house on April 26, 1834. See Pierre-Georges Castex's introduction to Balzac, *Le père Goriot,* xxv, and Heppenstall, *French Crime in the Romantic Age,* 101.

25. The Vidame de Pamiers's servant, Justin, reports that Ferragus had earlier been "un Lovelace capable de séduire Grandisson" [a Lovelace who would have succeeded in charming Grandisson himself]. *Pl,* 5:827.

26. Maulincour has a blind faith in the ability of the police to trace Ferragus. The Vidame de Pamiers counters, "La police, mon cher enfant, est ce qu'il y a de plus inhabile au monde" [The police, dear boy, are incomparably incompetent]. Ibid., 5:826. The fact remains that Maulincour will tell Desmarets that the man he is employing to trace Ferragus is "plus habile à découvrir la vérité que ne l'est la police elle-même" [better able to uncover the truth than the police themselves]. Ibid., 5:847.

27. Ibid., 5:831.

28. According to Le Bibliophile Jacob, the rue Fromentel, or Froidmanteau, was one of a number of Paris streets "affectées à la prostitution" [given over to prostitution]. "Les noms des rues," 90. The "rue Froidmanteau" is similarly highlighted in *Gambara.*

29. See the references to these works in Deaucourt, *Premières loges,* 125.

30. Michel Lichtlé draws a pertinent parallel between the prior presentation of Fromenteau in "Un espion à Paris" (*Le diable à Paris,* vol. 1, 1844) and the paragraph on the "spy" in *Ferragus.* Balzac, *Ferragus,* 315n32.

31. *Pl,* 5:813.

32. The origin of the munificent provision made for Jules Desmarets is never made explicit, though the fact that he becomes the absent Nucingen's stockbroker is an indication of the hidden nature of capitalist enterprise.

33. *Pl,* 5:815.

34. Ibid., 5:851, 1043–1044, 827.

35. He is Gratien, Henri, Victor, Jean-Joseph Bourignard.

36. No reference is made to Ida's father. It is possible to see an exaggerated emphasis in the text on her mother's status as a widow, and to deduce that we are meant to call it into question. It is revealing that Ida assumes that Jules and Clémence are not husband and wife. The theme of illegitimacy, and its disruptive influence, becomes still more evident in *La fille aux yeux d'or*.

37. Citron, *La poésie de Paris*, 2:205. Roger Caillois, "Balzac et le mythe de Paris," states, "à la cité innombrable s'oppose le héros légendaire destiné à la conquérir" [pitched against the city is the legendary hero whose destiny is to be its conqueror] (iv).

38. *Pl*, 5:816–817.

39. Ibid., 3:144.

40. Arlette Michel sees *La duchesse de Langeais* as a cross between the novels of Mrs. Radcliffe and the epic poems of Ariosto or Tasso. Michel, "*La duchesse de Langeais* et le romanesque balzacien," 93.

41. See Tilby, "Balzac et le jeu parodique dans *Gambara*."

42. See Petitier, "La mélancolie de *Ferragus*," 50, 56.

43. *Pl*, 5:826, 1071, 1066, 849, 1057; 3:51.

44. Ibid., 5:793. In *Le père Goriot*, the narrator famously declares, "Paris est un véritable océan" [Paris is a veritable ocean]. Ibid., 3:59.

45. "Quelques rues, ainsi que la rue Montmartre, ont une belle tête et finissent en queue de poisson" [Certain streets, among them the rue Montmartre, possess a beautiful head yet terminate in the form of a fishtail]. Ibid., 5:793. This descriptive detail is echoed in the grotesque portrait of Paquita's elderly mother in *La fille aux yeux d'or*. Ibid., 5:1080. There was an actual ruelle de la Sirène in Paris at this time, situated opposite the church of Saint-Barthélemy.

46. Ibid., 5:794.

47. Ibid., 5:796.

48. Bachelard, *L'eau et les rêves*.

49. *Pl*, 5:815.

50. Ibid., 5:1050. Rose Fortassier explains that Lutetia was derived from a Celtic name meaning "lieu des marais." Ibid., 5:1538n2.

51. Petitier relates the rain to the theme of degradation that is all-pervasive in the novel and observes neatly: "La pureté n'est qu'un des modes de l'eau, le résultat d'une de ses innombrables transformations, et non plus son essence" [Purity is only one of the modes of water, the result of one of its innumerable transformations and no longer its essence]. "La mélancolie de *Ferragus*," 48. The same critic sees *Ferragus* as a novel of melancholy, presided over by Saturn, who was also, we are reminded, "une divinité de la pluie ou de la mer, responsable des innondations" [the god of rain and the sea, instigator of floods] (52).

52. *Pl*, 5:901.

53. See Lyon-Caen, "Configurations identitaires et poétique," 94.

54. *Pl*, 5:791. The correct spelling is Trelawny.

55. Ibid., 5:787; 6:330.

56. Ibid., 5:823, 875, 1052.

57. Ibid., 3:50.

58. Ibid., 5:795.

59. In *Ferragus,* the rue Soly is said to be "la plus étroite et la moins praticable de toutes les rues de Paris" [the narrowest and least traversable of all Paris streets], with the result that Madame Jules's *fiacre* has to wait for her in the rue des Vieux-Augustins. Ibid., 5:796.

60. When, in *Le contrat de mariage,* de Marsay looks back on his participation in Montriveau's expedition to "spring" the Duchesse de Langeais from her Spanish convent, he describes it as "un tour en Orient" [an Oriental jaunt]. Ibid., 3:641. His own adventure, as featured in *La fille aux yeux d'or,* might be regarded as an attempt to construct the Orient in Paris. This is what Balzac himself had done in the apartment he had recently rented in the rue des Batailles, which, by his own admission to Madame Hanska, was the model for his description of Paquita's boudoir. See also Bordas, "L'orient balzacien," and, on Paquita's interior surroundings, Delon, "Le boudoir balzacien."

61. For a complementary discussion of this passage (and of *La fille aux yeux d'or* as a whole) in terms of Balzac's fascination with vision, but one that strangely leaves aside the ways in which this composition may be regarded as a prototype of the detective novel, see Goulet, *Optiques,* 61–81, especially 79.

62. The narrator opines, "Une bien belle chose est le métier d'espion, quand on le fait pour son compte et au profit d'une passion" [The business of a spy is a fine thing when undertaken for a purpose that is one's own and in the service of an amorous passion]. *Pl,* 5:812–813. As for Desmarets's use of a hole in the wall to spy voyeuristically on Clémence and Ferragus, it has parallels in Balzac's other novels from this period; see Massol, *Une poétique de l'énigme,* 150–151.

63. *Pl,* 5:795.

64. The narrative allows the reader to entertain the notion initially that it is the as-yet unnamed Paquita who is de Marsay's Iberian half-sister, that "la fille aux yeux d'or" who resides in the rue Saint-Lazare is, in other words, the previously described Marquise de San-Réal. It is perhaps only on a re-reading that it is immediately clear that it is the latter who is the subject of Paul de Manerville's eulogy, and that "la fille aux yeux d'or" is the "jeune créole des Antilles" Madame de San-Réal has brought with her to Madrid from Havana.

65. "L'espace urbain [in *Ferragus*] opère un détachement du réel qui fait de lui un matériau déjà littéraire; le décrire ou le raconter, c'est faire de l'art sur de l'art" [The urban space performs a detachment from the real that transforms the latter into an element that is already literary; to describe or narrate it is to engage in art that is a reflection on art]. Petitier, "La mélancolie de *Ferragus,*" 54.

SIX

The Landscapes of Eugène Fromentin and Gustave Moreau

BARBARA WRIGHT

"JE DOIS PLUS À MOREAU QU'IL NE ME DOIT," EUGÈNE FROMEN-tin told Jules Breton; "c'est lui qui m'a appris à émailler la croupe d'un cheval" [I owe more to Moreau than he owes me; it is he who taught me how to put the shine on a horse's rump].[1] This is borne out by the fact that in the late 1850s, Gustave Moreau regularly touched up Fromentin's pictures before they were exhibited in the shop of the art dealer Adrien Beugnet. On December 8, 1856, Moreau specifically referred to such alterations.[2] He and Fromentin are generally agreed to have met when Moreau was preparing *Les Athéniens livrés au Minotaure*[3] (Bourg-en-Bresse, Musée de Brou) for the *Exposition universelle* of 1855.[4] Geneviève Lacambre notes that Fromentin played a major role in Moreau's career by encouraging him to exhibit in the provinces, finding commissions for him, and introducing him to dealers like Beugnet, Hector Brame, Paul Tesse, and Georges Petit.[5] Despite being six years his junior, Moreau was Fromentin's artistic mentor, described by him as "le meilleur et le plus exigeant des maîtres" [the best and most demanding of masters].[6] Too impoverished to establish himself anew in Paris, Fromentin, with his wife, Marie, settled in Saint-Maurice, close to La Rochelle, where Fromentin had been born and brought up, and where his daughter Marguerite was born in 1854. It was a period of domestic happiness for the rising Orientalist painter, despite the cramped working conditions (a bedroom had to double as a studio) and, more significantly, despite the frustration of being away from Paris and his friends at this crucial stage in his career. Fromentin shared Moreau's studio, renting it for himself during Moreau's trip to Italy from 1857 to 1859.

Although Moreau's *Cavalier écossais*,[7] long thought to have been a prototype of Fromentin's Arab horsemen, can now be dated to the early 1870s, various compositions with horses by Moreau executed around 1854 testify to the way in which these two men worked together after Fromentin's return from his third and last journey to Algeria in 1853.[8] Moreau also loved horses and was skilled at representing them, as in his *Diomède dévoré par ses chevaux* (c. 1875; Musée Gustave Moreau, Paris, Rouleau 38, no. 1). He showed them being ridden by Arab, Persian, and Indian hunters, and finally, with the addition of a horn in the middle of their foreheads, they became the unicorns of his paintings of the 1880s. Geneviève Lacambre notes that Moreau was influenced in his picture of Diomedes by two images of the Barberi race in Rome by Théodore Géricault.[9] Fromentin subsequently became almost obsessive about his depiction of Arab horses, claiming in the summer of 1874 that he would have to start afresh in order to learn how to draw a horse and buying a little Arab horse for this purpose in Saint-Maurice.[10]

A friend of Moreau's since the late 1840s, Narcisse Berchère was also part of this small circle of friends.[11] He and Fromentin had met in the studio of the academic painter Jean-Charles Rémond, though Fromentin left after a few months to enter the studio of Louis Cabat. Berchère's work was more directly useful to Moreau, since he was by far the most widely traveled of the three, and some of his studies of Oriental architecture served as models for Moreau's paintings, as did his costume chest.[12] When Berchère complained that he found the area around his native town of Étampes uninspiring, Moreau responded:

> Il y a quelque chose à tirer de tout. On n'a pas besoin d'aller promener son ins-
> piration ou d'aller la chercher sur des rives lointaines. Elle est en nous. On peut
> faire une ample moisson, en voyageant de Paris à Saint-Cloud. J'irai à Étampes
> et je montrerai à Berchère que la nature est partout bienveillante à l'artiste
> puisqu'elle n'est, en somme, pour lui, que l'occasion d'exprimer son âme.

> [There is something to be gained from everything. We don't need to wheel out
> our inspiration or seek it on distant shores. It is within us. A simple journey
> from Paris to Saint-Cloud can yield a rich harvest. I shall go to Étampes to show
> Berchère that nature beckons the artist everywhere, being merely the pretext for
> him to give voice to his soul.][13]

What linked Fromentin and Moreau most of all was the central role of landscape in their work. The backgrounds of the two men were very different. Moreau, brought up in Paris, admitted to the awakening of nature for him in the course of his journey to Italy,[14] whereas for Fromentin it was the most salient feature of his childhood in the countryside near to La Rochelle.[15] They each responded, however, by sketching landscapes: Moreau in Italy, as later, when visiting his uncle in Honfleur and when visiting Berchère in Étampes (notably in 1879 and 1885); Fromentin in Paris and its surroundings in the early 1840s. For the most part, these sketches bear inscriptions, giving details of location, season, dates, or even the hour of day. Moreau's early sketches included watercolors and painted oil studies as well as drawings, whereas Fromentin's early sketches were exclusively drawings. But Moreau later incorporated these early landscapes into his finished paintings in a way that Fromentin did not.

Elements of Moreau's future symbolism can be detected in these early Italian sketches, which make great play of distant horizons and atmospheric effects. The watercolor *Rome, le Colisée vu de l'Angelicum des Dominicains* (1858) shows horizontal layers of light and shade leading to the architecture silhouetted against the calm sky.[16] Another watercolor, *Rome, Villa Pamphili* (1858), exchanges the browns and greys of the view of the Coliseum for a range of tonal variations of green.[17] Fromentin's early sketches, by contrast, are more reminiscent of the seventeenth-century Dutch landscape school, with one drawing, *Montmartre*, actually incorporating elements of Rembrandt's famous etching of *Three Trees*, of which Fromentin sketched a copy.[18] What both men shared was a love of stasis. "J'aime peu ce qui court, ce qui coule, ou ce qui vole," Fromentin admitted when he was twenty-four; "toute chose immobile, toute eau stagnante, tout oiseau planant ou perché, me cause une indéfinissable émotion" [I don't like things that run, or flow or fly; anything that is immobile, stagnant water, a bird hovering or on a perch, causes me an indefinable emotion].[19] Autumn was their favorite season.

This love of stasis chimed in with the classical formation of Fromentin and Moreau. Both were well versed in classical literature and both received their initial training in the studios of neoclassical painters. However, whereas Moreau was a pupil of François-Édouard Picot (who also taught Alexandre Cabanel and William Bouguereau) and never swerved from his self-appointed goal of breathing new life into history painting, Fromentin's artistic training was seriously, if not fatally, compromised by the complex nature of his relationship with his father, a distinguished medical man who was himself a talented amateur painter. The question turned not merely on whether Fromentin would follow paternal advice in becoming a lawyer, rather than a painter, but also on what kind of a painter he would become. As a student in Paris, Dr. Fromentin had studied landscape and portrait drawing under Victor Bertin and had frequented the studios of Gros and Gérard. His Empire-style self-portrait and his large copies of eighteenth-century landscapes exhibit painstaking care; his topographical drawings were praised by Jacques Foucart for their poetic charm, notwithstanding their somewhat archaic "stylisation."[20] Dr. Fromentin recommended the studio of the archconservative Rémond for his son, where the young painter felt that he was being asked to make works which ended up looking like those of other artists, though all he wanted was to learn their methods and apply them to his own work.[21] Subsequently, Fromentin was to plunder his second master, Cabat, together with Alexandre Decamps and, to a lesser extent, Prosper Marilhat, in a quest for his own style. Cabat had, since the late 1830s, been the most advanced and consistent practitioner of natural landscape, apart from a few Barbizon artists, such as Théodore Rousseau and Jules Dupré. Cabat reinforced Fromentin's budding enthusiasm for the Dutch school and encouraged his aspirations toward the high ideals of the finest Classical art.

Many of the locations visited by Fromentin overlapped with the haunts of the Barbizon painters in the forest of Fontainebleau. They, too, noted topographical details and were sensitive to atmospheric changes of time and season. Indeed, before establishing himself as an Orientalist painter, Fromentin tried his hand at peasant painting, at Le Tremblay in 1851, and on his prolonged honeymoon at Saint-Raphaël in 1852. Had he continued in this vein, in which he showed considerable promise, his work might have developed in ways similar to that of Jean-François Millet or Jules Breton.

But this was not to be. Chance, in the shape of an invitation to the wedding of the sister of his friend Charles Labbé, led Fromentin to Bli-

dah in 1846. He was stunned by the light and beauty of Algeria. Art
dealers bore in on him the potential of the new market in Orientalist
painting, arising out of the recent French conquests. Furthermore, in
Moreau, Fromentin found a soulmate whose ideas on aesthetics were
close to his own and indeed constituted a natural evolution from the
neoclassicism that he associated with the rigid conservatism of his father.
But, whereas Moreau never deviated from the path of history painting,
Fromentin's devotion to neoclassicism was complicated by the memory
of earlier tensions with his father and by the inherent incompatibility of
neoclassicism and Orientalism.

It is only in recent years that Fromentin has been given his due as a
theorist of Orientalism.[22] A theorist, rather than an apologist, since, in
the exposition of his views in *Une année dans le Sahel,* he puts his finger
on the "curiosity" factor as being both the originality and the potential
pitfall of Orientalism, in terms of lasting, universal art. He tells how his
teacher Cabat described the Seine as "un fleuve," thus emphasizing its
general rather than its specific qualities.[23] Looking at some boys playing
a ball-and-stick game on the Market Square in Blidah,[24] he reflected that
the "impressions multiples" [multiple impressions] of the real-life situation—the heat, the shouts, the vivid colors—all needed to be transmuted
by the painter away from the scene, in the studio, where "le vrai relatif"
[relative truth] would be abandoned in favor of "un ordre de vérité plus
large, moins précise et d'autant plus absolue qu'elle est moins locale" [a
wider order of truth, less precise and the more absolute for being less
localized].[25] Local color, the trademark of exoticism, was, Fromentin
thought, contrary to the universality of art. These views, analogous to
Moreau's disparagement of "ethnography" in art, were outlined by Fromentin as early as his "Salon de 1845," before he ever set foot in Algeria.[26]
They were developed in his last work of published prose, the "Salon de
1876," where, in relation to Jean-Léon Gérôme's *La mosquée,* Fromentin
mocked the detailed accuracy with which the slippers of the faithful had
been depicted, exclaiming: "Et l'on s'extasie sur la vérité avec laquelle
cette cordonnerie est imitée. J'ai pourtant entendu un spectateur difficile
s'étonner que toutes ces babouches fussent également neuves. Il ne trou-
vait pas cela vraisemblable" [And people wax lyrical over the precision
with which this footwear is replicated. Yet I heard a fussy bystander mar-

vel that all these slippers were equally new. He found that improbable].[27] Both Fromentin and Moreau were gifted conversationalists, and their discussions almost certainly informed the views on aesthetics expressed by Fromentin in *Une année dans le Sahel*.[28]

With the gradual abandonment of neoclassical hierarchy at the end of the eighteenth century, the senses and the intellect came to be perceived as opposites, with the implication that, of these two forces, the senses contained greater and hitherto unexplored strengths. Moreau reacted by seeking inspiration in the "principes exquis immuables" [exquisite and immutable principles] of the Italian Renaissance.[29] As corroborated by Fromentin's closest friend, Armand Du Mesnil,[30] it was Moreau who strengthened Fromentin's belief in all that was "sublime" in the art of Leonardo da Vinci, Raphael, and Andrea del Sarto, "ces païens" [those pagans].[31] Towering over their subject matter, these masters focused on "la beauté plastique" [plastic beauty] as "l'apothéose de l'homme" [the apotheosis of man].[32] Taking two different examples in the Louvre, Poussin's *Les Philistins frappés de la peste* (1630–1631), in the case of Moreau, and Titian's *The Entombment of Christ* (1523–1525), in the case of Fromentin, they each stress that, far from looking for servile accuracy in their representations, these masters universalize the import of their work by the use of anachronisms in time or place: Titian has Christ being mourned by red-headed Lombard women; Poussin invests the architecture in his painting with an archaeological wealth such that he was able to "fondre ensemble . . . les civilisations les plus opposées" [blend together . . . the most divergent civilizations].[33] For both men, the conclusion was clear: "Être beau, tel était le premier et le dernier mot, l'alpha et l'oméga d'un catéchisme que nous ne connaissons plus guère aujourd'hui" [To be beautiful, that was the first and last word, the alpha and the omega of a catechism which is scarcely recognized today].[34]

These views derive essentially from the teaching of Roger de Piles, whose *Cours de peinture par principes* (1708) became a standard text for more than a century, updated by Pierre-Henri de Valenciennes's *Élémens de perspective pratique à l'usage des artistes* (1799). Roger de Piles identified three distinct phases in artistic perception: first, the simple truth, or faithful imitation; second, the ideal truth, the blending of several models (including the antique), in order to produce a degree of perfection oth-

erwise unattainable; finally, the composite truth, an amalgam of simple
and ideal truth, representing a credible beauty that often appears more
true than truth itself.[35] Piles did much to emphasize the dignity of the
landscape painter among artists, a recognition that was enhanced by
Valenciennes, who, like his predecessor, was an advocate of open-air
painting. In both cases, however, the open-air study, or "étude," was
recommended as a method of strengthening the artist's sense of visual
fidelity and of enabling him to select and compose a pictorial image from
the bewildering variety of perceptual experiences—but never to constitute a finished painting for public display. "Il est vrai que ces études ne
forment pas des tableaux," wrote Valenciennes, "mais on les garde dans
le portefeuille pour les consulter et en faire son profit dans l'occasion"
[It is true that these studies are not paintings, but they can be kept unpublished, for consultation and to be used as the occasion requires].[36]

The drama for Fromentin was that some of his most imaginative
work was executed in the form of just such oil studies. In July 1853 in
Laghouat, toward the most southerly point of his expedition in the Sahara, he pushed himself to the limit, physically and aesthetically. He
found himself confronted with monumental oppositions of rock and sky,
devoid of the trappings of conventional landscape composition, such as
framing trees or recessional paths. Two painted sketches of Laghouat
are unique examples of this phenomenon—dated, as were his drawings
of Paris and its surroundings, though in all other respects unrecogniz-
ably different. The more striking of the two, *Laghouat, 20 juin 9 heures,*
gives a worm's-eye view of the steep slope of a sandy, rocky hill.[37] The
curve of the buildings on top of the hill conveys a distorted, wide-angle
eccentricity, anticipatory of the unexpected viewpoints of a Degas or
a Caillebotte. Moving dramatically away from the one-point perspective sanctioned by Alberti, a fifteenth-century convention that had been
breached on more than one occasion, this work by Fromentin was far
ahead of its time. Being a sketch, it had the vivacity and color intensity
that Fromentin, in the tradition of Valenciennes, could not countenance
in a full-scale painting. Bereft of human association, it is almost abstract
in its simplicity. It is a nineteenth-century counterpart of some of the
works of Ruisdael, Fromentin's favorite landscapist, in that it is totally
self-sufficient: its dimensions are its secret and it has no message, no

communication to make. This oil sketch, along with its companion work, *Laghouat, 22 j[uin] 10 heures,* which offers sunken slopes in place of bulging height, is the closest that Fromentin ever came to painting the void, conceived not as negative emptiness but as an empowering force.[38] He seems to have taken fright, fearful perhaps of being unable to sustain such innovation, certainly not daring to pursue it further. In any case, the new experience needed to be filtered through his memory. It was not until he wrote it up, in *Un été dans le Sahara,* that Fromentin came to terms with what he had discovered. There he described the combination of sun, space, and solitude at Laghouat as exceptional.[39] Literature, being less hidebound than painting at this time, gave Fromentin greater freedom to express himself on this subject. The visual and the textual were, however, inseparable, representing two different phases or aspects of the same phenomenon: the challenge of rendering the metamorphosis and ultimate dissolution of the tangible world under the dazzle of the southern light.

The vista view is more easily represented in horizontal format. It is not surprising, therefore, that Fromentin followed this tradition in nearly all of his early depictions of external nature, whether in the greater Paris area, Provence, or the wide, open spaces of Bedouin nomadic life in Algeria. However, the potential for drama, inherent in historical landscape painting, is a compelling motive for shifting on occasion to the vertical format, as Fromentin himself did in his 1853 drawing of *Laghouat, Bab-el-Gharbi.*[40] Here he depicted monumental oppositions of rock and sky, sun and shadow, with figures lying passive in torpid prostration. This work is a prelude to later developments on the theme, culminating in the 1859 Salon painting so greatly admired by Baudelaire, *Une rue à El-Aghouat* (Musée de la Chartreuse, Douai), and the 1867 Salon painting *Femmes des Ouled-Nayls; dans un village du Sahara* (Art Institute of Chicago).[41]

It is surely no coincidence that this evolution toward the vertical format of some of Fromentin's major paintings in the 1860s took place in Moreau's studio in the 1850s, and that *Une rue à El-Aghouat* was painted there during his friend's absence in Italy. The rocks and ravines, so characteristic of Moreau's major works in the 1860s—the *Chemin de croix* for Notre-Dame-de-Decazeville (the 1862 commission secured for him by Fromentin), *Œdipe et le Sphinx* (1864, Metropolitan Museum of Art,

New York), and *Hercule et l'hydre de Lerne* (1876, Art Institute of Chicago)—have their counterparts in Fromentin's 1868 painting *Arabes attaqués par une lionne* and his *Centaures et centauresses s'exerçant au tir de l'arc* of the same period.[42] In these works, the craggy V-like setting is intended to accentuate the drama of the lion hunt or to highlight the pastoral capers of the centaurs. The landscape is imaginary, rather than based on any precise geographical location. Moreau is known to have measured up Leonardo da Vinci's *Virgin of the Rocks* (Musée du Louvre, Paris) when working on *Œdipe et le Sphinx*. In *Hercule et l'hydre de Lerne*, as Julius Kaplan has pointed out, "the large rocky masses serve as visual extensions of the two confronting forces."[43] However, although these paintings by Moreau outstrip those by Fromentin in terms of virtuosity of technique and complexity of vision, they have in common a desire to establish a link between the mood of the picture and the setting in which it is cast. These works exemplify Moreau's advice to his pupil Henri Evenepoel: "Il faut copier la nature avec de l'imagination: c'est cela qui fait l'artiste" [You have to copy nature with imagination: that is what makes an artist].[44] Nature, as shown eloquently by Baudelaire in his "Salon de 1859," was thought to be insufficient on its own to produce a work of art, and needed to be modified by creativity and imagination.[45] Moreau and Fromentin, avid readers of Ovid's *Metamorphoses,* were wholly convinced of the need for this kind of transformation. The form ideally sought by Fromentin was "moitié réelle et moitié imaginaire" [half real and half imaginary].[46]

Despite a reigning theory that devalued landscape (Baudelaire called it a "genre inférieur" [an inferior genre] in his "Salon de 1859"),[47] despite the efforts of Moreau and his friends to save historical landscape painting (which was not so much dying as disintegrating into genre painting),[48] and despite the powerful art administration's robust measures to curb naturalism, landscape became a major focus of change in nineteenth-century art.[49] As it happens, Fromentin, who from 1864 until his death in 1876 was a member of the Salon jury, wrote a brief history of landscape painting in France, in *Les maîtres d'autrefois*. Drawing on his dual qualifications as a painter and writer, he credits eighteenth-century literature with the arousal of a new interest in nature—an interest, incidentally, already developed in England and Holland, where the Reformation ban on religious imagery was a catalyst for the development of innovative alternatives. Fromentin goes on to show how from 1816 to 1825, the torch was passed from prose writers to poets, and from 1824 to 1830, to the painters. "Vers 1828," writes Fromentin, "on vit du nouveau" [About 1828, something new was seen]: "Des paysages naïvement, vraiment rustiques, et des formules hollandaises. La Hollande . . . nous enseignait à voir, à sentir et à peindre" [Unaffected, truly rustic landscapes and Dutch formulae. Holland . . . taught us to see, to feel and to paint].[50]

"Voir," "sentir," "peindre": this progression marks the development of nineteenth-century French landscape painting in ways that far outstrip Fromentin's own pictorial output. "Voir" encompasses the Enlightenment emphasis on ocular awareness and the evidence of the senses; "sentir" adds to this the multisensorial approach to perception, implicit in synaesthesia; "peindre" announces Mallarmé's call to order in terms of the materiality of painting, "cet art fait d'onguents et de couleurs" [this art made of unguents and colors].[51] Fromentin concludes his schematic outline with the remark, "Je ne serais pas surpris que la Hollande . . . après nous avoir ramenés de la littérature à la nature, . . . nous ramenât de la nature à la peinture" [I should not be surprised if Holland . . . having returned us from literature to nature, . . . led us back from nature to painting].[52]

Fromentin's interdisciplinary approach to landscape was reflected in his own œuvre, where his literary descriptions (in *Un été dans le Sahara* and *Carnets du voyage en Égypte*) were often more original than many of his finished paintings. Even in the 1870s, by which time Fromentin's attempts at self-renewal in history painting had failed and he became repetitive and uninspired, his skies (as in the 1874 *Souvenir d'Algérie*, National Gallery of Ireland, Dublin) have an atmospheric quality that Moreau greatly admired.[53] From Rome, he wrote in 1859: "Depuis que . . . j'ai pu voir le ciel. . . . C'est du Fromentin! me suis-je écrié bien souvent" [Now that . . . I've been able to see the sky. . . . It's Fromentin! I've often said to myself].[54] Georges Rouault would later write how, in the work of Claude Lorrain, Moreau pointed out "les dégradations subtiles de l'atmosphère" [the subtle graduation of the atmosphere].[55] Many of the skies in his later landscapes, such as *Paysage* (Musée Gustave Moreau, Paris, cat. 658), testify to the domination of color and paint over any concern with direct representation as such. Something of this strength, this vigorous outreach toward pure painting, can be detected in Fromentin's *Attaque d'une caravane* (Musée des Beaux-Arts, La Rochelle), a work that the artist deliberately—and unusually—left unfinished.[56] In September 1871, Fromentin took time to advise one of his own students, Ferdinand Humbert, who had consulted him about a projected painting of Judith and Holofernes: "Pas de littérature, *soyez peintre,* et ne respirez que l'amour du grand, du beau, du simple" [Leave out all literature, *be a painter,* and breathe only a love for the great, the beautiful and the simple].[57] Moreau, for his part, was almost obsessive in his insistence on "cet ensemble plastique, très plastique, toujours plastique, uniquement plastique" [this plastic unity, very plastic, constantly plastic, uniquely plastic].[58]

The combination of word and image, central to the achievement of both Moreau and Fromentin, is a rich vein to tap in this connection. Of all pictorial art forms, historical landscape painting was, almost by definition, the one most dependent on words, the subject of the painting being given in the title—an epic or mythological topic, or a dramatic event, such as a tree struck by lightning. The coveted Prix de Rome for historical landscape painting was first awarded in 1817 to Michallon, the pupil of Valenciennes and the first teacher of Corot. Berchère failed once, and Moreau twice, in this competition. Although the prize ceased to be awarded after 1863, the year of the death of Delacroix, Moreau ended by transforming this particular art form, abandoning the theatricality of action traditionally associated with it for the contemplative stasis of symbolism. There was indeed a seismic shift. Long-established hierarchies were eroded and the well-defined categories of the past were collapsing. Furthermore, the "fraternité des arts" [fraternity of the arts], so much a feature of the 1830s and emblematized in the cover-page of the periodical *L'Artiste,* which showed a painter, a sculptor, a writer, and a musician grouped together, gave way in the latter half of the nineteenth century to a concern with the specificity of the different art forms. Fromentin felt the need to mark out clear lines of demarcation between painting and literature in the 1874 preface to the second edition of *Un été dans le Sahara,* and Moreau, plagued with critics accusing him of being too "literary" in his painting, never tired of praising painting as "ce langage muet" [this mute language].[59]

Notwithstanding these declarations, the work of both men is informed by their dual talents. Fromentin shone in both painting and writing. The "Notices" written by Moreau, in the first instance for the benefit of his deaf mother, reveal great rhetorical eloquence and, as Peter Cooke has shown, constitute not merely a valuable *post hoc* commentary on specific pictures but also, in some cases, an ongoing evolution in words, leading to an autonomous iconography quite separate from that of the paintings themselves.[60] Fromentin's decline in painterly originality in the 1870s was counteracted by a new spurt of literary vigor in his book of art criticism, *Les maîtres d'autrefois,* an art-form that he might well have developed further had he not died suddenly at the age of fifty-six. His verbal descriptions of the Dutch landscapes and of the concavity of the cloud formation in Ruisdael's skies are among his finest achievements. "Transposition" is central to the art of both Fromentin and Moreau: not in the sense of the "transposition d'art," as exemplified by Théophile Gautier, where the lines of demarcation between the two art-forms become merged, but rather with an ongoing potential for recreation in either medium—by the reader/spectator or by the artist himself.

BARBARA WRIGHT is professor emerita of French literature at Trinity College, Dublin, having taught previously at the Universities of Manchester and Exeter. She is a member of both the Royal Irish Academy and the Academia Europaea, and is an officer in the French National Order of Merit. She specializes in nineteenth-century French studies, with particular reference to the interconnection between literature and painting, and has published books and articles on the works of Charles Baudelaire, Eugène Fromentin, Gustave Moreau, and Edgar Quinet. She is the author, with James Thompson, of a monograph on Fromentin. Her edition of *Le désert de Suez: Cinq mois dans l'Isthme,* by the painter-writer Narcisse Berchère, focuses on the first phase of the construction of the Suez Canal. Wright's edition of the manuscript essays by Albert Aubert, *Du spiritualisme et de quelques-unes de ses conséquences,* pertains to intellectual life in the July Monarchy.

NOTES

I should like to acknowledge my debt of gratitude to the staff of the Rhys Carpenter Library, Bryn Mawr, where I was given unfailing support in the preparation of this chapter. I should also like to thank Marni Kessler of the University of Kansas for her invaluable comments on this paper, when she kindly read it in draft form.

1. Reported by Jules Breton in *Nos peintres du siècle*, 178.

2. Fromentin, *Correspondance*, 2:1014 (hereafter *CEF*).

3. See Sarda, *Paysages de rêve de Gustave Moreau*, fig. 62, 99. The work is the catalogue of an exhibition held at the Monastère Royal de Brou, Bourg-en-Bresse, June 12–September 12, 2004, and the Musée des Beaux-Arts de Reims, October 2004–January 2005.

4. Julius Kaplan establishes a parallel between the kneeling figure in *Les Athéniens livrés au Minotaure* and the shepherd in Poussin's *Et in Arcadia ego*. Kaplan, *Catalogue of Gustave Moreau Exhibition*, 12. The exhibition took place at the Los Angeles County Museum of Art, July 23–September 1, 1974, and the California Palace of the Legion of Honor, September 14–November 3, 1974. This painting by Poussin is also discussed by Fromentin in *Un été dans le Sahara*, in Fromentin, *Œuvres complètes*, 48 (hereafter *OC*).

5. Lacambre, *Gustave Moreau*, 52. This work is the catalogue of an exhibition held at the Grand Palais, Paris, September 29, 1998–January 4, 1999; the Art Institute of Chicago, February, 13–April 25, 1999; and the Metropolitan Museum of Art, June 1–August 22, 1999.

6. *CEF*, 2:1012.

7. See Sarda, *Paysages de rêve de Gustave Moreau*, fig. 114, 144.

8. Lacambre, *Gustave Moreau*, 121.

9. Ibid., 120.

10. See Wright, *Eugène Fromentin*, 477–478.

11. In the Musée Gustave Moreau there is a small painting by Narcisse Berchère of the Château de Bomy (Pas-de-Calais), the property of Moreau's mother's family. Berchère made the painting during a stay there in 1848 with Moreau and Anatole Nancy.

12. Moreau refers to "ma caisse à costumes de Berchère" in *L'Assembleur de rêves*, 127 (hereafter *AR*).

13. Quoted by Marie-Cécile Forest in Sarda, *Paysages de rêve de Gustave Moreau*, 10.

14. "Pour moi qui n'ai jamais mis le nez à ma fenêtre, et qui suis bien le plus affreux ignorant des choses de la nature que l'on puisse rencontrer, je ne me lasse pas de m'extasier sur tout ce qui m'environne" [I, who had never looked out the window and who must be the greatest ignoramus you could ever meet, as far as nature is concerned, am endlessly rapturous about all that surrounds me]. Moreau, *Correspondance d'Italie*, 87.

15. See *OC*, 868.

16. See Sarda, *Paysages de rêve de Gustave Moreau*, fig. 24, 42.

17. See ibid., fig. 25, 43.

18. See Thompson and Wright, *Eugène Fromentin*, 47, 38 (hereafter *ACR*).

19. *CEF*, 1:312.

20. *ACR*, 22; Jacques Foucart, preface to Lefrançois, *Eugène Fromentin au Musée des Beaux-Arts de La Rochelle*, 24.

21. See *CEF*, 1:223.

22. See Benjamin, *Orientalist Aesthetics*, 17–23.

23. That is, "a river." *OC*, 326.

24. See also Fromentin's painting *Les enfants arabes* (La Salle University Art Museum, Philadelphia; *ACR*, 260).

25. *OC*, 319.

26. Moreau deplored the deviation of his contemporaries into genre painting and ethnographic Orientalism, maintaining his belief in the traditional hierarchy of the genres; see Moreau, *Écrits sur l'art*, 2:349.

27. *OC*, 1223.

28. As Guy Sagnes has pointed out, to these also need to be related the contemporary "Notes sur le genre dans la peinture." Ibid., 921–924.

29. *AR*, 195.

30. See *CEF*, 1:985.

31. *OC*, 316.

32. Ibid., 922.

33. Ibid., 317; *AR*, 133.

34. *OC*, 317.

35. Piles, *Cours de peinture par principes*, 20–23.

36. Valenciennes, *Élémens de perspective*, 410.

37. *ACR*, 131.

38. Ibid., 130, b.

39. *OC*, 123.

40. *ACR*, 126.

41. Ibid., 190, 273.

42. See Sarda, *Paysages de rêve de Gustave Moreau*, fig. 15, 32; *ACR*, 275, 280.

43. Kaplan, *Catalogue of Gustave Moreau Exhibition*, 41.

44. Evenepoel, *Lettres à mon père*, 1:197.

45. For the derision of the unpurified and uninterpreted "culte niais de la nature" [idiotic cult of nature], see Charles Baudelaire, "Salon de 1859," in *Œuvres complètes*, 2:660.

46. *OC*, 295.

47. Baudelaire, "Salon de 1859," 660.

48. Fromentin spotted this as early as 1845, when he remarked on "l'empiétement du genre sur la grande peinture" [the invasion of history painting by genre painting]. *OC*, 879. In *Une année dans le Sahel*, he observes that "le genre a détruit la grande peinture et dénaturé le paysage même" [genre painting has destroyed history painting and altered the very nature of landscape painting]. Ibid., 315.

49. "Le paysage a tout envahi," Fromentin wrote in *Les maîtres d'autrefois*, "en attendant qu'il ait rencontré sa propre formule, il a bouleversé toutes les formules" [landscape has invaded everything . . . until such time as it finds its own formula, it has upset all formulae]. Ibid., 718.

50. Ibid., 711.

51. Mallarmé, *Écrits sur l'art*, 298.

52. *OC*, 719.

53. See Wright, *Eugène Fromentin*, chap. 30; *ACR*, 359.

54. Moreau, *Correspondance d'Italie*, 531–532.

55. Rouault, *Souvenirs intimes*, 23.

56. *ACR*, 206.

57. *CEF*, 2:1698.

58. Moreau, *Écrits sur l'art*, 1:121.

59. Ibid., 2:257.

60. Cooke, *Gustave Moreau et les arts jumeaux*, 207.

SEVEN

Translating the Aesthetic Impression: The Art Writing of "Marc" de Montifaud

WENDELIN GUENTNER

A WORD OF INTRODUCTION TO THE AUTHOR WHOSE ART WRIT-
ing is the subject of my study. "Marc" de Montifaud is the pseudonym
chosen by the controversial editor and writer of history and fiction
Marie-Amélie Chartroule de Montifaud (Madame Léon de Quivogne;
1849–1912). The titles of the fictional narratives she began publishing in
the late 1870s, such as *Les vestales de l'Église* [The Church's Vestal Virgins]
(1877) or *Entre messe et vêpres; ou, Les matinées de carême au Faubourg
Saint-Germain* [Between Mass and Vespers; or, Lenten Mornings in the
Faubourg Saint-Germain] (1882), give some indication of the daring and
provocative themes that she explored. Her first book, the 1870 historical
study entitled *Les courtisanes de l'antiquité: Marie-Magdeleine* [The Courtesans of Antiquity: Mary Magdalen], as well as Montifaud's later works
of fiction, challenged the religious beliefs and sexual mores of her day
and did not pass unnoticed.[1] In fact, on four occasions over the years her
writings were seized and censored, earning her fines and imprisonment
for "outrage aux bonnes moeurs par voie de la presse" [affronting public
decency through the press].[2] In addition, between 1865—when she was
only sixteen years old—and 1877, the precocious Montifaud authored
numerous critical essays on literature, music, and, most frequently, the
plastic arts for the influential journal of cultural life, *L'Artiste.* The oft-
condemned sensuality that informs her fiction and historical works
found further expression in Montifaud's "pagan" vision of art, which
she articulated in her art criticism.[3] However, my goal in examining her
art writing here is to identify the ways in which Montifaud conceptual-

ized both the production and reception of artworks as translation, and to illustrate how her art writing provided verbal equivalents not only of the paintings under consideration but, most especially, of the aesthetic impressions that she received from them.[4]

Montifaud's aesthetic beliefs remained remarkably consistent during the twelve years that she wrote art criticism for *L'Artiste*. Her vision was above all androcentric since of all creatures, she asserted, man is the only one endowed with the physical, moral, and spiritual prowess needed to conquer and dominate the world.[5] The critic articulated her aesthetic ideal in an 1865 essay on Michelangelo's *Last Judgment*:

> Que demandons-nous à l'art? d'être pour nous le traducteur, la révélation d'un ordre de choses plus parfait que celui dans lequel nous vivons, et que nous ne pourrions pas découvrir nous seul; en second lieu, que le langage soit approprié à l'idée, et que l'originalité de la forme caractérise, personnalise celui qui conçoit.

> [What do we ask of art? to be for us the translator, the revelation of an order of things that is more perfect than the one in which we live, and which we couldn't discover on our own; second, that the language be appropriate to the idea, and that the originality of the form characterizes, personalizes the one who conceives it].[6]

Montifaud presents the beautiful and the true as timeless universals that depend on an artist's individual temperament and mastery of pictorial language to become manifest. As the same sun shining on a number of objects illuminates them in different ways, so too do artists who attempt to bring to light various aspects of the same human subjectivity filter it through their own individual prisms: "Son interprétation, sa réflexion, plus ou moins harmonieuses, plus ou moins poétiques, dépendent maintenant de l'organisation qui la réfléchit, de l'instrument qui la met en action et constitue la personnalité artistique de celui qui l'exprime" [Now its more or less harmonious, more or less poetic interpretation and reflection depend on the organization that ponders it, on the instrument that puts it into operation and makes up the artistic personality of the one who expresses it] (137). Thus, she holds that a work of art should not only translate an artistic motif but also transmit a moral reality filtered through the particular—and ideally elevating—vision of the artist.

But for Montifaud a painting is a "complete" work, and its creator a genius, only when it also expresses the *cachet* of the period:

Il faut que l'artiste soit en même temps le miroir de son siècle, dont il manifeste les croyances, sans pour cela anéantir son individualité; il faut que nous ayons à la fois la société et l'homme dans une création quelconque, et que l'un et l'autre soient toujours en présence en toute œuvre.

[The artist must at once be the mirror of his age, whose beliefs he expresses, without, however, at the same time destroying his individuality; in any creation we must have society and the human being both at the same time, and one and the other must always be present in every work.] (137)

When in her 1867 salon essay Montifaud poses the identical rhetorical question that she had two years earlier—"Que demandons-nous à l'art?" [What do we ask of art?]—the answer she gives develops this social dimension of her aesthetic ideal. She writes that an artwork should be "la traduction infaillible de toute manifestation intellectuelle, de tout fait particulier ou social, car l'action, c'est l'humanité dans les péripéties progressives de ses transformations" [the unerring translation of every intellectual expression, of every private or social fact, because action is humanity in the continuous surprises of its transformations].[7] It is this tension between the universal and the particular, the static and the dynamic, the spiritual and the material, evident in Montifaud's two descriptions of a work of art as translation, that lies at the center of her profoundly humanist aesthetic.[8]

Another defining characteristic of Montifaud's aesthetic ideal, and one consonant with her conception of art as translation, is her acute awareness of the dialogical nature of artistic communication. This communicative process begins, according to Montifaud, when artists become attentive to the emotion that an external stimulus had provoked in them. It continues when, bringing to bear both their personal sincerity and technical skill, the artists attempt to accurately translate this impression through the language of their chosen medium. Montifaud formulated her conception of the dialogical and emotive nature of artistic communication most explicitly in 1868 when she wrote, "La commotion pathétique ou violente qu'on reçoit d'une oeuvre n'est que le contre-coup de celle déjà éprouvée par celui qui le traduit" [The touching or violent upheaval that we receive from a work is but the aftereffect of that already felt by the one who expresses it].[9] The emotive *commotion* that artists experience and that they then attempt to translate through pictorial language can originate not only in nature or in scenes of contemporary life, she contends: historical and mythological motifs can also provide a valid impetus to artistic creation. In 1865, Montifaud described what must occur for this to successfully happen by means of a scientific metaphor popular in critical discourse from the early nineteenth century on—that of electricity. She wrote, "Il faut qu'un courant électrique parti de lui-même traverse les siècles et les distances, afin qu'il s'établisse entre le peintre et son sujet une relation immédiate" [An electric current gone out from himself must cross centuries and distances, so that a direct relationship may be established between the painter and his subject].[10] The communicative chain is then completed when the artwork produces in the spectator both a visual impression and a subjective response.

If Montifaud's conception of the creation and reception of artworks is profoundly dialogical, this communication is the most complete and multidimensional in the case of the art critic. Like all spectators, she contends, critics must discern the nature of the "upheaval" that the artist had received from a stimulus. But in their status as privileged spectators, critics are also charged with evaluating whether the visual vocabulary the artist employed was successful in translating his or her emotive response to the initial stimulus.[11]

Furthermore, when critics communicate their own aesthetic responses to artists, they can influence the future direction of the artists' work. The critics' discourse thus constitutes, in the terms of J. L. Austin and John Searle's speech act theory, a "directive," that is, a type of illocutionary act whose purpose is to effect a certain result, to have the addressee *do* something.[12] This is also true when *salonniers* shared their responses to an artwork with the reading public, for their words could have the effect both of forming public taste and influencing trends in art acquisition. In order to carry out these functions successfully, the critic must find discursive means to translate into words both the motif depicted and the artist's interpretation of it, as well as to evaluate the artist's skill and pictorial technique. However, Montifaud was most interested in questions of reception at all stages of the communicative chain—the *commotion* the painter received from the motif, that which the critic received from the painting, and, ultimately, the one the reader would receive from the art writing.

I would now like to examine two stylistic techniques that Montifaud often adopted in an effort to confront some of the intersemiological
challenges inherent in art criticism. First, Montifaud was particularly
given to the nominalization of adjectives. The following four examples
all come from her 1866 salon essay. She writes, for example, of Madame
de Rothchild's landscapes that "il y a de la limpidité dans les eaux" [there
is limpidity in the waters], and praises Gérôme's execution technique in
his painting "Mosquée el Assaneyn au Caire," asserting that "dans cette
toile sont enfouies les virilités les plus hautes que nous connaissions" [the
highest virilities that we know are hidden in this painting]. In addition,
Montifaud claims that in Vidal's painting *Amours des anges,* "les éblouis-
santes sérénités des extases viennent dégager je ne sais quelle délicieuse
quiétude au fond de l'âme, qui plonge ses ailes sous les diaphanéités du
paradis" [the blinding serenities of transports come to free I don't know
what kind of delightful tranquility in the soul's depths, which plunges
its wings under the translucencies of paradise].[13] The formulation "je
ne sais" is an example of the *Unsagbarkeitstopos* [inexpressibility topos]
which expresses a realization that words cannot be found adequate to
their communicative task.[14] Thus, "je ne sais quelle délicieuse quiétude"
suggests that the substitution of nouns for adjectives is one way Montifaud chose to address the difficulties of translating, or, more accurately,
of communicating, through poetic language, the ineffable quality both
of angelic love and of the aesthetic impression to which the viewing of
this painting had given rise in the critic.[15]

"Limpidité" [limpidity] and "virilité" [virility] instead of "limpide"
[limpid] and "virile" [virile], "sérénités" [serenities] rather than "sérène"
[serene], and "diaphanéités" [diaphanities] rather than "diaphane" [di-
aphanous]—this preference Montifaud shows for substantives, characteristic, of course, of the Goncourt Brothers' *écriture artiste*, produces an
effect of strangeness by aestheticizing the traditionally descriptive and
evaluative language of art criticism.[16] Moreover, the abstract neologisms
coined from adjectives that often result from her practice of nominal
style appear to be yet another aspect of her attempt to address the challenges of her intersemiological task.

Montifaud's response the same year, 1866, to Théodore Rousseau's
landscapes illustrates how the nominal style facilitated her expression of

an aesthetic vision that embraces the Symbolist notion of synesthesia, the linking of different sensations inspired by a presumption of a fundamental correspondence between them. She wrote of his paintings *Bornage de la forêt de Fontainebleau à Barbizon* and *Coucher de soleil:* "Nous n'y avons pas constaté cette mordoration, ce satinage, ce perlé que la saison verse ordinairement en parcourant toutes les notes et demi-notes de son clavier" [We haven't noticed there this golden brown, this satinizing, this sparklingness, which the season usually pours out while following all the notes and half-notes of its keyboard].[17] In this sentence, Montifaud suggests a correspondence between visual and auditory sensations, between shades of color and musical notes or half-notes. However, two of the nouns with which she begins, "satinage" and "perlé," introduce visual, tactile, and musical elements. The *Dictionnaire de l'Académie française* of 1832–1835 offers six meanings for the adjective "perlé." Besides usages that are culinary and domestic, this dictionary identifies two others that are aesthetic. The first of these is decorative, with "le perlé" meaning "orné de perles" [decorated with pearls], the expression being useful to describe an ornate crown. The second aesthetic usage the *Dictionnaire* identifies is figurative and musical, and is perhaps the closest to the meaning Montifaud intended: "PERLÉ se dit figurément, en termes de Musique, pour qualifier l'exécution, lorsqu'elle est nette, égale, brillante. Un jeu perlé. Une cadence perlée" [With respect to Music, PERLÉ is used figuratively to describe execution when it is clear, steady, sparkling. A sparkling playing style. A sparkling cadence].[18] Nonetheless, Montifaud's transformation of the adjective "perlé" into a noun is lexicalogically unsettling, and creates an evocative but indistinct impression that allows the reader to hesitate between one of several possible meanings. Moreover, none of the categories of substance, form, or material consistency is respected in her formulation, for the personified season pours out ("verse") these objects—or, more precisely, the colors and tactile impressions associated with them—expressed indirectly and lyrically onto objects. The neologism "mordoration," from the adjective "mordoré" [golden brown] or the noun "le mordoré" ["the golden brown"], further aestheticizes her critical language. In Montifaud's writing, borders between objects and sensations appear to dissolve in something of a Baudelairian "ténébreuse et profonde unité" [gloomy and deep unity].[19]

Jules Lemaître's views on the Goncourt Brothers' style are enlightening in this regard. In the third volume of *Les contemporains* (c. 1887), he explains the Goncourt Brothers' *écriture artiste* by their desire to paint, for, he asserts, they considered things as much from the perspective of "des ouvriers des arts plastiques" [workers in the plastic arts] as from that typically held by writers or psychologists.[20] The brothers' experience of the world is double, he contends: they receive impressions resembling those of a painter who was "le plus fou de couleurs et le plus entêté de pittoresque" [the craziest for colors and the most obdurate with respect to the picturesque], as well as those to which literary writers would typically be sensitive (76). This causes Jules and Edmond to engage in what Lemaître describes as "une lutte du dictionnaire contre la palette" [a struggle of the dictionary with the palette] and "une transposition d'art enragée" [a furious transposition of art]:

> Les tons, les nuances, les lignes que le pinceau peut seul reproduire, ils font cette gageure de les rendre sensibles avec des phrases écrites; et c'est alors un labeur, un effort désespéré des mots pour prendre forme et couleur, . . . des phrases qui ont des airs de glacis, des substantifs qui sont des frottis, des épithètes qui sont des touches piquées, des adverbes qui sont des empâtements.

> [(The Goncourt Brothers) take on this bet to make palpable the tones, shades, and lines that only the brush can reproduce with written sentences, and it is then hard work, the word's despairing effort to take on form and color, . . . of sentences that have the appearance of glaze, of nouns that are frottis (thin transparent or semitransparent layers of pigment), of adjectives that are sharp strokes, of adverbs that are impasto.] (76)

Lemaître concedes that words can never adequately reproduce a painting; therefore, the Goncourts' attempt to enable a reader to visualize the image depicted with any kind of accuracy is necessarily doomed to failure. However, in spite of this, Lemaître continues, the brothers persisted in writing only for the eyes, disdaining anything in literary style that did not enable the reader to fully experience the artwork in question, both visually and emotively (78–79). Lemaître explains the Goncourts' penchant for neologisms by "ce désir inassouvissable d'une expression égale leur impression" [this unquenchable desire for an expression equal to their impression], as well as by their frustration at not finding existing words that were adequate to their task (80).[21]

Lemaître further asserts that since the Goncourts' viewpoint is pictorial, their first visual impressions are not of a subject—the motif—but rather are elements of pictorial language such as color and lines that would, therefore, best be conveyed by adjectives. But, he contends, dissatisfied with the fact that adjectives by definition always have a subordinate relationship to nouns, the Goncourts elect to nominalize them.[22] Being sensitive and poetic, Lemaître writes, the brothers "trouvent que la langue ordinaire, telle qu'elle est établie par l'usage même de grands écrivains, y est impuissante: ils l'enrichissent audacieusement de vocables nouveaux et de tournures imprévues, troublent toutes ses habitudes, la tendent et la violentent à la faire crier" [find that ordinary language, even as it is established by the use of great writers, is powerless with respect to it: they audaciously enrich it with new words and unexpected expressions, unsettle all its patterns, and stretch and assault it to the extent that it cries] (85).

When the only comment that Montifaud makes about a painting by M. Dupray—one, like others she is considering, that was inspired by the 1870–1871 Franco-Prussian War—is to note that it had failed to produce "cet effet si ingénieux, réalisé peut-être avec une valeur de blanc, une note de jaune, jetées dans la coloration spléenale d'une matinée d'hiver" [this effect that is so ingenious, produced perhaps with a white value, a yellow note, thrown into the splenetic coloration of a winter morning], she does something analogous.[23] We are not given the title of the painting nor the exact subject matter: rather, Montifaud's evaluation is limited to a comparison of the colors Dupray used to those successfully employed by another artist whose work she had just considered and who, in his view, had been able to create a certain visual—and melancholy—effect. The "étrangeté" [strangeness], the "excentricité" [eccentricity] that Lemaître associates with the Goncourts' écriture artiste is here produced not by the nominalization of an adjective but by the substitution of one noun for another more abstract ("coloration" replacing "couleur") and by the neologism "spléenale," which does transform an adjective into a noun. Lemaître believed that the Goncourts constantly struggled to make their style "adéquat à leurs sentiments et à leurs sensations" [appropriate to their feelings and sensations], and it would appear that Montifaud does the same thing.[24]

Another of Montifaud's stylistic trademarks—a technique already evident in the previous example—is her recourse to musical comparisons and metaphors. Montifaud chose music, the least intellectual and most suggestive of the arts, to express analogically both the art object and the aesthetic impression it produced in her. Thus, with reference to Monsieur Hébert's *Perle noire* and *Banc de pierre,* she writes,

> Pourvu qu'il y fasse intervenir la lumière, peu lui importe cette teinte verte des feuilles, il saura en parcourir toute la gamme, depuis la note la plus élevée, la plus foncée, jusqu'à la note la plus pale; il connaît la croissance et la décroissance de ses tons; comme le musicien sur son clavier, il en trouvera d'encore inconnus aux peintres modernes; il composera des symphonies en couleur comme un autre en composera avec des lignes.

> [Provided that he makes light come into play, this green tint of the leaves doesn't matter to him, he will know how to cover the whole scale, from the highest note, the deepest, all the way to the palest note, he knows the growth and decline of its tones; as a musician at his keyboard, he will find new ones still unknown to modern painters; he will compose symphonies in color as another will compose one with lines.][25]

In this example, Montifaud reiterates the comparative "comme" to make the meaning of her musical vocabulary transparent: a pleasurable arrangement of lines and colors in a painting is analogous to the pleasurable arrangement of sounds in a symphony. Here the aesthetic impression the critic receives is not from the representation of identifiable objects on the canvas but, rather, from the suggestive disposition of color. Thus, Montifaud's art writing does not transpose a painting but attempts to record—and recreate in the reader—an aesthetic response.

In 1873, Montifaud's enthusiasm for two genre paintings inspired her to a lyricism informed by synesthesia in which musical metaphors again play an important role. Employing a metaphor that associates linguistic, auditory, and visual modes of communication, she characterized Hébert's *Tricoteuse* as being "un vrai petit poëme de mélodie picturale" [a veritable little poem of pictorial melody].[26] After sketching a portrait of the woman in a single sentence, and asserting in another that the loose brushwork suggests that the woman knitting had been dreamed rather than seen, Montifaud tried to identify the source of the charm, which— to her eyes—the young woman's physiognomy exudes:

Quelle phrase de coloris la fait se modeler, palpiter, parler, dans le relief
adouci de ses ombres? Entre ces carnations de la figure, entre ces mains d'une
mordoration violente, le peintre, uniquement pour faire jouer un accent, a placé
le tricot d'un blanc de lumière; alors cet objet insignifiant par lui-même frappe
une consonnance éclatante au milieu de cette tonalité brune de la composition.
L'artiste fait résonner ainsi une note froide, une seule note claire qui chante
d'autant plus qu'elle est toute seule, c'est ce qui rend son tableau intéressant.
De même que dans un orchestre le violon vient donner la note agréable, la
phrase sympathique. Savoir faire vibrer à propos les consonnances froides dans
une gamme chaude, ne serait-ce pas là où résiderait une grande partie de la
puissance?

[What phrase of shade makes it shape itself, palpitate, speak, in the softened
relief of its shadows? Between these complexions of the face, between these
hands of a violent golden brown, the painter, simply to show a tone, placed the
knitted fabric of a whiteness of light; and so this object, insignificant in and of
itself, strikes a sparkling consonance in the middle of this brown tonality of the
composition. The artist thus makes a cold note ring out, a single clear note that
sings even more because it is alone, this is what makes his painting interesting.
Just like in an orchestra the violin comes to give the pleasing note, the pleas-
ant phrase. Knowing how to make cold consonances vibrate in a warm scale,
wouldn't that be where a great part of the power resides?] (276)

It is striking that Montifaud is not concerned with the subject matter—
"face," "hands," and "knitted fabric" are the only words that describe the
motif depicted—but rather with the aesthetic effect produced by the
painter's selection and application of color. The critic uses a sustained
musical metaphor ("jouer," "consonnance," "résonner," "note," "orchestra," "violon") in an attempt to communicate the aesthetic *commotion*
that she received from this painting to her reader, who is inscribed in
the passage by the rhetorical questions of the first and last sentences. She
also employs terms commonly used by musicians, which were initially
borrowed from other linguistic fields, just as "phrase" or "accent" had
been from verbal expression. In formulations such as "tonalité brune,"
"note froide," or "note chaude," Montifaud uses interchangeable sensations that are visual, auditory, and tactile. In addition, rather than
remaining in stasis, colors under her pen become animated through
the use of verbs of action or motion ("se modeler," "palpiter," "vibrer"),
allowing Montifaud to incorporate a temporal dimension into what is
most essentially a spatial art. This lively effect is underlined through
the trope of personification (the phrase of shade "speaks"). The fact that

Montifaud is not concerned with the choice of motif but rather in one particular component of pictorial language, color, brings to mind Maurice Denis's 1890 admonition: "Se rappeler qu'un tableau—avant d'être un cheval de bataille, une femme nue, ou une quelconque anecdote—est essentiellement une surface plane recouverte de couleurs en un certain ordre assemblées" [Remember that a painting—before being a battle horse, a naked woman, or whatever anecdote—is essentially a flat surface covered with colors combined in a certain order].[27] However, it also resonates with Stéphane Mallarmé's ideal, formulated in 1864, "Peindre non la chose mais l'effet qu'elle produit" [Paint not the thing but the effect it produces], doing so, moreover, in an indirect, suggestive, and nondescriptive way.[28]

Of course, the "correspondences" between visual and aural sensations had already been brilliantly explored by Charles Baudelaire. That Montifaud was not unaware of Baudelaire's poetry becomes clear when she finishes her 1873 discussion of genre painting, "comme on plaque un accord final après un morceau" [as we tack on a final chord after a musical piece], with a work that has music-making as its motif, Firmin Girard's *Toilette japonaise*. Montifaud briefly describes this exotic interior scene: the central figure is a young Japanese woman "rêveusement occupée à suivre les accords qu'elle tire d'un instrument placé entre ses mains" [dreamingly occupied with following the chords that she draws from an instrument placed in her hands].[29] However, Montifaud is particularly fascinated with the layered arrangement of the woman's ample hair, which, the critic imagines, a lover will soon loosen. This time Montifaud evokes her aesthetic response not through an analogy to music but rather to poetry, for it inspires her to quote the following taken from Baudelaire's prose poem "Un hémisphère dans une chevelure": "Tes cheveux contiennent tout un rêve, plein de voilures et de mâtures; ils contiennent de grandes mers dont les moussons me portent vers de charmants climats, où l'espace est plus bleu et profond; où l'atmosphère est parfumée par les fruits, par les feuilles et par la peau humaine" [Your hair contains a complete dream, filled with sails and masts; they contain great seas whose monsoons carry me toward delightful climates, where space is bluer and deeper; where the atmosphere is scented by the fruits, the leaves, and by human skin].[30] Just as objects attain privileged status through the *rêverie* to which they give rise, so, for Montifaud, a successful painting liberates the deepest level of the spectator's imagination, as poetry is often capable of doing. While she did not author this poetic passage but rather merely quoted it, Montifaud would seem to agree with Baudelaire's well known 1846 assertion that "le meilleur compte rendu d'un tableau pourra être un sonnet ou une élegie" [the best account of a painting could be a sonnet or an elegy].[31]

It is the genre of landscape, which I discuss elsewhere, that touches Montifaud most deeply.[32] However, with landscape painting, as with the other pictorial genres, her ideal is expressive rather than descriptive, the interest of a landscape residing in its potential to communicate a subjective state. Therefore, along with the Goncourt Brothers and Mallarmé, Montifaud's aesthetic vision also resonates with Paul Verlaine's "paysages d'état d'âme" [mood landscapes]. This is consonant, moreover, with Jules Lemaître's experience of Verlaine's poetry. He writes,

> Le monde sensible . . . vous entre, si je puis dire, dans les yeux. Le monde sensible cesse de vous être extérieur. Vous perdez subitement le pouvoir de "l'objectiver," de le tenir en dehors de vous. Vous éprouvez réellement qu'un paysage n'est . . . qu'un état de conscience.

> [The tangible world . . . enters into you, if I might say so, with the eyes. The tangible world stops being external to you. You suddenly lose the power to "objectify" it, to hold it outside of you. You really feel that a landscape is only a state of consciousness.][33]

And, Lemaître continues, Verlaine's reader begins to believe that describing one's sensations and communicating one's feelings are the very same thing. For her part, through her use of evocative language, Montifaud attempted to produce in her readers an aesthetic experience analogous to the one that she herself had received when she initially viewed the painting. Thus, the critic translates into prose not the landscape but the state of *rêverie* that her viewing of the painting had induced in her, as well as the subjective state that the landscape had initially provoked in the artist and that he had felt keen to communicate.

In the "Notice" with which Montifaud opens her 1884 edition of the *Aventures de l'abbé de Choisy habillé en femme,* she writes that some writers leave to posterity the secret of two or three of their master strokes ("maîtresses touches"). To make her point she evokes the type of aesthetic effect produced by the Goncourt Brothers' prose:

Vous possédez soit un morceau d'ambre, soit les fils d'or d'une étoffe merveil-
leuse transpercée de soleil, soit un effet d'harmonie gris-bleu; ou bien vous
croirez, en froissant cette page entre vos mains, opérer le rapt des plus adorables
couleurs que la terre possède. Au bout des doigts on gardera le chatoiement
laiteux du satin: à l'oreille on aura comme un grésillement de mouches de feu.

[You either possess a piece of amber, or the gold threads of a marvelous fabric,
which is shot through with sun, or an effect of grey-blue harmony; or again
you will have the impression, in crumpling this page between your hands, of
carrying out the abduction of the most adorable colors that the earth possesses.
Our fingertips will keep the milky tickling of the satin: we will have in our ears
something like a chirping of fireflies.][34]

As is so often the case in her art criticism, Montifaud transposes into
words not the semantic content but rather an aesthetic effect, here produced by the Goncourt Brothers' characteristic stylistic techniques,
their "maîtresses touches." In particular, she suggests the *recherché* quality of their *écriture artiste* by identifying a series of correspondences.
Montifaud likens their unusual lexicon, syntax, and sonorities to a series
of refined sensations that are alternately visual ("un morceau d'ambre,"
"les fils d'or," "transpercée de soleil"), tactile ("[a]u bout des doigts,"
"le chatoiement . . . du satin"), and auditory ("à l'oreille . . . un grésillement"). While the Baudelarian fascination with the olfactory is lacking
here, two sensations—colors and sounds—nevertheless do correspond
to each other, expressing in two cases synesthetic experiences: "un effet
d'harmonie gris-bleu" and "le chatoiement laiteux."[35]

Marc de Montifaud's art writing begs the question: was she a Symbolist art critic "avant la lettre"? Montifaud characterized herself as both
an idealist and a pagan; while she reacted against the materialism of the
Realist and Naturalist traditions, she believed that it was by renewing the
pre-Christian sensuality of the early Greeks that art could rediscover its
true nature and purpose. And yet, many aspects of her critical prose—
the search for linguistic novelty, the privileging of the irrational (often
suggested through analogies to music), the use of synesthesia and otherwise aestheticized language to connote, to suggest, rather than to name
or describe—are all traits of Decadent and Symbolist writers as well.
Verlaine, Mallarmé, and Arthur Rimbaud remained largely unknown
until the early 1880s, but in 1865, the year after Montifaud began writing
for *L'Artiste,* Mallarmé published in this review a prose piece entitled
"Symphonie littéraire," in which he evokes the "landscape" he experi-

ences when reading Baudelaire's poems.[36] Already in 1862, Mallarmé had published in *L'Artiste* another prose piece, "Hérésies artistiques: L'art pour tous," in which he argues that art, like religion, should envelop itself in mystery.[37] It is thus likely that Montifaud would have been exposed to at least these articles by Mallarmé, as well as two of his early poems, "Le guignon" and "Le sonneur," which also appeared in *L'Artiste* in 1862.[38] Moreover, from 1864 until several months before his death in October 1872, Théophile Gautier published articles on painting in *L'Artiste* as well. And Arsène Houssaye, the longtime editor of the influential art revue *L'Artiste,* was not only a good friend of Gautier but also served as an important mentor to the youthful and precocious Montifaud.[39] Note that it was in 1862, during the period in which Houssaye served as literary director for the newspaper, *La Presse,* that Baudelaire dedicated the *Petits poèmes en prose* to him.

Thus, through reading and discussion, Montifaud would have had many opportunities to familiarize herself with the constellation of issues preoccupying the cultural avant-garde. Giving a verbal equivalent to paintings and sculptures was considered central to art criticism in France as it developed into a literary genre in the eighteenth and nineteenth centuries.[40] As the author of numerous salon reviews for the influential revue *L'Artiste,* with which Gautier was so intimately involved, Montifaud was certainly aware of this discursive tradition and was no doubt influenced by its literary aspirations. However, it is clear that Montifaud's conception of artistic communication had deep affinities with notions that would be expressed by Symbolist writers and theoreticians more than a decade later. Thus, although she was not a Symbolist herself, at least in the years before her cessation of art criticism in 1877, various aspects of her artistic vision, as well as her personal style of art writing, seem to point to beliefs and practices that would be adopted in the 1880s and 1890s by such Decadent and Symbolist writers on the arts as Emile Hennequin, Maurice Denis, and Albert Aurier.[41] For them, as for Montifaud, the critic was not a sterile eunuch or parasite, as some contended, but rather someone who was capable of creating an autonomous work of art through words, just as a painter or a sculptor could do through the language of the plastic arts.[42] And Montifaud, like them, believed that art criticism was a literary genre, one that fully justified calling an art writer a "poet," at least in the way Baudelaire used the term: "Or, qu'est-ce qu'un poète (je prends le mot dans son acceptation la plus large) si ce n'est un traducteur, un déchiffreur?" [What then is a poet (I take the word in its widest usage) if not a translator, a decipherer?].[43]

WENDELIN GUENTNER is professor emerita of French literature and culture at the University of Iowa. She is the author of *Stendhal et son lecteur: Essai sur les* Promenades dans Rome and *Esquisses littéraires: Rhétorique du spontané et récit de voyage au XIXe siècle,* and editor of *Women Art Critics in Nineteenth-Century France: Vanishing Acts.* She has published widely on the history and rhetoric of the travel narrative, interpretative strategies and reader reception, photography and book illustration, the discourse of the preface, and salon criticism and the literary fragment. She is currently engaged in projects on the pictorial sketch in literary and aesthetic discourse, and on the late nineteenth-century man of letters Jules Claretie.

NOTES

1. The *Larousse XIXe* characterizes it thus: "Oeuvre audacieuse qui valut à son auteur les plus vives attaques et aussi les plus chaleureuses approbations. L'ouvrage saisi, ou arrêté à la frontière, n'obtint l'autorisation de paraître qu'en 1870, à l'arrivée de M. Emile Olivier au ministère" [Audacious work that earned the author the most heated attacks and also the warmest approbations. Seized or stopped at the border, the work did not obtain the authorization to be published until 1870, when Mr. Emile Olivier became minister]. Cited in Montifaud, *Marc de Montifaud,* 109.

2. Heather Dawkins recounts Montifaud's legal problems in *The Nude in French Art and Culture,* 134–140.

3. For more on Marc de Montifaud's life and aesthetic beliefs, see my biographical sketch in Guentner, ed., *Women Art Critics in Nineteenth-Century France,* 295–305. I argue that the defense of the Classical nude made in her art criticism demonstrates a personal, materialist vision, one that distinguishes itself from the conventions of the academy.

4. Françoise Lucbert gives a useful definition of art criticism as translation and transposition. She writes that both are forms of what Roman Jakobson calls "la traduction intersémiotique" [intersemiotic translation], that is, a passage from a system of nonlinguistic signs to a system of linguistic signs. However, Lucbert also distinguishes the two. The goal of "translation," she writes, is to describe a work of art in such a way as to permit readers to represent it mentally for themselves, even if they have not seen it. But the difficulty of translating an image into words results in what Lucbert calls a topos of art criticism, "l'intraductibilité de la peinture" [painting's untranslatability], which she defines as "des énoncés par lesquels un critique évoque un tableau par une prose poétique qui s'attache à en restituer les effets visuels" [utterances through which a critic

conjures up a painting through a poetic prose which strives to restore the visual effects (of it)]. Lucbert, *Entre le voir et le dire,* 200.

5. Montifaud, "Salon de 1867," *L'Artiste,* June 1, 1867, 448.

6. Montifaud, "Michel-Ange: *Le jugement dernier,*" *L'Artiste,* March 15, 1865, 137. Subsequent references are given in the text.

7. Marc de Montifaud, "Salon de 1867," *L'Artiste,* July 1, 1867, 112.

8. I discuss Montifaud's original and nuanced approaches to history, genre, portrait, and landscape painting, as expressed in more than a decade of her art writing, in my essay "'Marc' de Montifaud: The *'esprit critique'* of an *'esprit fort,'*" in Guentner, ed., *Women Art Critics in Nineteenth-Century France,* 203–235. Both similarities and differences exist between Montifaud's conceptions of art and art writing and that of major critics of the time such as Théophile Gautier. Thus, while both Montifaud and Gautier privileged the ideal of antique beauty and referred to themselves as "pagans," they also demonstrated suppleness in their approaches to modern artists. Montifaud remained open to the artistic techniques of the early Impressionists, such as Edouard Manet. Similarly, she could praise Camille Corot for having renewed the Classical tradition without trite academic conventions and, at the same time, for being "le premier des impressionnistes" [the first of the Impressionists]. See Montifaud, "Salon de 1877, I," *L'Artiste,* May 1, 1877, 339. Gautier, however, was less tolerant. See Drost, "Pour une réévaluation de la critique d'art de Gautier," 417–418.

9. Montifaud, "Salon de 1868," *L'Artiste,* June 1, 1868, 408–409.

10. Montifaud, "Salon de 1865," *L'Artiste,* May 1, 1865, 197. On the use of this metaphor in nineteenth-century critical discourse in France, see Bouverot, "La métaphore dans le langage de la critique d'art," 186–189.

11. Marge Käsper has used the translation from French to Estonian of Montifaud's 1874 account of the first Impressionist exhibition in her analysis of the semiological process of translating art criticism from one language to another. Käsper coined the term *polyphonie traductionnelle* [translational polyphony] to express the many-stranded process of translating texts describing paintings when the translator is separated by time and culture from the author of the target text. If the artwork is available so that the reader can compare the painting and the art writing it inspired, she calls it a "co-texte," while she terms "pro-texte" those cases of descriptive text where the artwork is no longer extant, thus making such a comparison impossible. See Käsper, "Sur des propos à propos des impressionnistes," 577, 580. This terminology is useful for identifying the challenges faced by the nineteenth-century *salonniers,* as they wrote for two publics. The first was made up of salon-goers, for whom their essay would constitute a "co-texte," whether they read the review before, during, or after their salon visit. The second included those readers who had no visual point of reference, either because they had never viewed the works exhibited in the salon or had never even seen lithographic or photographic images of them. For these readers the critics' words constituted a "pro-texte."

12. See Kerbrat-Orecchioni, *Les actes de langage dans le discours,* 8.

13. Montifaud, "Salon de 1866, II," *L'Artiste,* June 15, 1866, 201, 200.

14. E. R. Curtius identifies this *topos,* which he applies to cases in which a writer finds that language is inadequate to its task. Curtius, *European Literature and the Latin Middle Ages,* 159–162.

15. Françoise Lucbert has identified the "intraductibilité de la peinture" as a topos of art criticism, given that writers often cite the impossibility of translating an image into words. See Lucbert, *Entre le voir et le dire,* 202.

16. For a discussion of *l'écriture artiste,* see Sabatier, *L'esthétique des Goncourt,* 400, and Ullman, *Style in the French Novel,* 121. We do not know whether Montifaud had read the Goncourts' novels, but the six novels the brothers authored together appeared between 1860 and 1869. Given Montifaud's age—she was seventeen when she wrote her 1866 salon review—and the intellectual milieu that she frequented, it is entirely conceivable and even likely that she was familiar with their writings. If so, it would support the notion that her style was on some level imitative, whether consciously or unconsciously.

17. Montifaud, "Salon de 1866, I," 171.

18. *Dictionnaire de l'Académie française,* 6th edition (Paris: Imprimerie et Librairie Firmin Didot Frères, 1832–1835), 2:394, http://artfl.atilf.fr/dictionnaires/ACADEMIE /SIXIEME/sixieme.fr.html.

19. Charles Baudelaire, "Correspondances" from *Les Fleurs du Mal,* in Baudelaire, *Oeuvres complètes,* 1:11.

20. Lemaître, *Les contemporains,* 3rd series, 76. Subsequent references are given in the text.

21. Besides neologisms (*les mots inventés*) and adjectives transformed into neuter nouns, Lemaître also identifies the linking of two words with the same root, "pleonasms, the doubling up of synonyms, abstract words and the imperfect tense as being characteristic of *l'écriture artiste.*" Ibid., 79–85.

22. "Pour nous rendre cette première vue saisissante, mais sommaire, ce premier éblouissement d'un tableau réel, ils commencent donc, instinctivement, par en abstraire les teintes, les lignes, les mouvements; et comme ils veulent leur donner dans la phrase la place d'honneur et les faire jaillir uniquement, ils ne les expriment point par des adjectifs, qui seraient toujours subordonnés à un nom, mais par des substantifs nécessairement abstraits. Et ayant ainsi traduit l'impression générale, qui correspond au premier moment de la vision, ils la précisent par les mots qui viennent ensuite et qui marquent ce qu'on distingue au second coup d'oeil" [In order to restore for us this first piercing but cursory glance, this first dazzling sight of a real painting, they begin thus, instinctively, by removing the colorings, lines, movements; and since they want to give them the place of honor in the sentence and only have them burst forth, they do not express them through adjectives, which would always be subordinated to a noun, but necessarily by abstract nouns. And having thus translated the general impression, which corresponds to the first moment of vision, they specify it with words that come afterward and that show what we distinguish in the second glance]. Ibid., 83.

23. Montifaud, "Salon de 1872," *L'Artiste,* June 1, 1872, 244.

24. Lemaître, *Les contemporains,* 3rd series, 81, 87, 85.

25. Montifaud, "Salon de 1865, II," *L'Artiste,* May 15, 1865, 220.

26. Marc de Montifaud, "Salon de 1873," *L'Artiste,* June 1, 1873, 276.

27. Maurice Denis, "Le symbolisme: Définition du néo-traditionnalisme," in Denis, *Du symbolisme au classicisme,* 33.

28. Stéphane Mallarmé to Henri Cazalis, October 30, 1864, in Mallarmé, *Correspondance,* 137.

29. Montifaud, "Salon de 1873," 278.

30. Charles Baudelaire, "Un hémisphère dans une chevelure," from *"Le spleen de Paris,"* in Baudelaire, *Oeuvres complètes,* 1:300. The poem appeared in *La Presse* on September 24, 1862, at a time when Arsène Houssaye, Montifaud's future mentor, was editor.

31. Charles Baudelaire, "Salon de 1846," in Baudelaire, *Œuvres complètes,* 2:418.

32. See Guentner, "'Marc' de Montifaud," 216–229.

33. Lemaître, *Les contemporains,* 4th series, 75.

34. Choisy, *Aventures de l'abbé de Choisy,* 37.

35. Recall that in "Correspondances," Baudelaire asserts that "les parfums, les couleurs et les sons se répondent" [scents, colors, and sounds answer each other]. See *Les Fleurs du Mal* in Baudelaire, *Œuvres complètes,* 1:11.

36. *L'Artiste,* February 1, 1865, 57–58.

37. *L'Artiste,* September 15, 1862, 127–128.

38. *L'Artiste,* March 15, 1862, 132.

39. Montifaud recognized Houssaye's benevolent guidance as does the *Dictionnaire Larousse* and Aliquis, the author of an 1877 article on Montifaud. See Montifaud, *Marc de Montifaud,* 7, 105, 109.

40. This is evident in Denis Diderot's dramatic descriptions of paintings in his eighteenth-century salon essays, and in the evocative art writing of Théophile Gautier and Charles Baudelaire. Indeed, it was in his 1859 essay on Gautier's style, one that served as a reflection of the latter's passion for the beautiful, that Baudelaire wrote his famous assertion: "Manier savamment une langue, c'est pratiquer une espèce de sorcellerie évocatoire" [To handle a language skillfully is to perform a kind of magical invocation]. Baudelaire, "Théophile Gautier [1]," in Baudelaire, *Oeuvres complètes,* 2:117–118. For a discussion of the rivalry between image and word from antiquity to the art criticism of Théophile Gautier, and Baudelaire's appreciation of the latter, see Benda, "Sur les 'expressions macaroniques'," 63–86. For a fuller discussion, see Hamrick, *The Role of Gautier in the Art Criticism of Baudelaire.* On Gautier's practice of "transposition d'art," see Montandon, "Ecritures de l'image chez Théophile Gautier."

41. According to Françoise Lucbert, Symbolist critics rejected the narration of a depicted anecdote in favor of an effort to create an atmosphere or a general visual impression: "la suggestion et l'évocation sont les mots d'ordre d'une génération de critiques qui préfère la création à la copie, la production à la reproduction, la transposition créatrice à la traduction fidèle" [suggestion and evocation are the watchwords of a generation of critics who prefer creation to copy, production to reproduction, creative transposition to faithful translation]. Lucbert, *Entre le voir et le dire,* 214. For the creative aspect of Symbolist art criticism, see also Symington, "Poétique de la critique picturale symboliste."

42. Françoise Lucbert discusses the nineteenth-century perception of the art critic as eunuch and parasite in *Entre le voir et le dire,* 180. David Scott contends that *L'Artiste* was predicated on the notion of "inter-art correspondances," where poetry and other creative writing were juxtaposed with historical or critical essays. See Scott, "Writing the Arts," 66.

43. Charles Baudelaire, "Réflexions sur quelques-uns de mes contemporains: I. Victor Hugo," in Baudelaire, *Oeuvres complètes,* 2:132.

EIGHT

Zola's Transpositions

ROBERT LETHBRIDGE

IF THE *TRANSPOSITION D'ART* HAS A LONG HISTORY, IT OCCU-
pies, as David Scott has shown, a privileged place in nineteenth-century
French culture.[1] His own emphasis on transpositional practice, rather
than merely the identification of borrowed subjects and themes, informs
the present chapter. And the process it explores is, in a sense, itself exemplary. For it both brings together two models of contemporary "intertextual" cross-fertilization and is emblematic of a modern rethinking of
the relationship, in more general terms, between literature and the visual
arts. In the very first issue of that other 1980s milestone, the advent of the
journal *Word and Image,* Robert Bruce's inaugurating essay (*"Orbis pictus
redivivus"*) asked of the transposition some crucial questions: "Does it
ignore, distort, betray, mock, make ironic, counter-point, endorse, underscore, cause to resonate, justify, or draw justification from the visual
image?" Does the transposition, as he put it, "add, or merely enact"? Or,
as he stresses, does the re-reading "re-enact"?[2] In a more specifically
nineteenth-century frame, the principle of transposition has been seen
as the major contribution to the period's interaction among the arts,
with a new insistence on creative reworking—substituted for analytical response—famously captured in Charles Baudelaire's remark, in his
"Salon de 1846," that the best criticism of a painting might be a sonnet.
If its ramifications are far-reaching, with transposing among the arts
invading critical discourse itself to the extent of servicing mediation
by inviting the reader to become a surrogate artist given access to the
pictorial experience, what characterizes the practice is that the textual
announces and explores its *own* procedures rather than simply reworking

similar motifs, with the original image, indeed, often left far behind. In other words, many of the writers of the period preoccupied by the visual arts are ultimately engaged, consciously or self-consciously, in a specular activity that involves a particularly acute perception of the possibilities of their own. This is what David Kelley called a "deliberate misreading" within which the tensions between word and image are foregrounded, whether in the *limitations* of the pictorial—in its inability to convey certain sensations (sound or smell) and its temporal freeze-frames and narrative constraints—or the *possibilities* of language in its accommodation of inner lives and the rich ambiguities of referencing sensory and moral (or abstract) qualities as well as playing with the seen and the unseen.[3]

It is further evidence of how far our understanding of the period has moved on since the 1980s that it is precisely those tensions that must be the focus of any critical return to transpositional practice. We were alerted to them by Mario Gamboni's *La plume et le pinceau* (1989). But we might have restricted these to the erosion of distinct cultural fields in the *fin de siècle* had it not been for Alexandra Wettlauffer's more recent *Pen vs Paintbrush* (2001), which amply demonstrates that the comforting notion of the so-called sister arts—even in the earlier post-revolutionary half of the century—simply will not survive serious scrutiny. It is with those tensions in mind that I want to approach the specificity of Émile Zola's transpositions, while remembering that the pioneering critical work on the writer and the visual arts (in the 1960s or thereabouts), which consisted of identifying precise pictorial sources for textual moments in his fiction, was inflected by the more general rehabilitation of the author of *Les Rougon-Macquart* in the service of which his early championing of Édouard Manet and the Impressionists supposedly underlined his modernist credentials. That such *superimpositions* remain visible on so many paperback covers of his novels should not be dismissed as a mere marketing strategy. For they also speak of a French critical celebration of an artistic solidarity that reached its apogee in Henri Mitterand's summary of Manet's portrait of Zola: "On ne saurait mieux signifier," as he puts it, "la consubstantialité du scriptural et du pictural" [It would be impossible to better signify the consubstantiality of the visual and the textual].[4] What I propose to do here, in exploring different kinds of transposition, is to take issue with that kind of perspective and adopt instead the mind-set of an Edgar Degas (ironically, given how often his *Blanchisseuses* adorn editions of *L'assommoir*) in his alleged remark that Zola had written *L'œuvre* "pour prouver la grande supériorité de l'homme de lettres sur l'artiste" [in order to prove the great superiority of the man of letters over the artist].[5] But that also encourages us to track back, long before *L'œuvre*, the ways in which engagements with particular paintings tell us much, more generally, about Zola's positioning vis-à-vis the painters of his time and, indeed, about the pictorial fabric of his own writing.

That is not to deny that Zola's transpositions often do register an avant-garde solidarity, and moreover one recognized by contemporaries. Reviewers of *Thérèse Raquin,* in the polemically charged context of 1867–1868, noted that his picturing of its heroine prompted analogies with Manet's technique: "Il voit la femme comme M. Manet la peint, couleur de boue avec des maquillages roses" [He sees Woman as Manet paints her, mud-colored with pink makeup].[6] That this provocative formulation by Louis Ulbach, with its allusion to objections to the "dirty skin" of *Olympia,* was in fact the result of collusion between a supposedly vitriolic critic and a publicity-seeking young novelist is consistent with Zola's admission, in a letter of May 8, 1867, that "jamais je n'ai si habilement travaillé à ma réputation qu'en cherchant à mettre le nom de Manet sur une de mes oeuvres" [the best thing I ever did for my reputation was to link Manet's name with one of my works].[7] In that sense, the transposition is the equivalent of Zola's endeavors to secure pictorial collaboration for editions of his texts and, occasionally, a quid pro quo. The explicit referencing of Pierre-Auguste Renoir's *Le bal du Moulin de la Galette* (1876) in chapter 8 of *L'assommoir* is a case in point. For the 1878 illustrated edition of the novel, Renoir provided three drawings: one of them is a duplicated reference back to Lantier's and Gervaise's visit to the *café-concert,* while another (an engraving overwritten by Zola's hand indexing its location) takes as its subject Nana and her young friends, parading their dresses on a sunny street.[8] The opening of *L'œuvre* contains a description of the sleeping Christine through the painter's eyes, which seems to transpose Renoir's 1869 *Femme demi-nue couchée: La rose.* Some of the fictional Claude's Provençal pictures bear a clear resemblance to Paul Cézanne's.

While allowing for this both sincere and self-interested dimension of the transposition, the latter is seldom merely such a marker. In this respect, it is worth returning to the relationship between Manet's *Nana* and Zola's verbal descriptions in his novel of the same name, which have long figured in scholarly commentary on both text and image. By virtue of the awkward fact that Manet's picture was painted during the winter of 1876 1877 (whereas Zola's *Nana* was planned in 1878 and the first installment appeared in October 1879), there has been much scholarly juggling of chronology to justify the possibility that the painting was inspired by episodes in *L'assommoir*, in which Gervaise's daughter begins her career as a Parisian "cocotte," notwithstanding the equally awkward fact that there is no textual moment in that earlier novel which allows us to confirm that hypothesis.[9] The consensus is that the painting owes only its title to Zola and that it is considerably more likely that it was the writer who was inspired by Manet's image, both in the preparation of his own *Nana* and its subsequent theatrical adaptation in 1881.[10] Much has been made of that transposition, by art historians and literary critics alike. Hollis Clayson, for example, has argued that "acknowledging and looking into the intertextuality of the works by Manet and Zola appears crucial to understanding the rejection of the painting by the Salon [of 1877]."[11] Her assertion that "the closest subject parallel to Manet's picture" is to be found in chapter 5 of Zola's novel, in the scene in which the actress performs her toilette in the company of Count Muffat, the prince, and the Marquis de Chouard, is now a commonplace.[12] Peter Brooks, on the other hand, has juxtaposed the painting with the episode in chapter 7 of the novel, in which Muffat is transfixed by the sight of a naked Nana watching and caressing herself narcissistically in the mirror.[13] In practice, neither scene corresponds precisely with Manet's. Brooks's most interesting suggestion remains that, in engaging with the problematic status of the mirror in relation to viewed and viewer,[14] Zola's writing might be a "narrative response" to Manet's preoccupations.[15] For it is, indeed, in such an emphasis on narrative that Zola's transpositions are genuinely revealing.

Before detailing some of the ways in which this particular example might reinforce that emphasis, it is instructive to turn to Zola's own art criticism. For his "transcriptions," or (to evoke the related theme of this volume) what he himself repeatedly calls his "translations," are better understood in the light of his 1865 essay in which he writes, "l'objet ou la personne à peindre sont les prétextes; le génie consiste à rendre cet objet ou cette personne dans un sens nouveau, plus vrai ou plus grand" [the object or the person to be painted is the pretext; genius consists in rendering this object or this person in a new way, truer or greater].[16] This anticipates, of course, his oft-quoted definition of a work of art as "un coin de la création vu à travers un tempérament" [a corner of creation seen through a temperament].[17] As he was to praise Gustave Courbet in 1878 for his "transcription puissante et fidèle de la nature" [powerful and faithful transcription of nature],[18] or repeat, in the case of Manet, that "la traduction qu'il nous donne est une traduction juste et simplifiée" [the translation he gives us is an exact and simplified one],[19] there is a very real sense in which Zola's own transpositions of paintings are *au second degré*. They are, in other words, a translation of a pictorial *reality* filtered through the originality of his own individual talent and marked by the same "improvisations" he had singled out for praise in Gustave Doré's rendering of prior biblical and other representations.[20]

If Manet's *Nana* is the "pretext" for Zola's rewriting, it is in the differentiating refractions of the image that the novelist asserts the specificities of his own practice. Their scope is illuminating, starting with the fundamental difference that while Manet's portrait of Henriette Hauser was refused entry to the Salon of 1877 (almost certainly on the grounds that its "outrage to morality" included its overtly, if uneasily, inscribing the male spectator), Zola's scene provocatively brings into a similarly theatricalized and intimate space a veritable male *audience,* thereby reduplicating in microcosm the collective and eroticized fascination with the initiating spectacle of Nana on stage. Second, there may still remain a relationship between Manet's single painting and Zola's *two* mirror scenes in, precisely, the narrative *prolongation* that has the partial viewing of chapter 5 as a phase in the "narrative striptease" (as Janet Beizer has underlined) which extends over a *durée* the movement from dressed to undressed originating in Zola's text—unlike Manet's painting—in the male spectators finding Nana naked to the waist with a bodice that only half-hides her breasts.[21]

The other differences between fictional scene and pictorial image are self-evident:[22]

Cette fois, Nana ne se retourna point. Elle avait pris la patte de lièvre, elle la
promenait légèrement, très attentive, si cambrée au dessus de la toilette, que
la rondeur blanche de son pantalon saillait et se tendait, avec le petit bout de
chemise. Mais elle voulait se montrer sensible au compliment du vieillard, elle
s'agita en balançant les hanches.

   Un silence régna. Mme Jules avait remarqué une déchirure à la jambe droite
du pantalon. Elle prit une épingle sur son coeur, elle resta un moment par terre,
à genoux, occupée autour de la cuisse de Nana, pendant que la jeune femme,
sans paraître la savoir là, se couvrait de poudre de riz, en évitant soigneusement
d'en mettre sur les pommettes. Mais, comme le prince disait que, si elle venait
chanter à Londres, toute l'Angleterre voudrait l'applaudir, elle eut un rire
aimable, elle se tourna une seconde, la joue gauche très blanche, au milieu d'un
nuage de poudre. Puis, elle devint subitement sérieuse; il s'agissait de mettre le
rouge. De nouveau, le visage près de la glace, elle trempait son doigt dans un pot,
elle appliquait le rouge sous les yeux, l'étalait doucement, jusqu'à la tempe. Ces
messieurs se taisaient, respectueux. . . . Elle avait trempé le pinceau dans un pot
de noir; puis, le nez sur la glace, fermant l'oeil gauche, elle le passa délicatement
entre les cils. Muffat, dérrière elle, regardait. Il la voyait dans la glace, avec ses
épaules rondes et sa gorge noyée d'une ombre rose. Et il ne pouvait, malgré son
effort, se détourner de ce visage que l'oeil fermé rendait si provocant, troué de
fossettes, comme pâmé de désirs. Lorsqu'elle ferma l'oeil droit et qu'elle passa le
pinceau, il comprit qu'il lui appartenait. (2:1212–1214)

[This time Nana didn't turn around. She had picked up the hare's paw and was
lightly stroking it over her skin with great concentration, arching her body over
the dressing-table so that her white trousers stretched tightly over her plump
round bottom with the little tag of her shift showing above. She did however try
to express her appreciation of the old man's compliment by wiggling her hips.

   There was a pause. Madame Jules had spotted a tear in the right leg of the
trousers. She took a pin from the array on her bodice and knelt down for a moment beside Nana's thigh while the young woman, apparently not noticing what
she was doing went on covering herself with rice-powder, taking care not to put
any on her cheek-bones. But when the prince said that if she were to come and
sing in London the whole of England would go to applaud her, she gave a friendly
laugh and turned round for a second in a cloud of powder, with her left cheek
very white. Then her face suddenly took on a very earnest expression: she was
about to apply her rouge. Once again, holding her face close to the mirror, she
began dipping her finger in a jar and rubbing the rouge under her eyes, spreading
it gently along to her temples. The gentlemen maintained a respectful silence. . . .
She had dipped the brush in a jar of [black] mascara and, with her nose pressed
hard against the mirror, closing her left eye, she stroked it gently between her
lashes. Muffat was standing behind her, watching. He could see her in the
mirror with her plump shoulders and her breasts bathed in pink shadows. And
despite all his efforts, he couldn't take his eyes off this face, so provocative with
its dimples and one closed eye making her seem overcome by desire. When she

closed her right eye and again passed the brush over it, he knew that the die was cast: she had him in her power.] (128–130)

For while Zola may wittily gesture toward that "pinceau dans un pot noir" ["brush in a jar of [black] mascara"] integral to Manet's suppression of semi-tones, those differences are not limited to the number of figures involved, expanded here to include Madame Jules at work on Nana's costume. Nor are interpolated snatches of conversation, laughter, indirect speech, and interior monologue the most telling of the novelist's variations on a theme. What really marks the latter is the animation (as opposed to the stasis of the painting) of the makeup ritual: in the modulations of pose, manual dexterity, and facial expression; in the movement of fingers in jars, turned cheeks, momentarily applied brushes, rouge and creams; in the sensory dynamics of clouds of powder and alternative coloration. And, as opposed to that possibly grumpy, if enigmatic and disengaged, cropped figure in the Manet, Zola's intimations of the perversities of male response traverse a spectrum of moods from seduction to transferred surrender.[23]

This is not the place to judgmentally compare the two images, let alone express a preference for painterly indifference over authorial overdetermination. My main point is that this kind of transposition has to be viewed within a longer dialogue between Manet and Zola, in particular, but also between Zola and the visual arts, and indeed more generally between writers and painters of the period. At its most fundamental, that dialogue is not about the sensorial, temporal, or psychological dimensions of one art form or the other, but about the discursive capacities of painting. So obdurately formalist is Zola's art criticism, for example, that he finds himself discounting perceived affinities between Baudelaire and Manet[24] on the grounds that the latter's refined arrangement of colors is evidence that he has decidedly not put "des idées dans sa peinture" [ideas in his paintings], a predilection maintained right through the next thirty years and underlying his distaste for the Symbolist codifications of an Odilon Redon or a Gustave Moreau.[25] As I have argued elsewhere, Manet's *Portrait d'Emile Zola* (1868) is the most eloquent refutation of Zola's unwillingness to grant the painter a degree of intentionality, with its own iconography and pictorial wit taking issue with the implication, in all Zola's commentaries on Manet since 1866, that only writing can articulate meaning.[26] And Zola's own partial transposition of *Olympia*, in *Thérèse Raquin*, highlights the contradictions and ambiguities of such a strategic relegation of subject to form, which simultaneously occludes a more personal response to painting.[27]

Such transpositions are by no means limited, however, to his engagement with Manet. Renoir's *La balançoire* provides us with an example of Zola's narrativization of the visual image even more extended than in the case of *Nana*. But it also offers a more radical challenge on the part of the writer, in the shape of what looks like a deliberate verbal appropriation of the painting's descriptive fabric, thereby questioning the exclusivity of its visual properties. *La balançoire* was shown at the Third Impressionist Exhibition, which Zola visited in April 1877. And, as Joy Newton pointed out long ago, it almost certainly inspired the portrait of Hélène, on her *balançoire,* in the novel that Zola started that same spring, namely *Une page d'amour.*[28] For in the equally dappled sunlight of the scene in part 1, chapter 4, precise color values can be superimposed on chronological coincidence: "Ses cheveux châtains, aux reflets d'ambre, s'allumaient; et l'on aurait dit qu'elle flambait tout entière, tandis que ses nœuds de soie mauve, pareils à des fleurs de feu, luisaient sur sa robe blanchissante" [Her chestnut hair, with amber highlights, lit up and one would have said that her whole body was burning as the knots of mauve silk on her dress shone like flowers of fire on her whitening dress] (2:843). And these impressionistic effects are so precisely elaborated that this particular passage has often been exploited to substantiate Zola's oft-cited reported remark about his own descriptions testifying to his being "en contact et échange avec les peintres" [in contact and interchanges with painters].[29]

What has not been remarked upon, however, is the way in which this single *transposition d'art* has been developed through successive pages (2:839–844) and the novel as a whole. The virtuoso performance may well include an expression of solidarity—altruistic or not[30]—in response to an astonishing contemporary critical hostility toward this apparently innocuous painting.[31] Whether or not it gestures toward sympathetic alignment, what is significant is the direction of Zola's reworking of the image in *Une page d'amour.* For he invests it with a symbolic weight patently at odds with the stance adopted in his art criticism. Above all, by transforming pictorial stasis into a full-fledged "épisode," the novelist demonstrates the richer capacities of the text.[32] Through metaphorical substitutions, erotic connotations, and semantic slippage—"la passion de voir sa mère s'envoler" [the excitement of seeing her mother take off] (2:841)—Zola's narrative unmistakably tracks taboo, transgression, and the Fall as synonymous with an ultimately proscribed sexual emancipation.[33] And he does so to an extent which suggests, at the very least, that Zola may have read *La balançoire* in ways which prefigure modern questioning of Renoir's denial of legibility in the interests of an art-for-art's-sake "pure" painterly pleasure.[34]

That he may have done so, as his reworkings of *Olympia* or *Nana* also suggest, points to a related feature of Zola's transpositions. For beyond demonstration of writing's superiority or the polemical deflection away from scandalous subject-matter, their narrative directions imply an approach to the originating image that is essentially literary. This is particularly evident in Zola's unease with any painting depicting a social situation or human figures, as opposed to his less contradictory appraisals of landscapes (from Daubigny to Pissarro), seascapes (Monet), Parisian views (Jongkind), or *natures mortes* [still-lifes], all of which offer less temptation to the storyteller.[35] By contrast, of Monet's *Camille*, Zola writes (in his 1866 essay), "Son tableau me conte toute une histoire" [His painting tells me an entire story].[36] It may seem paradoxical that in his "Salon de 1875," he should castigate the "préoccupations littéraires" [literary preoccupations] of the Romantics,[37] or admit, in his own 1866 evocation of the work of Jean-François Millet, that "je parle en poète, et les peintres, je le sais, n'aiment pas cela" [I speak as a poet, I know the painters don't like that].[38] Yet such self-deprecation is explicitly rehearsed in the pages of *L'œuvre*, in which his surrogate, Sandoz, "malgré lui, était parfois tenté d'introduire de la littérature dans la peinture" (4:47) ["often found himself being tempted to introduce literature into painting" (39)].[39] If an underlying theme of Zola's art-historical discourse is the necessity of separate cultural spheres (with an implied hierarchy, of course, making it unsurprising that *L'œuvre* juxtaposes failed painter and successful writer), his novels consistently encroach on the spatial autonomy of the pictorial in ways which illuminate that otherwise enigmatic reflection in the *Ebauche* [Draft] of *L'œuvre:* "Un art mangé par l'autre et ne produisant rien" [One art eaten by another, producing nothing].[40]

It is in that novel, too, that a more curious transposition is effected in the case of Manet's *Le déjeuner sur l'herbe,* which scholars have repeatedly overlaid on, or seen beneath, Claude's painting entitled simply *Plein air.* As Peter Brooks writes, for example, "Claude's *Plein Air* closely resembles *Le Déjeuner sur l'herbe,* with a fully clothed male, two women wrestling in the background and a reclining nude woman in the centre foreground."[41] It would be equally interesting in the margins to compare what Zola wrote about Manet's original painting, on the one hand and its fictional counterpart on the other. For this exemplifies, at one level, another kind of transposition that it would be worth exploring in detail, namely those segments in *L'œuvre* in which Zola transposes—but at a crucial twenty years' distance—a number of his critical texts of the 1860s, while layering over his original journalistic evocation of a painting a not quite verbatim fictional retranscription of it. In the case of the imagined *Plein air,* Zola's elaboration (as it had been in his analysis of *Le déjeuner sur l'herbe*) almost willfully ignores its human figures, except to the extent that they provide a structure of colors set off against the foliage of the sunlit clearing. But again, in comparing real and fictional paintings, one is struck not by exact correspondences of the kind toward which Brooks tends, but rather by calculated difference at odds with the generality of reference. This starts most obviously with the fact that Claude's work has only one male figure in it and that, in contradistinction to Manet's, he is turned away from the viewer rather than staring directly at us. But if Manet's painting can still be vaguely discerned (though corresponding neither in size[42] nor layout) as the prototype, the differences as they appear in three separate textual segments charting the successive phases of the composition of *Plein air* do not stop there:

C'était une toile de cinq mètres sur trois, entièrement couverte, mais dont quelques morceaux à peine se dégageaient de l'ébauche. Cette ébauche, jetée d'un coup, avait une violence superbe, une ardente vie de couleurs. Dans un trou de forêt, aux murs épais de verdure, tombait une ondée de soleil; seule, à gauche, une allée sombre s'enfonçait, avec une tache de lumière, très loin. Là, sur l'herbe, au milieu des végétations de juin, une jeune femme nue était couchée, un bras sous la tête, enflant la gorge; et elle souriait, sans regard, les paupières closes, dans la pluie d'or qui la bagnait. Au fond, deux autres petites femmes, une brune, une blonde, également nues, luttaient en riant, détachaient, parmi les verts des feuilles, deux adorables notes de chair. Et, comme au premier plan, le peintre avait eu besoin d'une opposition noire, il s'était bonnement satisfait, en y asseyant un monsieur, vêtu d'un simple veston de velours. Ce monsieur tournait le dos, on ne voyait de lui que sa main gauche, sur laquelle il s'appuyait, dans l'herbe. (4:33)

[It was a big canvas, five metres by three, all planned out, although parts of it were still hardly developed beyond the rough stage. As a sketch it was remarkable for its vigour, its spontaneity, and the lively warmth of its colour. It showed the sun pouring into a forest clearing, with a solid background of greenery and a dark path running off to the left and with a bright spot of light in the far distance. Lying on the grass in the foreground, among the lush vegetation of high summer, was the naked figure of a woman. One arm was folded beneath her head, thus bringing her breasts into prominence; her eyes were closed and she was smiling into space as she basked in the golden sunlight. In the background, two other nude women, one dark and one fair, were laughing and tumbling each other on the grass, making two lovely patches of flesh-colour against the green, while in the foreground, to make the necessary contrast, the artist had seen fit to place a man's figure. He wore a plain black velvet jacket, and was seated on the grass so that nothing could be seen but his back and his left hand upon which he was leaning.] (25)

Le monsieur en veston de velours était ébauché entièrement; la main, plus poussée que le reste, faisait dans l'herbe une note intéressante, d'une jolie fraîcheur de ton, et la tache sombre du dos s'enlevait avec tant de vigueur que les petites silhouettes du fond, les deux femmes luttant au soleil, semblaient s'être éloignées, dans le frisson lumineux de la clairière; tandis que la grande figure, la femme nue et couchée, à peine indiquée encore, flottait toujours, ainsi qu'une chair de songe, une Eve désirée naissant de la terre, avec son visage qui souriait, sans regard, les paupières closes. (4:47)

[The man in the black velvet jacket was now completely brushed in; his hand, which was farther advanced than the rest, showed up well against the grass, while the dark patch of his back stood out with such force that the two little shapes in the background, the two women tumbling each other in the sunshine, looked as if they had withdrawn far away into the shimmering light of the forest clearing; the big reclining female figure, however, was still only faintly sketched in, still little more than a shape desired in a dream, Eve rising from the earth smiling but sightless, her eyes still unopened.] (39)

Les fonds, la clairière sombre trouée d'une nappe de soleil, n'étaient toujours qu'indiqués à larges coups. Mais les deux petites lutteuses, la blonde et la brune, presque terminées, se détachaient dans la lumière, avec leurs deux notes

si fraîches. Au premier plan, le monsieur, recommencé trois fois, restait en
détresse. Et c'était surtout à la figure centrale, à la femme couchée, que le peintre
travaillait: il n'avait plus repris la tête, il s'acharnait sur le corps, changeant de
modèle chaque semaine, si désespéré de ne pas se satisfaire, que, depuis deux
jours, lui qui se flattait de ne pouvoir inventer, il cherchait sans document, en
dehors de la nature. (419a)

[The background and the dusky forest clearing, broken by a patch of sunshine,
were still only roughly sketched in, but the two little female figures, one dark,
the other fair, were practically finished and stood out remarkably clearly in
the sunlight. In the foreground the man had been attempted three times and
then left unfinished. It was the central figure, the reclining woman, that had
received most attention. The head Claude had left untouched, but he had worked
persistently on the body, using a fresh model every week until at last, despairing
of ever finding one to his satisfaction, for the last two days he had been working
from memory instead of from nature, in spite of his contention that his power of
invention was non-existent.] (84)

As we can see here, Zola also replaces the figure of the seated and
inscrutable woman gazing directly out of Manet's painting with that
of a naked female, "enflant la gorge" ["bringing her breasts into prominence"] and unequivocally smiling, who lies back with her eyes closed
("sans regard"). Were it not for that last detail, which blanks out the
brazen stare so distinctive of *Le déjeuner sur l'herbe,* the arm behind her
smiling head makes her more akin to the full-frontal availability of a
Cabanel or an Ingres rather than one of Manet's more troubling nudes.
In her almost disembodied imprecision ("flottait toujours" ["still only
faintly sketched in"]), she seems to have less in common with the figure
nearest the viewer in *Le déjeuner sur l'herbe* than with the ungrounded
bather in the distance. And Zola puts in his own background *wrestling*
women (which they are patently not doing in the Manet). Indeed, Michael Fried has speculated that this may be an indirect transposition of
Frédéric Bazille's wrestling *men* in his *Summer Scene* of 1869. Fried goes
on to suggest that the fictional painting is made more "Courbet-like," or
at least an amalgam of Courbet and Manet, by virtue of the elimination
of that "facingness," which he detects as the necessary marker of Manet's
achievement in the 1860s.[43] At the same time, it is also worth noting that
there is a sense in which *Plein air* and, behind it, *Le déjeuner sur l'herbe*
are recomposed, later in *L'œuvre,* in Fagerolles's significantly entitled *Un
déjeuner,* in which the spectacle—much admired by the viewing pub-

lic—of two men and three women under some trees derives from, and inverts, Claude's earlier failure.

These kinds of transpositional amalgams and recompositions are integral to the more general strategies of *L'œuvre,* which consciously frustrate recuperative moves to specific artists and their works. They substitute for the risks of the *roman-à-clef* the composite portrait (for painters) and a heterogeneous range of styles (for paintings) that has Claude move through, even to the extent of superimposing one style on another, every artistic realization from Cézanne to Monet, and from Manet to the Symbolists.[44] This is emblematic of the autobiographical and creative distortions (*déformation*) of the kind valorized by post-Realist aesthetic imperatives.[45] For the key point is surely that Sandoz (the quasi-anagrammatic Zola) poses for the male figure in the fictional transposition with his face turned away from recognition: "On ne voyait de lui que sa main gauche" (4:33) ["nothing could be seen but . . . his left hand"] (25). This important but hitherto unnoticed detail seems to have its origin in an earlier conception of the painting, in which there was to be, as Zola put it in his notes, "un batelier . . . vu de dos en bras de chemise, les bras nus" [a boatman . . . seen from behind, bare-armed in shirt-sleeves].[46] No wonder that Sandoz, volunteering to sit for him, protests to the painter: "Elle n'est pas commode ta pose" (4:35) ["Confound this pose! It's breaking my wrist"] (27). Given the dematerializing immobility to which it condemns him, it replicates the transformation into a *nature morte* that Zola remembered from the experience of having his portrait painted by Manet.[47] There is a specific echo, indeed, in the asides in *L'œuvre:* "La main, plus poussée que le reste, faisait dans l'herbe une note très intéressante" (4:47) ["his hand, which was farther advanced than the rest, showed up well against the grass"] (39); "décidément, . . . la main seule était belle" (4:127) ["the best thing about him was his hand"] (118). So too, in his Salon review of his own portrait, Zola singles out the hand for comment: "Je recommande tout particulièrement la main placée sur le genou du personage" [I particularly appreciate the hand placed on the figure's knee]. He goes on to say that if the whole portrait had similar qualities, "on eût crié au chef-d'oeuvre" [it would have been a master-piece].[48] The pragmatic result of Sandoz's differentiating pose is that he is no longer recognizable: "Au premier plan, le monsieur recommencé trois fois, restait en détresse" (4:92) ["In the foreground the man had been attempted three times and then left unfinished"] (84). Ultimately, the immobility impossible to sustain becomes a metaphor for the novel as a whole, as the preparatory dossier of which ("Moi, fatalement, je suis immobile" [I am fatally immobile]) had vainly hoped to position Sandoz as no more than an authorial mouthpiece, resolutely not integrated into the fiction itself.

Specific in its application to the transpositions between *L'œuvre* and *Le déjeuner sur l'herbe*, and mediated by Manet's 1868 portrait of the novelist, such a perspective nevertheless opens up a number of others. In relation to the fictional Sandoz, Zola noted, "Mon portrait modifié" [My portrait modified]. From the anagrams, onomastics, pastiches, and disguised models, as much as in the scrambling of titles and paintings (both recognizable and not),[49] there emerges a bigger and related subject, which is the transposition of the self and others. This is consistent with what has been termed "une poétique de la transposition" [a poetics of transposition], a "processus de refiguration du vécu ... dans la fiction romanesque" [process of reconfiguring lived experience as novelistic fiction],[50] nowhere more interesting than in the case of Cézanne whose transposition in *L'œuvre* determined the views of his personality and paintings retailed by an entire generation of critics and admirers.[51] Without extending this essay into that enormous supplementary dimension of Zola's transpositions, suffice it to conclude that even the most identifiable of his pictorial models are neither stable reference points in a *musée imaginaire*, nor even successive repositionings in another medium or another key. They testify instead to a critical, imaginative, and creative reworking in which the original citation is merely the starting point in a complex dynamic. And if the insights offered by interdisciplinarity are posited on difference rather than similarity, it is also that dynamic, in the case of Zola's transpositions, which allows us to see the original differently.

ROBERT LETHBRIDGE recently retired as Honorary Professor of French and Master of Fitzwilliam College at the University of Cambridge. His work is focused on late nineteenth-century France and, in particular, the relationship between literature and the visual arts in that period. He was made Chevalier dans l'ordre des Palmes Académiques in 1998, and Commandeur in 2013, for services to French culture and scholarship, and is Honorary President of the Society of Dix-neuvièmistes. He has published widely on Zola and on nineteenth-century French literature and art, including important collective volumes such as *Zola and the Craft of Fiction: Essays in Honour of F. W. J. Hemmings* (with Terry Keefe), and *Artistic Relations: Literature and the Visual Arts in Nineteenth-Century France* (with Peter Collier). He is currently preparing a new edition of Zola's *Écrits sur l'art*.

NOTES

1. David Scott, "The Art of Transposition," in his seminal *Pictorialist Poetics,* 88–115.
2. Bruce, *"Orbis pictus redivivus,"* 109.
3. See Kelley, "Transpositions."
4. Mitterand, "Le musée dans le texte," 15.
5. Cited in Reff, "Degas and the Literature of His Time," 197–198, 198n71.
6. Cited in the Garnier-Flammarion edition (1970) of *Thérèse Raquin,* 41.
7. Zola, *Correspondance,* 1:496–497.
8. See Thibaut, "Renoir illustrateur de *L'assommoir.*"
9. And even in relation to *L'assommoir,* the chronology is problematic. The painting was begun in October or November 1876; chapter 11 of the novel, which features Nana, was also serialized that November, but her "career" at this stage was far less well-advanced than that of Manet's courtesan. For a contrary view, intermittently persuasive but speculating that the painter's belated insertion of the cropped gentleman coincides with Nana subsequently securing a "protector," see Briggs-Lynch, "Manet's *Nana.*"
10. See Tintner, "What Zola's *Nana* Owes to Manet's *Nana,*" and Best, "Portraits d'une 'vraie fille'."
11. Clayson, *Painted Love,* 67–75, 70 (quotation).
12. Ibid., 71. See Roger Clark's useful recent summary in his *Zola: "Nana,"* 33–42.
13. Brooks, *Body Work,* 123–161. See also Berg, *The Visual Novel,* 67–68, who invokes both scenes.
14. For one of the most succinct and penetrating analyses of its implications, see House, *Impressionism,* 132–134.
15. Brooks, *Body Work,* 145. On the mirror as narrative catalyst, see my "Le miroir et ses textes."
16. Zola, *Écrits,* 52.
17. Ibid., 81.
18. Ibid., 379. Chapter 11 of *Thérèse Raquin* has a description that may be a transposition, *en hommage,* of Courbet's *Demoiselles près de la Seine.*
19. Ibid., 153. Elsewhere in this same *brochure* for Manet's one-man 1867 exhibition, Zola writes, "On n'est pas habitué à voir des traductions aussi simples et aussi sincères de la réalité" [We are not used to seeing such simple and sincere translations of reality]

(152); and, in 1876, he refers to the painter's "traduction d'une justesse littérale" [literally exact translation] (349).

20. Ibid., 55.

21. Beizer, "Uncovering *Nana*," 52–53.

22. All interpolated textual references are to Henri Mitterand's five-volume (Pléiade) edition of *Les Rougon-Macquart* (Paris: Gallimard, 1960–1966). English translations are from Douglas Parmée's edition (Oxford: Oxford World's Classics, 1992).

23. Unless one is willing to subscribe to the certainties of Tamar Garb's reading of "her lecherous companion who leers suggestively at her swollen buttocks, his cane placed strategically in his lap"; see Garb, *Bodies of Modernity*, 139.

24. "Et je profite de l'occasion pour protester contre la parenté qu'on a voulu établir entre les tableaux d'Edouard Manet et les vers de Charles Baudelaire" [I'm taking this occasion to protest against the relationship that some have wanted to establish between the paintings of Edouard Manet and the poems of Charles Baudelaire]. Zola, *Écrits*, 152.

25. See my "Zola and Contemporary Painting," 76–77.

26. Lethbridge, "Manet's Textual Frames."

27. See Cousins, *Zola*, 20, and Andrew Rothwell's excellent "Introduction," xxx–xxxiii.

28. Newton, "Émile Zola impressionniste (II)," 137.

29. "Je n'ai pas seulement soutenu les Impressionnistes. Je les ai traduits en littérature, par les touches, notes, colorations, par la palette de beaucoup de mes descriptions. Dans tous mes livres . . . j'ai été en contact et échange avec les peintres" [I have not only supported the Impressionists. I have translated them into literature with the strokes, colorations, and the palette of many of my descriptions. In all my books . . . I have been in contact and interchanges with painters]; see Hertz, "Emile Zola, témoin de la vérité," 32–33.

30. It coincides, almost exactly, with Renoir's illustrations for *L'assommoir* (see note 8, above).

31. For selected extracts from that critical reception, see Moffett, ed., *The New Painting*, 234–235.

32. See the preparatory notes for the novel in which Zola reminds himself: "Rappeler l'épisode de la balançoire" [Remember the episode with the swing] (MS, N.a.f., 10,318, fol. 458, Bibliothèque Nationale, Paris).

33. See my "Le jeu des formes."

34. See Stephen Kern's persuasive reading in his *Eyes of Love*, 40; Pointon, "Biography and Body in Late Renoir"; and Green, *French Paintings of Childhood and Adolescence*, who erroneously claims that Renoir's *Parapluies* (c. 1881 and c. 1885) is "the only instance in [his] work of the child overtly aware of and specularising adult sexuality" (110). It is precisely that presence in *La balançoire* which may even have inspired Zola's triangulation of heroine, lover, and child. As he later explained of the preparation of *Une page d'amour*, "le drame m'a été donné par l'invention de l'enfant, qui meurt de l'amour de la mère" [the drama was suggested to me by the invention of the child who dies for love of her mother]. See his letter of June 8, 1892, in Zola, *Correspondance*, 7:289. This "invention" dates from exactly the moment he saw the painting in the spring of 1877.

35. Even in his description of *Le déjeuner sur l'herbe*, Zola deflects attention away from the human figures to the "paysage entier." Zola, *Écrits*, 159.

36. Ibid., 122.

37. "Nos peintres ont voulu écrire des pages d'épopée ou de roman" [Our painters wanted to write pages of epics or novels]. Ibid., 286.

38. Ibid., 129.

39. All textual references to *The Masterpiece* are from Roger Pearson's revised edition of Thomas Walton's translation (Oxford: Oxford World's Classics, 2006).

40. MS, N.a.f., 10,316, fol. 295, Bibliothèque Nationale.

41. Brooks, *Body Work,* 134.

42. *Le déjeuner sur l'herbe* measures 208 x 264 cm, the fictional *Plein air* "cinq mètres sur trois."

43. Fried, *Manet's Modernism,* 249.

44. "J'ai horreur du roman à clef," Zola wrote in an article in *Le Voltaire,* May 3, 1886, "où l'on prend des personnages sur le vif; cela me semble une mauvaise action" [I'm horrified by the *roman à clef,* where the characters are taken from life; to me, that seems to be the wrong thing to do]. Quoted in Patrick Brady, *"L'œuvre" d'Émile Zola,* 237. This is also a judicial preemptive move against the kinds of attacks to which Maupassant's *Bel-Ami* had recently been subjected. On posterity's judgment of *L'œuvre* in this respect, see Pagès and Morgan, *Guide Émile Zola,* 280–282.

45. See Schiff, *Cézanne and the End of Impressionism,* 37.

46. In the first detailed plan for chapter 2 (see 4:1409).

47. Zola, *Écrits,* 198–200.

48. Ibid., 200. On the ramifications of the portrait itself, see Katz, "Photography versus Caricature."

49. Bongrand's work and personality, for example, have been "identified" as those of Courbet, Delacroix, Manet, Millet, and Daubigny. On this recuperative anarchy, see Henri Mitterand's remarks in the critical apparatus for *L'œuvre* (4:1353–1359).

50. Baudille, "Du vécu dans le roman."

51. See Newton, "Cézanne's Literary Incarnations."

NINE

Transposition and Re-Invention: Rodin's Vision

SONYA STEPHENS

TALKING WITH PAUL GSELL ABOUT THE BEAUTY OF THE HU-
man figure, particularly the female form, Auguste Rodin is moved to
quote Victor Hugo:

> Chair de la femme! argile idéale! ô merveille!
> O pénétration sublime de l'esprit
> Dans le limon que l'Être ineffable pétrit!
> Matière où l'âme brille à travers son suaire!
> Boue où l'on voit les doigts du divin statuaire!
> Fange auguste appelant les baisers et le cœur.
> Si sainte, qu'on ne sait, tant l'amour est vainqueur,
> Tant l'âme est vers ce lit mysterieux poussée,
> Si cette volupté n'est pas une pensée,
> Et qu'on ne peut, à l'heure où les sens sont en feu
> Étreindre la beauté sans croire embrasser Dieu!

> [A woman's flesh! ideal clay! O, wonder!
> O sublime penetration of the mind
> In the alluvium that the ineffable Being shapes!
> The soul shines through the shroud of matter!
> Mud in which is seen the hand of the divine sculptor!
> August mire that invites both kisses and the heart.
> So saintly that we cannot know, so vanquishing the love,
> And so irresistibly drawn is the soul to this mysterious bed,
> Whether this exquisite delight is not a thought,
> Nor whether, in this moment of fiery sensuality,
> Beauty can be embraced without, it seems, embracing God!][1]

In these lines from "D'Ève à Jésus," Rodin, with Hugo, evokes the translation of form, transposing flesh and clay, word and matter, desire and
thought, as well as multiple stories of creation.[2] As subject and object

fold into one another, and action embraces thought, what emerges is Beauty, but a beauty very much concerned with the specific possibilities of artistic representation.

Interdisciplinary and cultural studies have in the last twenty years spawned a number of accounts that have attempted to bring into sharper focus interart relations and ekphrastic practice. David Scott's *Pictorialist Poetics* was perhaps the first to go beyond thematic comparisons to tackle the question of "how transpositional poets . . . succeed in creating (to borrow Prévost's terms) 'une sorte de connaissance plastique et d'immobilité, une sorte de masse plastique immobile autour de laquelle erre longuement la rêverie' [a sort of plastic knowledge of immobility, a sort of immobile, plastic mass around which imagination wanders timelessly]."[3] Murray Krieger has traced the evolution of the genre from antiquity to the present, and W. J. T. Mitchell continues to influence our thinking on the subject, in *Iconology: Image, Text, Ideology,* by considering images from the perspective of language.[4] David Kelley's essay in *Artistic Relations* finds indeterminacy to be a key factor in the transpositions of Théophile Gautier and Charles Baudelaire.[5] Other studies, notably those by James Heffernan and Didier Maleuvre, have placed the emphasis on the role of the museum, which increased access to great works of art, thereby prompting transpositional responses in the cultural field.[6] Henry Majewski considers the problem in a strictly Romantic context in *Transposing Art into Texts,* though he considers not only French ekphrastic texts but also pictorial symbolism more broadly,[7] while Peter Wagner's collection of essays on the subject, *Icons-Texts-Iconotexts* argues for something beyond ekphrasis, for a theoretical system that would allow intertextuality to break out of a single medium through means of intermediality.[8] And Rosemary Lloyd's own discussion of the subject, "The Art of Transposition," in *Baudelaire's World,* shows how the poet-critic seeks out intimate thought in the visual as the subject fades into "the symbolic dimension of the work of pure art."[9]

If ekphrasis is, simply put, "the verbal representation of a visual representation," then the *transposition d'art,* although originally conceived by Gautier as a poetic text in relation to a work of visual art, offers itself as a more malleable concept, one that lends itself to permutations in that exchange. Indeed, it is generally interpreted to mean simply (though enacted complexly) translation into another medium. Rodin's citation of Hugo is significant because, in intermedial terms, the sculptor, in conversation with Gsell about female beauty and thus limited by language, reaches for a poetic analogy but one marked by transposition, by the language of sculpture. It is this coming together of discourses in the nineteenth century, the enrichment of all forms through such mutual borrowings and correspondences, that makes such transpositions culturally so central after Romanticism.

The Hugo poem takes the traditional theme of the beauty of the female form and translates it, much as the *transposition d'art* does, not only into words that can express form but into a question of representational, or formal, limits. The "boue," "limon," and "matière" [mud, alluvium, and matter] reveal respectively the manipulation ("les doigts," "pétrit" [fingers, knead]) and the conception of the artist ("l'âme brille" [the soul shines through], "pénétration sublime de l'esprit" [the sublime penetration of the mind]), so that in its divine and beauteous transformation, the sculptor-poet is no longer able to distinguish between "volupté" [pleasure] and "pensée" [thought], since both are presumed to be aesthetic, and, as we shall see in due course, libidinal. What is, in effect, translated in the poem is the creative *process* through which flesh becomes eternal and ideal beauty, its intrinsic self already present in the "argile idéale" [ideal clay].

Rodin's quotation of "D'Ève à Jésus" is just one way of apprehending the sculptor's transpositions, translating as it does into discourse, and so intermedially, a narrative present in, for example, *La main de Dieu* [The Hand of God] (fig. 9.1). In a photograph taken in 1902 (fig. 9.2), Rodin, who demystified the studio and thought of it both as *chantier* [construction site] and as museum, poses next to *La main de Dieu*. Rodin's sculpture shows the very process by which form emerges from raw material, so that in this work, there is a meaningful conjunction of art and its creation, representational finish, and the unfinishedness of the creative act. Taken from one of the *bourgeois de Calais* [burgers of Calais], the hand emerges from the block of matter to find its meanings radically redefined: here it is the powerful hand of the Creator, manipulating in its palm the fetal figures of Adam and Eve, born as a sensual, embracing couple. The subtle combination of highly finished, polished aspects, evidence of tool work,

Figure 9.1. *La main de Dieu* [The Hand of God]. Marble, 1896? Photograph by Christian Baraja. Courtesy Musée Rodin, Paris (s.988). 78 × 54 × 94 cm.

Figure 9.2. *Rodin coiffé d'une casquette avec* La main de Dieu [Rodin, in a hat, with the *Hand of God*]. Anonymous aristotype. Courtesy Musée Rodin, Paris (Ph. 76). 8.3 × 10.8 cm.

and unhewn matter make this a particularly eloquent example of a narrative of translation and transposition. Whether in bronze or stone, Rodin balances the composition with unhewn material at the base and apex, the perfectly formed hand emerging from formless matter, evidence of what has been called "primeval roughness."[10]

When set alongside the photographic image, what results is a meditation on art as transposition. For this photograph, beyond a mere portrait of the artist alongside an unfinished act of divine/artistic creation, makes clear the blurring of the boundaries not only between creator and creation but between media. The work no longer stands in for the artist here; instead, the artist stands alongside it *as its creator.* Here is the same allegory of creation we find in Hugo's poem, with humankind emerging barely formed, still entwined in fetal suggestiveness, from the matter held by the creative hand. The foot is still entrenched in the rock, incomplete (it has no toes), emerging but arrested in the process of becoming by the sculptor's decisive unfinishedness. Just before his death, a cast was

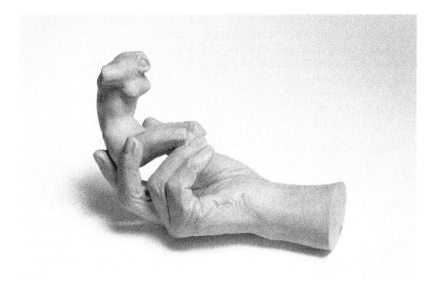

Figure 9.3. Rodin, *Main de Rodin, avec torse feminine* [Hand of Rodin Holding a Torso].
Plaster. Courtesy Philadelphia Museum of Art, Bequest of Jules E. Mastbaum, 1929.
6 ¼ × 9 × 3 ¾ inches (15.9 × 22.9 × 9.5 cm).

made of Rodin's own hand. Weakened and almost inactive, the hand of
the sculptor nevertheless invites comparison with *La main de Dieu,* and
with the Hugo poem, as what emerges from it in an assertion of creative
power is sculpture's ideal, the torso of a woman (fig. 9.3).

Alain Montaudon describes the process of transposition as it occurs
in Gautier's work in a way similar to this, emphasizing the constant move
toward the creative—away from the product to the process:

> Le "spécialiste" de la transposition d'art a en effet dans ses œuvres mis en place
> un discours de type narratif qui au fur et à mesur de son évolution démasque ce
> que Lyotard appelle *le dispositif libidinal* de l'œuvre d'art. De la correspondance
> à la transposition, de la transposition au jeu de la surface et de la profondeur, le
> créateur évolue d'une conception allant de l'œuvre à son faire, de la création à
> l'acte créateur . . . .
>
> Le rêve secret de l'artiste serait pour Gautier de dépasser les conditions
> matérielles de la réalisation, les contraintes de divers ordres pour une expression
> s'épanouissant dans la plus totale liberté.
>
> [The specialist of the "transposition d'art" has, in effect, through his works, put
> in place a kind of narrative discourse, which, as it evolves, reveals what Lyotard
> has called the works' *libidinal dispositive.* From analogy to transposition, from

transposition to the play between surface and depth, the creator evolves from
the work to its making, from the creation to the creative act . . . .

The secret dream of the artist is, for Gautier, to go beyond the material conditions of production, the constraints of every order, in order to discover absolute
freedom of expression.][11]

Both in Gautier and in Baudelaire, transposition is related to art criticism. In this volume, we have seen this phenomenon in the work of Marc
de Montifaud and Émile Zola. Transposition begins, then, with a visual
experience and passes through commentary into the creative response
of the "transposition d'art."[12] If I raise these points, it is because I want
to trace a similar process in Rodin's work, a process that represents conscious intermediality (invoking, as it does, *la poésie*, both symbolically
and concretely), and one that plays out the kinds of freedoms that transpositional interplay not only allows but encourages, both in form and
subject matter.

Before turning to Rodin's increasingly erotic transpositions, I want
to offer as a kind of cameo another example, also elaborated in one of
Rodin's conversations with Gsell—the one on nature and beauty—
conversations that themselves elaborate, as we shall see, Rodin's transpositional, and intermedial, impulse. The example is Rodin's *La belle
Heaulmière* (fig. 9.4), which dates from the early 1880s (1880–1883). Gsell
evokes Rodin's transpositional practice, demonstrating how closely the
bronze resembles François Villon's poem, which he quotes at length.
He then goes on to address to Rodin remarks about the public's (negative) reaction to this statue in the Musée du Luxembourg, which prompt
Rodin first to laugh, and second to embark on an exposition of his understanding of modern beauty, a beauty, according to Rodin, greater in
art "the more poignant the martyrdom of the conscience lodged in the
grotesque body" is.[13] Gsell immediately thinks of Donatello's penitent
Magdalene, in whose renunciation he sees radiance, in contrast to Rodin's *Belle Heaulmière*, who is anguished by her cadaverous body. Gsell
describes it as such:

Le sculpteur n'est point resté au-dessous du poète. Au contraire, son œuvre dans
l'effroi qu'elle inspire est peut-être plus expressive encore que les vers si trucu-
lents de maître Villon. La peau tombe en nappes flasques sur le squelette apparent: les cerceaux de la carcasse s'accusent sous le parchemin qui la récouvre: et
tout cela branle, flageole, se racornit, se recroqueville.

Figure 9.4. Rodin, *Celle qui fut la Belle Heaulimière; ou, La vieille Heaulimière* [She Who Was the Helmet-Maker's Once Beautiful Wife; or, The Old Courtesan]. Bronze, 1887. Photograph by Adam Rzepka. Courtesy Musée Rodin, Paris (s.1148). 50 × 30 × 26.5 cm.

[The sculptor is in no way inferior to the poet in realism. On the contrary, his work, in the horror that it inspires, is perhaps even more impressive than the truculent verses of Maître Villon. The skin hangs in flaccid folds on the skeleton; the ribs stand out beneath the parchment that covers them, and the whole figure seems to totter, to tremble, to shrivel, to shrink away.][14]

Rodin's own theory, much like Baudelaire's, hinges on the alchemist's transformation of ugliness into beauty, that is, into art, and on the relationship between fearless apprehension of exterior truth and creative encounter with inner truth. So the Baudelairean quest to transform "volupté en connaissance" [pleasure into knowledge] is, in Rodin's version, a transformation of "volupté en vérité" [pleasure into truth], where "le caractère" [character] is a "double vérité" [double truth]—the inner truth translated by the outer truth. Invoking other manifestations of such *transfiguration,* as he calls it, he turns to Velasquez, to Millet, and, finally, to Baudelaire's "Charogne," unequalled for Rodin in "cette terrible opposition de la Beauté qu'on voudrait éternelle et de l'atroce désagrégation qui l'attend" [its terrible juxtaposition of beauty, which we could wish eternal, and the atrocious disintegration that awaits it].[15]

Rodin's transpositional strategy, in other words, reaches beyond the translation of one medium (Villon's poem) into another (his own *Belle Heaulmière*). It embodies, in Rodin's understanding of it, a broader concept of art—one that he chooses to locate in *caractère*—apprehended intermedially through two poems, two paintings, and through Shakespeare's and Racine's investigations of "la laideur morale" [moral ugliness]. While *La belle Heaulmière* does not betray these intertextual references, or to use Norman Bryson's more measured term for the visual arts, these mutual interpenetrations, Rodin's remarks disclose such a system of intermediality, a system closely related in his work with a transpositional impulse.[16] Bryson takes issue with the notion of intertextuality in visual media on the grounds that paintings "possess embodiment,"[17] a concept that in his view deconstructs the opposition between matter and information, and which finally accounts for the fact that paintings offer a resistance to intertextuality.[18] Others, however, have demonstrated that, despite formal differences which usually lead to the faltering analyses in the "correspondence-of-the-arts" approach, "there is, *semantically* speaking (that is, in the pragmatics of communication, symbolic behavior, expression, signification) no essential difference between texts and images."[19]

What I would like to suggest is that Rodin's visual poetics (the term generally accepted to refer to ekphrasis in reverse)[20] is dependent, as are his conversations with Gsell, on such intertexts, or intermediality, and that the texts he often turns to are iconotexts, or texts that themselves work with images.[21] Here Rodin's notion of inner and outer truth, of surface and depth, becomes significant too, for if recent studies point to the rise of the museum as a factor in transpositional practice (and Rodin was an avid collector of artifacts), what also appears to be descriptive of the engagement with other arts is the notion of theater. This is because of the role the studio plays in Rodin's encounters and, etymologically, because it derives (as does theory) from the Greek *theasthai,* meaning to look at, contemplate, or behold. The artist who transposes is a spectator-theorist who views the representation (of the world) from within the theater of artistic production.

This goes some way to elaborating Rodin's sculptural engagement with poetry, but it does not address the question of different trans-positional practices. How should one, for example, measure *La belle Heaulmière* in relation to Rodin's illustration of Gallimard's copy of *Les Fleurs du Mal* (1887) or his collaboration with Octave Mirbeau on his salacious text *Le jardin des supplices* (1902)? Indeed, is illustration even to be considered transpositional? Much theoretical inquiry has foun-dered here, privileging text over image or vice versa, but rarely treat-ing the two as potentially separate and coexistent. Eric T. Haskell, to take just one example, considers Baudelaire's *Fleurs du Mal* in the illus-trated *édition de luxe,* describing various artists' renderings of the text and concludes:

> The numerous studies critics have devoted to *Les Fleurs du Mal* find their correspondence in the extraordinary variety of images created by artists to picture them. These representations not only elucidate the text; they extend it. The corpus of illustrated editions of this monumental nineteenth-century text constitutes an inexhaustible resource for the study of image/text aesthetics. The present essay serves only to indicate the scope inherent in such investigation and to chart the variety of illustrated visions available. *Les Fleurs du Mal* remains the very personal message of its creator. On the graphic plane, this fact is indicated by the multiplicity of Baudelairian portraits which assure him the central role in his textual scenario. The poet's struggle between good and evil, beauty and ugliness, *Idéal* and *Spleen,* harmony and discord, order and chaos, elevation and precipitation, and heaven and hell endlessly places the reader on the brink between dream and nightmare. This privileged space, itself an equivalent of the human condition, is inevitably shared by the viewer of images as he, too "reads" them concurrently with the text.[22]

Haskell recognizes here the scope of the question, and specifically refers at one point to illustration as transposition. Although he focuses
on the Baudelairean text, seeking in the illustrations confirmation of
established critical views, he sees the images as *visionary* illuminations
of the Baudelairean aesthetic. While text and image might be mutually
illuminating, how does the iconotext transcend this limiting framework
to become other? The problem is already present in the terminology.
The illustrated edition still foregrounds the text and makes the images
subservient to it, while the *livre d'artiste* and the *édition de luxe* tend to
emphasize the book's appearance, its exteriority.

In this respect, Rodin also offers examples—the illustration of *Les
Fleurs du Mal* and of Mirbeau's *Jardin des supplices*—that help us to come
to a better understanding of the transpositional impulse, or the iconotext. The development of the "livre d'artiste," especially in this period
under the patronage of Ambroise Vollard, offers an alternative way of
thinking about illustration transposition and its equivalent paradigm to
that of the museum. Indeed, Vollard's enterprise is "a sort of museum of
great texts as seen by great painters," according to Jean Bruller. Writing
in 1937, he notes,

> Vollard is a special case, as he only uses major painters, or those regarded as
> such. He is interested in seeing the reactions of an important painter confronted
> with an important text. . . . Collectors of paintings will be happy with them, but
> a true bibliophile will not. Rather than find an illustrator who best fits the text,
> Vollard only has his half-dozen of artists from whom to choose. The result is that
> his books lack the unity and spiritual homogeneity that would cause them to be
> classified as books of the first order. But they are too beautiful and important
> to be considered of the second order. They belong to some entirely different
> category.[23]

A special case, an entirely different category, indeed, for Vollard's conception of the "livre d'artiste" led him to create what is effectively *le livre de
dialogue,* and to be ever more adventurous in his presentation of such
books, challenging bibliophiles' notions of what such books should
be. By *livre de dialogue,* I mean, with Yves Peyré, the *rencontre conjugée*
[conjugated encounter] of two artists using different media.[24] Peyré explains in terms specifically related to poetry and painting, but that are
enlightening for our concerns: "Jamais le peintre et le poète n'ont été

retenus comme le pivot central faute duquel le phénomène n'existerait pas. Le plus souvent le parti qui a triomphé dans l'approche a eté celui de l'amalgame et de la confusion" [Never before had poet and painter been brought together in such a central way, without which the phenomenon of the artist's book would not exist. Most frequently, what prevailed in this approach was amalgam and confusion].[25] Vollard sought precisely to enable such dialogue, and it would be no exaggeration to say that many of the greatest interart collaborations in this period were a result of his acute understanding of the possibilities of such encounters.

By February 1899, that is, before Vollard's first such published work appeared in 1900, Rodin and Mirbeau had already approached him to work together on *Le jardin des supplices.* On February 10 the contract was signed, and Rodin—who was notorious for not delivering contracted works in a timely fashion (or indeed at all)—delivered ten of his fifty designs to the master printer just two weeks later. Vollard's edition, a *livre de dialogue,* was published in 1902. Mirbeau's text, although most often discussed in terms of cruelty and torture, frames a consideration of contemporary aesthetics, and illustrates his beliefs about art and the roles of the artist and art critic. As Christina Ferree Chabrier has recently shown, *Le jardin des supplices* also elaborates Mirbeau's espousal of the Baudelairean aesthetic, particularly in relation to "Une charogne," a poem that appears as specific intertextuality as Clara becomes the *charogne* and that Mirbeau described as "la pièce la plus spiritualiste des plus spiritualistes des poètes" [the most spiritualist work of the most spiritualist of poets],[26] even adopting the poem's philosophy as a closing for his 1895 defense of Oscar Wilde.[27] The passion in a torture garden, where the blooms are nourished by blood and excrement, figures, like Baudelaire's *charogne,* as a form of aesthetic rebirth.[28]

The Vollard edition was the culmination of a series of exchanges. In 1897, Mirbeau wrote the preface to the first published edition of some of Rodin's drawings, the edition now known as the Album Goupil. In 1899, Rodin did the frontispiece for the first edition of Mirbeau's *Jardin des supplices,* the 1899 Charpentier edition. Then, following the success of this, Rodin completed twenty illustrations for the luxurious Clot edition later that year. What emerges from this extended, ever-growing body of collaborative work between the two men is a real dialogue, one that, in a concise and intermedial way, demonstrates the power of the true iconotext. As Peyré describes this, in the *livre de dialogue,*

> La peinture attend la poésie, mieux, elle l'atteint, l'ayant rejoint dans un mouve-ment de nécessité qui dépasse d'assez loin la seule volonté. De même la poésie vis à vis du fait plastique. C'est dans le livre, à travers lui, dans le jeu de vertige et de foi de la double page qu'une telle intrépidité se donne libre cours.

> [Painting attends to the poetry, or rather, it reaches it, having met it in necessity, which goes beyond desire. And so it is with poetry, in terms of the plastic. It is through the book, and only the book, in the play of vertigo and faith represented by the double-page spread, that such intrepid enterprise finds its way.]²⁹

Ten years before this, in 1887, Gallimard had approached Rodin to illus-trate his own copy of a first (1857) edition of *Les Fleurs du Mal.* The book was to be rebound by another great artist, Marius Michel. In addition to illustrating the margins of the text, Rodin added a few *lavis* [wash draw-ings] on *papier japon* [Japanese tissue] that were subsequently bound in by Michel. Although not a dialogue in the same sense as the collabo-ration with Mirbeau, Rodin profoundly admired Baudelaire and was motivated, no doubt as much as Baudelaire was to transpose sculpture, by what Rosemary Lloyd has called regarding the latter case "a desire to meet a rhetorical challenge."³⁰ Rodin's drawings in the margins of the text, especially in the original (rather than in the facsimile) edition, create a sense of depth and volume that one might expect in a sculptor's drawing but that also complement perfectly the semantic density of the Baudelairean aesthetic.

In "La Beauté," for example, the "rêve de pierre" [dream of stone] is alluring, the contours of the nude echoed by the flowing lines of hair that constitute contrasting movement against the folds of the background, which mirror the statuesque figure (fig. 9.5). The "austères études" [aus-tere studies] that Beauty requires are challenged by Baudelaire's son-net form, and by Rodin's sketchily decisive shaping of the image that surrounds it, just as they are in Rodin's "Baiser" [Kiss]. This sculpture, inspired by song V of Dante's *Inferno,* is also inscribed with the first qua-train of "La Beauté," and captures the moment in which the lovers yield to temptation having read of Lancelot's and Guinevere's love (the book is just visible in Paolo's hand). It, too, like the *lavis,* gives volume to the "rêve

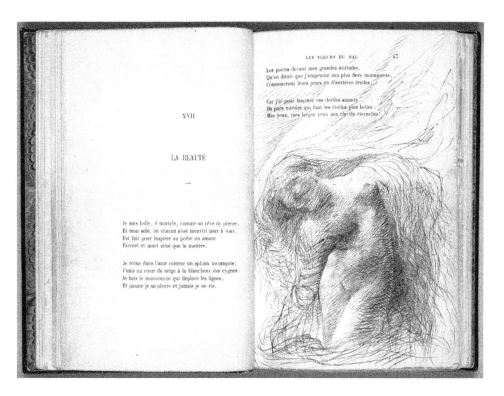

Figure 9.5. Rodin, illustration for Paul Gallimard's 1857 copy of *Les Fleurs du Mal*, "La Beauté." Graphite. Photograph by Jean de Calan. Courtesy Musée Rodin, Paris (d.7174(e)). 18.6 × 12 cm.

de pierre" and, in the way in which it translates passion through tensed toes and raised thigh, speaks with and over the muteness of Baudelaire's "matière" [matter]. The symbiosis we see in these examples, both iconotexts, brings to the fore not just mutually illuminating aspects of the text and image, and wider intermediality, but the transcendental power of a third art, something more than the sum of the individual parts—spiritually beyond form itself. Rainer Maria Rilke describes Rodin's response to Baudelaire in far more poetic terms but ones that also reach for a formulation of Rodin's transpositional practice:

> Et dans ces vers il y avait des passages qui sortaient de l'écriture, qui ne semblaient pas écrits, mais formés, des mots, et des groupes de mots qui avaient fondu dans les mains chaudes du poète, des lignes dont on palpait le relief, et des sonnets qui portaient comme des colonnes aux chapiteaux confus le poids d'une

pensée inquiète. Il sentait obscurément que cet art, là ou il s'arrêtait brusque-
ment, touchait au commencement d'un autre art dont il avait eu la nostalgie.

[And in those lines there were passages that went beyond writing, that seemed
less to be written than formed, words, and groups of words which had melted
in the warm hands of the poet, lines whose contours could be felt, sonnets that
carried within them, like complicated decorative columns, the weight of worry.
He sensed, obscurely, that where that art ended began another, for which he felt
some nostalgia.][31]

The example of "La Beauté": also brings into sharp focus the way
in which Rodin *reinvents*—further translates—not only in relation to
the textual encounter but in new encounters with his own work. So, for
example, in the Gallimard text, Rodin erotically adorns "Femmes damnées" with a lesbian embrace, framing the text with the open thighs of
the lovers, thighs in which their sex is also suggestively sketched:

> Beauté forte à genoux devant la beauté frêle,
> Superbe, elle humait voluptueusement
> Le vin de son triomphe, et s'allongeait vers elle,
> Comme pour recueillir un doux remerciement.
>
> Elle cherchait dans l'oeil de sa pâle victime
> Le cantique muet que chante le plaisir,
> Et cette gratitude, infinie et sublime
> Qui sort de la paupière ainsi qu'un long soupir.[32]

> [Strong and yet bowed, superbly on her knees,
> She snuffed her triumph, on that frailer grace
> Poring voluptuously, as though to seize
> The signs of thanks upon the other's face.
>
> Gazing, she sought in her pale victim's eye
> The speechless canticle that pleasure sings,
> The infinite gratitude that, like a sigh,
> Mounts slowly from the spirit's deepest springs.][33]

This theme predates the Gallimard illustration: an early version of the
"Femmes damnées" (1885) embrace is to be found on the right pilaster
of the Porte de l'Enfer (1880–1917) and is reincarnated in *Métamorphoses
d'Ovide* (1884), a piece that has also been identified under the title of *Les
Fleurs du Mal* and *Volupté*. Taking these transpositions a stage further,
and at about the same time, Rodin had a vertical version of the plaster
photographed, inscribing the image with the word "Désir."

Figure 9.6. Rodin, illustration for Paul Gallimard's 1857 copy of *Les Fleurs du Mal*, "Les femmes damnées." Brown ink. Photograph by Jean de Calan. Courtesy Musée Rodin, Paris (d.7174(d)). 18.6 × 12 cm.

"Femmes damnées" is the most illustrated of all of Baudelaire's poems, not always with happy results, but Rodin had a unique capacity to develop the subject. Indeed, it is a theme to which he returned repeatedly after 1900, and as Mahuzier points out, "his treatment of the sapphic subject is different from the usual postcard or peep-show representation of the topic," this difference "appear[ing] in the supple posture of the figures and in the paradoxical way that the illustrations make the viewer feel privy to the scenes without suffering the sense of performing voyeuristic invasion."[34] Indeed, in their movement, their sketchy sublimity, their questioning of what woman is and what she wants, they evoke Baudelaire's own transposition of Constantin Guys's women:

> Tout ce qui orne la femme, tout ce qui sert à illustrer sa beauté, fait partie
> d'elle-même; et les artistes qui se sont particulièrement appliqués à l'étude de
> cet être énigmatique raffolent autant de tout le *mundis muliebris* que de la femme

elle-même. La femme est sans doute une lumière, un regard, une invitation au bonheur, une parole quelquefois; mais elle est surtout une harmonie générale, non seulement dans son allure et le mouvement de ses membres, mais aussi dans les mousselines, les gazes, les vastes et chatoyantes nuées d'étoffes dont elle s'enveloppe, et qui sont comme les attributs et le piédestal de sa divinité.[35]

[All that adorns woman, all that serves to illustrate her beauty, is a part of her, and those artists who have applied themselves to the study of this enigmatic creature take pleasure in all that is a part of this *mundis muliebris* as if it were woman herself. Woman is without a doubt an illumination, a glance, an invitation to happiness, and sometimes a verbal expression, but mostly, she is a general harmony, not only in the way she looks and in her movements, but also in the silks, the gauze, all the vast and titillating fabrics in which she envelops herself, and which are both the attributes and pedestal of her divinity.]

Rodin's sapphic drawings, watercolors, and cutouts, richly suggestive and powerfully erotic, develop a theme begun as illustration and transposition and remain, intermedially, connected to those intertexts. But what occurs is a constant reinvention of the theme, as if the vision cannot be grasped, could never be captured. So that the sketches of sapphic couples appear in different postures or positions, light and airy, melded in the activity of (auto-) eroticism.[36] Rodin referred himself to this struggle to capture movement, by which he means ephemerality, and described his graphic technique as "drawing in depth," which develops progressively into vibrating outlines, wash drawings, and representations in Indian ink, watercolor, and gouache.[37] Rodin described his quest in these drawings as very much a part of his aesthetic of modeling. This is how Ludovici transcribes it: "Don't you see that for my work of modelling, I have not only to possess a very complete *knowledge* of the human form, but also a deep *feeling* for every aspect of it? I have, as it were, to *incorporate* the lines of the human body, and they must become a part of myself, deeply seated in my instincts. I must become permeated with all its contours, all the masses that it presents to the eye, I must feel them at the end of my fingers."[38]

The self-transposition becomes more urgent, and Rodin returned to drawings again and again, pursuing subjects movements, and ideas, cutting and pasting in a process of collage and montage to create new versions, to transpose figures from one context into another. In this transpositional practice, Rodin revealed how intermediality works. Using his

Figure 9.7. Rodin, "Couple saphique" [Sapphic Couple]. Watercolor, graphite, and estompe. Photograph by Jean de Calan. Courtesy Musée Rodin, Paris (d. 5713). 32.5 × 50.6 cm.

own drawings and sculptures "like a stock repertory," or like intertexts, he created new encounters from within his own work. At the same time, he appropriated plaster pieces, placing them in new situations, attaching them to antique goblets or vases, photographing "assemblages" as new compositions.[39] Perceiving affinities between them, Rodin moved to create new conjunctions within his own work that operate in imaginative unions and in transpositional dialogue, but most significantly represent the making as powerfully as the renewed subject. Rodin replaced Baudelaire's "culte des images" [cult of images] with what he called his "culte pour le nu" [cult of the nude], but what is clear in this theater, this choreography of nudes, is that the female body, like intermediality and transposition, is a means to an end, the source of art and an invitation to it.

What I have tried to suggest is that Rodin's engagement with illustration, with transposition, with iconotextuality and intermediality, offers a particularly privileged vantage point from which to survey questions of interart relations. Jean-Francois Lyotard's description of the transformations of the libidinal band is a theoretical fiction that provides an account

Figure 9.8. Rodin, "Deux femmes enlacés" [Two Women Embracing]. Watercolor and graphite. Photograph by Jean de Calan. Courtesy Musée Rodin, Paris (d. 5197). 32.5 × 25 cm.

Figure 9.9. Rodin, "Assemblage: Torse feminine agenouillé dans une coupe" [Female Torso Kneeling in a Goblet]. Plaster and antique ceramic. Photograph by Christian Baraja. Courtesy Musée Rodin, Paris (s.3611). 23 × 25.7 × 18.5 cm.

of how intense libidinal energies meet stable structures which exploit
and dampen their intensity.[40] Artistic conventions and frontiers present
somewhat stable systems and structures, which, despite their own intrinsic energies, inhibit change. The energy within such structures, however,
is released when brought into contact with competing interpretations
and dispositions. Rodin's intermediality—his experimentation across
structures, his reinvention through drawing and "assemblage"—is, like
Lyotard's, metaphorically libidinal in terms of its processes and engagement, and causes such new energies to be released, resulting in often
unexpected outcomes, complementing and complicating the explicit
source and the energized new work, and sometimes resulting in complex
distillations of both aesthetic and spiritual otherness.

SONYA STEPHENS is professor of French and acting president
at Mount Holyoke College having taught previously at Indiana
University, Bloomington, and Royal Holloway, University of
London. She has published widely on nineteenth-century French
poetry and its relation to visual culture, and is currently working on
questions of process and iconicity in modern France, as well as on
a study of illustrated editions of *Les Fleurs du Mal*. She is the author
of a book, *Baudelaire's Prose Poetry: The Practice and Politics of Irony*,
and editor of *A History of Women's Writing in France, Ebauches/
Esquisses: Projects and Pre-Texts in Nineteenth-Century France*, and
coeditor of *Birth and Death in Nineteenth-Century French Culture*.

NOTES

1. Gsell, *Auguste Rodin*, 156. See Rodin, *Art*.
2. "Le sacre de la femme," in Hugo, *La légende des siècles*, stanza 4, lines 146–156, 27–
28. Gsell's punctuation of the poem, presumably as Rodin quoted it, varies from Hugo's
own.
3. Scott, *Pictorialist Poetics*, 93.
4. Krieger, *Ekphrasis*; Mitchell, *Iconology*.
5. Kelley, "Transpositions."
6. See Heffernan, *Museum of Words*, and Maleuvre, *Museum Memories*. Notable
examples of this phenomenon would be Gautier's *España*, as much influenced by the
Louvre's acquisitions as by his trip to Spain, and the British Museum's acquisition of the
Elgin Marbles, which, Heffernan argues, influenced John Keats and Percy Shelley. See
Heffernan, *Museum of Words*, 94–134, and Majewski, *Transposing Art into Texts*, 7.

7. Majewski, *Transposing Art into Texts.*

8. Wagner, ed., *Icons-Texts-Iconotexts,* 17–18.

9. Lloyd, *Baudelaire's World,* 188–208, 197 (quotation).

10. Robinson-Valéry, "The 'Rough' and the 'Polished'," 65.

11. Alain Montaudon, "Écritures de l'image chez Théophile Gautier," in Wagner, ed., *Icons-Texts-Iconotexts,* 105–106.

12. See Lloyd's account of this process for Baudelaire in *Baudelaire's World,* 192–206.

13. Gsell, *Auguste Rodin,* 39ff.

14. Ibid., 43. The full conversation is translated in Rodin, *Art,* 15.

15. Gsell, *Auguste Rodin,* 48; Rodin, *Art,* 18.

16. Bryson, "Intertextuality and Visual Poetics," 187.

17. Ibid., 192.

18. See Wagner, *Icons-Texts-Iconotexts,* 18.

19. W. J. T. Mitchell, *Picture Theory,* 161.

20. Wagner, *Icons-Texts-Iconotexts,* 18.

21. For a definition of iconotext, see ibid., 16–17.

22. Haskell, "Illustrations for Baudelaire's *Les Fleurs du Mal,*" 194.

23. Cited in Rabinow, ed., *Cézanne to Picasso,* 202–203.

24. See Peyré, *Peinture et poésie,* 6. Peyré specifically understands this to be poetry and painting; he writes, "La rencontre conjuguée à l'exact de la peinture et de la poésie, cet attrait irrépressible des contraires" [The absolutely true and conjugated encounter of painting and poetry, that irresistible attraction of opposites].

25. Ibid., 6.

26. Chabrier, "Aesthetic Perversion," 359–360.

27. Mirbeau, *Les ecrivains,* 2:52.

28. Chabrier, "Aesthetic Perversion," especially 359–360.

29. Peyré, *Peinture et poésie,* 8–9.

30. Lloyd, *Baudelaire's World,* 198.

31. Rilke, *Auguste Rodin,* 26.

32. Charles Baudelaire, "Femmes damnées: Delphine et Hippolyte," in Baudelaire, *Œuvres complètes,* 1:152.

33. Huxley, *The Cicadas and Other Poems,* 20–21.

34. Mahuzier, "Rodin's Sapphic Designs," 402.

35. Charles Baudelaire, "Le Peintre de la vie moderne. X. La Femme," in Baudelaire, *Œuvres complètes,* 2:714.

36. See Rodin, *Images of Desire,* especially plates 79, "Temple à l'amour" (Musée Rodin, D. 6906), and 80, "Sapphic Couple" (fig. 9.7; Musée Rodin, D. 5713). For examples of "montage" and "collage," see plates 85–205, especially 85–92; plate 85, "Two Female Nudes, Semi-Recumbent" (Musée Rodin, D. 5192), and plate 88, "Two Women Embracing" (Musée Rodin, D. 5197).

37. Conversation with Jardin-Beaumetz, quoted in Anne Marie Bonnet, "Introduction," in *Auguste Rodin,* 12.

38. Ludovici, *Personal Reminiscences of Auguste Rodin,* 138.

39. See, on this subject, Goldscheider, "Assemblages et métamorphoses dans l'œuvre d'Auguste Rodin," 137–140.

40. See Montandon's explanation of how this operates within the artistic sphere in "La seduction de l'œuvre d'art chez Théophile Gautier."

PART THREE
SELF-TRANSLATION

TEN

The Mummy's Dance: Staged Transpositions of Gautier's Egyptian Tales

JULIANA STARR

IN NINETEENTH-CENTURY FRANCE, THE DISPLAY OF EGYP-
tian mummies in museums, and their public unwrapping at Universal
Exhibitions—something that Théophile Gautier himself witnessed—
embodied in a literal way the Western desire to unveil and pierce the
"secrets" of the "Orient."[1] In keeping with this vogue, figures of feminine
sexuality at the fin de siècle and beyond were often depicted as both
exotic and veiled.[2] Two such representations were controversial adaptations of Gautier's Egyptian tales. In 1907, fifty years after the publication
of his *Roman de la momie* (1857), the vaudeville actress and future writer
Colette performed at the Moulin Rouge a sketch called *Rêve d'Égypte,* in
which she played the role of a mummy brought back to life by an Egyptologist, a sketch that followed the plot of Gautier's prologue. Perhaps
the controversy was not so much caused by the striptease, in which the
mummy's bandages were gradually unwound, but by the fact that she enthusiastically kissed the Orientalist scholar, played by a woman in drag,
her real-life lover, Missy de Belbeuf.[3] So it was that the sketch which
would become known simply as "The Scandal of the Moulin Rouge"
violated taboos surrounding the exposure of the female body and the
display of lesbian sensuality.

Two years later, in 1909, the Russian Ida Rubinstein performed on
the stage of the Théâtre du Châtelet the title role in Sergei Diaghilev's ballet *Cléopâtre,* an adaptation of Gautier's short story *Une nuit de Cléopâtre*
(1838).[4] The fact that this performance, unlike Colette's, was hailed as a
revelation was due perhaps to its formal innovations, coupled with its

deft accommodation of the logic of the male gaze, a logic that sees art and femininity as visual representations of male genius and male sexual desire. I examine how all three women—Colette, Missy, and Ida—used Gautier's stories as a springboard to subversively lay bare sexual differences and resist regulatory norms of feminine behavior.

Around the time of her father's funeral in 1905, Colette's marriage began to fall apart, and unable yet to live off her writing, she began, like many women of her time, to consider acting as a means to more economic independence. In these aspirations, she was coached by Georges Wague, a man who had revolutionized the art of pantomime. Traditional mime, like Japanese No theater, used gestures and facial expressions codified and repeated by generations of mimes. Wague broke with tradition and invented a more realistic body language. Colette was greatly interested in this form of silent art, part dance, part acting.[5] She asked Wague if he would also teach pantomime to her lover, Mathilde de Morny, known as Missy de Belbeuf.

Colette and her husband, Willy, while still together, had been on the editorial staff of a new magazine, *Le damier,* which was launched at an exclusive club, Le Cercle des Arts et de la Mode. Missy was the club's main sponsor. Her great-grandmother was Empress Josephine, her grandmother Queen Hortense, her uncle Napoleon III, her father the Duke of Morny; on her mother's side, she was descended from the Romanovs of Russia.[6] She was France's most notorious cross-dresser, and was attracted to Colette who, encouraged by Willy, reciprocated. Missy wore grey or navy tailored suits, ties, a grey felt hat, and a monocle; carried a stick with a gold knob; and smoked cigars. She was perceived as outrageously shocking, yet took care not to shock. For social engagements she wore a long hooked-on skirt. When visiting friends, she would take it off to reveal a full, tailored suit with trousers. At her club, she would unhook the skirt and leave it in the cloakroom, as a man would leave a cape. Ten years Colette's senior, she had candidly crossed the gender border and forgotten all about it; her servants addressed her as "Monsieur le Marquis," and she liked to be called "Uncle Max" by her young friends, although she was referred to in the newspapers as "La Marquise."[7]

The performance took place on January 3, 1907, and became part of the great French tradition of opening-night riots like *Hernani, Ubu Roi, Le sacre du printemps,* and *Pelléas et Mélisande.* It was a fifteen-minute, one-act pantomime for two characters written by Willy, Wague, and Vuillermoz, with music by Édouard Mathé, starring Colette as a beautiful Egyptian mummy and "Yssim" as the archaeologist who discovers her.[8] "Yssim" was Missy's stage name, and of course it is "Missy" spelled backward. The name is a clever one in that not only is it Arabic-sounding, evoking the sketch's Orientalist themes, but it also plays on her gender ambiguity: spelled forward, she is a woman; spelled backward, she is a man. We can also turn the "M" upside down to form a "W," making a play on "Willy." The name ingeniously signifies that gender is a construct forming two sides of the same coin.

It is interesting to note that the poster for the play, as indicated by "Une pantomime de la Marquise de Morny," refers, quite erroneously, to the marquise as the author, as did the master of ceremonies, suggesting that the theater management cared less about correctly attributing authorship than about taking full economic advantage of Missy's fame and impressive pedigree. Indeed, the event was exploited with a cynicism worthy of tabloid television. Not only was the de Morny coat of arms printed on the placard, but it was posted at the entrance of the theater. In addition, in order to create a buzz, the event was leaked weeks ahead to several papers. Missy's brother, the Duke de Morny; her ex-husband, the Marquis de Belbeuf; and the leading Bonapartist, Prince Murat, took the bait: "They bought a large block of orchestra seats and filled them with their friends from the Jockey Club and a hundred and fifty hired thugs. When Willy appeared, accompanied by his girlfriend Meg, this throng turned to mumble threats."[9]

The curtain rose at 10:45 to a full house. The stage was immediately bombarded with coins, orange peels, seat cushions, tins of candy, and cloves of garlic, while the catcalls, the blowing of noisemakers, and shouts of "Down with the dykes" drowned out an orchestra of forty musicians. Incredibly, none of these missiles actually struck Missy or Colette, who went ahead with the performance despite the continuing riot, and they played with such unwavering courage that they earned the sym-

Figure 10.1. Colette, photographic still by Leopold Reutlinger for *Rêve d'Egypte*, 1907. Album Reutlinger de portraits divers, vol. 55, vue 55. B 12342. Bibliothèque Nationale de France. http://gallica.bnf.fr/ark:/12148/btv1b85969549/f55.item.r=Reutlinger ,%20Colette.zoom.

pathy and respect of their more impartial spectators, who stood up to applaud them.[10]

In a publicity still for the performance (fig. 10.1), we find yet more proof that the club's management fully exploited the sketch as a media event—but also an indication that Colette, more than willing to pose for the photograph, was quite complicit in that exploitation. Her "mummy" costume, with its jeweled bra, Egyptianesque collar necklace, and armband in the shape of a snake, owed quite a bit to fin-de-siècle iconography of Salomé.

During the performance, the mummy came back to life, slowly and seductively unwound her transparent wrappings, and at the climax of the dance—one reminiscent of Salomé's dance of the seven veils—passionately embraced the archaeologist. Here, we are reminded of Gautier's tale *La morte amoureuse* (1836) in which the deceased Clarimonde, compared at times to both Cleopatra and a mummy, is revived through a kiss from

Figure 10.2. Colette and Missy in *Rêve d'Egypte*, 1907. Photograph courtesy Centre d'Études Colette.

her beloved.[11] Another photograph (fig. 10.2) pictures the two actors moments before the kiss. Note that, if we were not told that the scholar is a woman, we would certainly not know. One source writes that the only thing that gave Missy away was her tiny feet.[12]

This image sets up an interesting power relationship between the two actors. At first glance, we could consider Colette as the more passive, since she is prone while Missy is standing above her. But Missy appears more timid—indeed, she seems to be drawing back almost in fear—while Colette, more centrally placed and bold, is the quintessential femme fatale, compared to both the Sphinx and the proverbial serpent. When the scholar took the unwrapped mummy in "his" arms to give her a lingering kiss, an element not present in Gautier's story, the uproar reached a fever pitch. As the curtain fell, a mob began to move on Meg and Willy, chanting, "Cuckold, cuckold." Willy struck out at them with his cane, Meg with her fists, "and they fought their way out into the hall, she punching one man in the nose, and scratching another with her ring. The police arrived to escort them from the theater, and four of their friends joined the police to do battle with the oncoming hordes, who backed off long enough for the couple to reach the manager's office and lock themselves into it."[13]

The next day, Missy's relatives asked the prefect of police to close the show. The theater management refused, and a large crowd gathered at the Moulin Rouge on January 4 for the second performance. At the last moment, however, a producer appeared onstage to inform the audience that by order of the police, there would be certain "modifications" to the play: it had a new title, *Songe d'Orient,* and Georges Wague, much to the disappointment of the spectators, would replace Yssim. "The performance began, and so, once again, did the riot. Stomping, whistling and pelting the stage, the crowd never stopped shouting for the marquise. Once again, Colette was applauded for her extraordinary courage."[14] The management had had enough, but it was the police commissioner who finally settled the matter with a total ban on the sketch.[15]

It is interesting to note that when Missy was replaced with a man, reestablishing traditional gender roles and removing the subversive elements, people were actually disappointed—proof that what they really wanted was scandal. I would like to suggest that she was triply subversive. First is her disruption of behavior seen as appropriate to her class. Here was an aristocrat of almost incredible pedigree, one of the wealthiest women in France, appearing on the country's most famous boulevard stage. Second is her lesbianism and gender ambiguity. Like the childless dandy Lord Evandale of Gautier's novella, described as "almost too beautiful to be a man," Missy questions the idea of fixed categories of gender.[16] Indeed, in both her real and stage lives, which could easily be confused, the idea of a stable identity gives way to one that is more performative, disaggregated, and mercurial.[17] In this sense, she is reminiscent of the androgynous Madeleine, the protagonist of Gautier's groundbreaking novel *Mademoiselle de Maupin* (1835), with its themes of homosexual desire, gender roles, and cross-dressing.

While her subversion of class and gender is somewhat obvious, I would like to suggest that Missy also challenged one of the most important and prevailing myths—that of Pygmalion, the *male* genius who turns stone beauty into flesh. In the original myth, it is Pygmalion, an artist king, who makes a statue of a woman and falls in love with it, but it is a woman, the goddess Aphrodite, who brings the statue-woman, later named Galatea, to life. Hence both man and woman participate in the artistic process. Many depictions of the myth, however, tend to portray the male artist as not only the creator of the woman/art object but also as the person who, through the quasi-magical powers of his genius, breathes life into that object. It could thus be argued that many writers and painters, in ignoring Aphrodite's contribution to the story, represented the myth in such a way as to diminish woman's power as artistic creator while accentuating male powers of creativity.

Part of what makes Gautier so revolutionary is the way in which he challenges these notions, empowering his female characters, and thus restoring to them the status held by Aphrodite in Ovid's original myth. In a story like *Le roi Candaule* (1844), for instance, the male protagonist is an artist king, like the first Pygmalion. However Nyssia, the beautiful Oriental princess who marries him, openly protests her unpleasant situation as a nude model and returns his gaze in a definitively powerful way.[18] The same could be said of Gautier's other Egyptian story, *Le pied de momie* (1840), in which the female mummy adamantly refuses to be used as bric-à-brac, and ingeniously restores her own integrity and wholeness. To the extent that these texts endow feminine characters with all the necessary intelligence and resolve to defy the male aesthete's gaze, and thereby to break the seemingly endless chain of the commodification of women, they join a very small number of texts that do so.[19] And here, at the Moulin Rouge, as the supposed author of the play as well as the life-giving archaeologist who revives the mummy through discovery and passion, Missy functions as both an intra- and extra-diagetic Pygmalion figure, and in so doing, challenges prevailing notions of gender roles vis-à-vis the creation of art. In fact, in her dual role as both scholar and lover, she represents both Pygmalion and Aphrodite, knowledge and love, forming an amalgam of the two central characters of Gautier's prologue, the intellectual Rumphius and the lover Evandale.

In contrast, as Cleopatra in Diaghilev's ballet of the same name—a work choreographed by the renowned Michel Fokine and designed by the innovative Léon Bakst—Ida Rubinstein was the embodiment of the modern muse, the ideal instrument of male artistic vision and genius. An exotic, wealthy Russian with only a few months of dance training, she joined Diaghilev's Ballets Russes, with dancers from the Imperial Russian Ballet, in her debut in the Western world on June 2, 1909. Here, Egyptian themes left the music hall to enter the newly renovated and sumptuous Théâtre du Châtelet, a haven of high art that introduced in the same season such legends of dance as Fokine, Vaslav Nijinski, Anna Pavlova, and Tamara Karsavina.[20] Among the more famous spectators that night were the composers Gabriel Fauré, Camille Saint-Saëns, and Maurice Ravel; the painter Jean-Louis Forain; the esthete Robert de Montesquiou (so taken by the work that he came back for virtually every performance); and, finally, a nineteen-year-old Jean Cocteau, who would become one of the regular backstage hangers-on.[21]

The ballet recounts the tale of the young hunter Amoun, danced by Fokine, who despite his betrothal to Ta-hor, danced by Pavlova, is mesmerized at the sight of Cleopatra, to whom he sends a message of love through the intermediary of an arrow, then offers his life in exchange for one night of love. Torn between his fiancée and a sensual adventure, Amoun ends up in the royal bed, but subsequently, the queen makes him drink a mortal poison, and Ta-hor, heartbroken, collapses over his dead body.[22] While Gautier's story concentrates on the monarch and her ill-fated admirer, exploring how the two become more equal partners through love, the ballet exploits the dramatic possibilities of a love triangle, while at the same time transforming the character of Cleopatra to conform to turn-of-the-century tastes and sensibilities.

Indeed, Gautier's tale depicts a multidimensional monarch, one torn between her royal duties and her need to be genuinely loved, not just admired and respected, as an individual and as a woman.[23] Her attraction to Amoun (Méïamoun in the text) is less problematic, as he is unattached. In fact, he has no fiancée, only a distant admirer (Nephté), who is not a developed character and remains totally unaware of his illicit love. Thus, absent is the ballet's dramatic dénouement, as well as the "shock" of the fatal poison. In Gautier's tale, it is understood beforehand that Méïamoun will have to take the poison, something he does quite willingly, and with no urging from the queen. Genuinely touched by her lover's courage, moreover, she is just about to spare his life, just about to say, "Vis encore pour m'aimer . . ., je le veux" [Live a while longer to love me . . . I wish it], when her husband, Mark Anthony (absent from

the ballet), abruptly returns, reestablishing patriarchal order and un-
derlining her vulnerability as a guilty wife and transgressor of domestic
law.[24] The only tear shed in the story is Cleopatra's own, as she is truly
saddened to have lost the only man who loved her for herself. The ballet
thus replaces the lonely, merciful, and melancholic queen with a fatal,
even sadistic enchantress who, after allowing her court to indulge in a
full-blown bacchanal, insists that her lover take poison as the penalty for
his infatuation. The punishment thus meted out, she coldly and callously
departs, leaving his real love to weep over his corpse.[25] Diaghilev dramatically modified Gautier's plot in order to create an iconic, decadent
monarch—the triumphant victor in a good girl versus bad girl rivalry.

As with *Rêve d'Égypte* two years before, the opening night performance was sold out, while audience reaction, though more positive, was
similar in its enthusiasm. To heighten the artistic effect, a musical score
with passages by Sergei Taneyev, Nikolai Rimsky-Korsakov, Aleksandr
Glazunov, and Modest Mussorgsky had been successfully pieced together. As soon as the curtain opened, a shiver ran through the house—
one caused by Bakst's impressively original décor. "Du jamais vu sur une
scène parisienne" [Never seen on a Parisian stage], writes Depaulis.[26]
Although the set echoed the monumental dimensions of the palace described by Gautier, it revealed a debauchery of violent colors, a startling
interpretation of the interior of an ancient Egyptian temple, with huge,
pink-colored statues of Egyptian gods along the sidewalls and a pro-
pylon four columns wide on both sides and two columns deep. And in
stark contrast to the parched, brownish landscape depicted in Gautier's
text, the backdrop revealed the lavender banks of a bright green Nile.[27]
Toni Bentley astutely points out the originality of the colors: "Bakst had
replaced the pale, pastel world of nineteenth-century classic ballet with
the violent, sexual hues of an imagined Orient—sapphire blue, oceanic
turquoise, blazing yellow, burning orange, and shocking pink filled the
stage."[28]

First, Karsavina and Nijinski interpreted a dance of veils that fascinated the public.[29] Then, after a long, ritualized procession of musicians
playing cithara and flutes, followed by dancing fauns, beautiful maidens,
slaves, and attendants, the prize was presented. Six black slaves entered
through the back portal of the set, holding aloft a gold and ebony casket

that they set down in the center of the temple, facing the audience. They unsealed its doors to expose an immobile mummy swathed in silk, which they lifted and placed center stage.[30]

Here, Salomé's seven veils were increased to twelve to denote her graduation from princess to queen of all Egypt.[31] To the beautiful but terrifying music of Rimsky-Korsakov's *Mlada*, four slaves began unwinding the veils, removing the first one (red with silver lotuses and crocodiles), then a second (green with the history of the dynasties of the Pharaohs in gold filigree), then a third (bright orange with prismatic stripes). As the Nubians ritualistically removed the twelve layers, each of a brilliant hue and sacred meaning, the standing figure of Rubinstein gradually emerged. The twelfth veil of deep blue released her, and she let it fall with a sweeping circular gesture.[32] On her head she wore a powder-blue wig with short golden braids, a wig "designed by Bakst to complete the vivid polychromatic fantasy of the decors."[33] Her grey eyes, enlarged by makeup, had a snake-like appearance, while her entire body, including her face and hands, was covered in turquoise body paint, for heightened decorative effect.[34] From Cocteau's description, it is easy to see how this woman of extraordinary beauty captivated the audience:

> Mme Rubinstein était debout, penchée en avant, avec un peu la bosse des ailes de l'ibis, bouleversée d'attente, ayant, dans son coffre obscur, subi comme nous l'intolérable et sublime musique de son cortège, instable sur ses hauts patins.... Elle était là, démaillotée, l'oeil vide, les pommettes pâles, la bouche entrouverte ... en face du public stupéfait, trop belle, à la manière d'une essence orientale qui sent trop fort.

> [Madame Rubinstein stood before us, perched unsteadily on her patterns, slightly bent forward with something of the movement of the Ibis's wings, having suffered like us from the confines of her dark coffin the intolerable and sublime music of her procession ... and so she stood with vacant eyes, pallid cheeks, and open mouth, before the spellbound audience, penetratingly beautiful, like the pungent perfume of some exotic essence.][35]

But when the queen of Egypt wrapped her snake-like body around that of the muscular Amoun-Fokine, performing a dance of love that culminated on a divan, the house exploded, even though the servants conveniently pulled a curtain that obscured the couple. The distinguished public lost all control, standing, shouting, stomping, and momentarily drowning out the music, as was the habit of the more lowbrow Moulin

Rouge audiences. The refined ladies of the Faubourg Saint-Germain enthusiastically smashed their fans on the railings of the box seats, while the men fought to storm the stage as soon as the curtain fell, mixing with the dumbfounded and frightened dancers.[36] And the subsequent audiences that packed into the Théâtre du Châtelet, even sitting willingly on the stairs, never ceased to be stunned.[37]

One should note that Gautier's story is set in Cleopatra's time, presenting her as a contemporary, living character, not as a mummy. Diaghilev's adaptation thus illustrates the enduring appeal, not only of Salomé and the dance of the seven veils, but also of the mummy-brought-to-life narrative. In *Le roman de la momie,* furthermore, the mummy's quiet tomb is pillaged and her bandages violently removed by two men—an act perhaps resembling rape more than striptease. And in *Une nuit de Cléopâtre,* the queen dances for her lover while fully clothed, taking off only her cape and crown, which she replaces with a crown of flowers. Her removal of her royal accoutrements can be seen as emblematic of her desire to be viewed as a woman rather than as a monarch. Hence, both staged adaptations, though vastly different, exploit the central character's sex appeal by turning Gautier's metaphoric plot elements into a mummy's striptease.[38]

A photographic representation of Rubinstein backstage in her Cleopatra costume (fig. 10.3) is unfortunately before the advent of color photography, and thus we can only imagine her blue wig. With her great height; slim, boyish hips; and long legs, she presented a startling image, an early metaphor for the athletically powerful woman. She had arrived barefoot in the land of the toe shoe, her dance thus embodying the integration of the music hall Salomé of Maud Allen and Mata Hari, and the improvisational sensibility of the new modern dance as presented by Loie Fuller, Ruth St. Denis, and Isadora Duncan, with ballet, the most classical of dance forms. Hence, for a ballet company with a centuries-old tradition, she presented a modern novelty. There were "no tutus, no pointe shoes, more turn-in than turn out, and bare midriffs glowing with body paint."[39]

She was infiltrating the shores of *Swan Lake,* the land where promises of eternal love dominate the aesthetic, with her own version of romance, the one-night stand. This infusion of veils into the world of

Figure 10.3. Auguste Bert, backstage photograph of Ida Rubinstein as Cleopatra, 1909. Courtesy Bibliothèque Nationale de France, Kochno Collection.

tiaras represented the sexualizing of the virgin ballerina, a transition illustrated within the ballet itself, where Pavlova, the Dying Swan incarnate, danced the role of the faithful woman who loses her fiancé to Cleopatra's insatiable sexual appetite.[40] The public was enthralled by this display, and underscoring the point, Rubinstein's success eclipsed that of Pavlova—quite remarkable when we consider that Rubinstein's role was essentially a static one in which a mere series of poses intended to evoke Egyptian bas-reliefs were used to convey the irresistible but cold and cruel fascination exercised by Cleopatra.[41] Clearly, then, the great success of the ballet was due not only to its dramatic exploitation of the good-girl-versus-bad-girl rivalry but also to its deft mix of classical and modern dance.

As an untrained dancer performing with a ballet company, Rubinstein thus personified the enlivening influence of modern dance on a classical tradition, which, prior to Diaghilev, had fallen into a period of decadence, repetition, and dullness. Hence, she carried the mantle of this extraordinary transition, bridging the gap not only between modern dance and classical ballet, but also between burlesque and ballet. It was as if Diaghilev had borrowed liberally from glitzy dance-hall numbers, replaced their pageantry with dancing, the showgirls with highly trained dancers, and "produced the ultimate burlesque ballet, squeezed into a brief and tumultuous twenty minutes."[42] At its center stood Rubinstein in her jewels and pale blue hair—the ultimate showgirl, surveying the scene first from her sarcophagus, then from her satin divan, with the ambiguous and proud expression of a mummified Mona Lisa. "Paris adored *Cléopâtre,* and it was hailed as a revelation, the greatest theatrical achievement in twenty-five years. Ida, with her vacant eyes and pallid cheeks, became an overnight sensation."[43]

Like Colette and Missy, Ida *was* somewhat exploited. Fokine and Bakst, after all, had chosen her partly because her notoriety was good for publicity. Besides, with her money, they thought they could count on her to work for free.[44] But at the same time, she willingly and actively strove to build her public image. Encouraged by friends like the outrageous dandy Robert de Montesquiou and the famous actress Sarah Bernhardt, she became a fashion icon; deliberately fed gossip about herself; commissioned a full-length, nude portrait; and cultivated her eccentricities, such as drinking champagne out of Madonna lilies and walking her tiger cub on a leash.[45] Like Colette and Missy, then, she did not confine her entrances and exits to the theater but treated all of life as her stage. Paris, with its grand avenues and sweeping vistas, provided the perfect docor for all three women, who took part in a new turn-of-the-century boulevard world that encouraged urban participants to showcase the self and to act for others. Their performances disrupted the liberal notion of the self as rooted in the sober variables of family, class, and profession, while transforming "identity" into a much more casual matter of display, appearance, and merchandizing.[46] Gautier's short stories, with their depictions of creative, powerful women and their provocative, revolutionary notions of gender identity, served as ideal sources.

Central to both transpositions was the striptease, *Rêve d'Égypte,* what we might today call a guilty pleasure. Performed at a popular music and dance hall and steeped in scandal, this low-budget sketch could perhaps be dismissed as shoddy art. However, Diaghilev's sumptuous production—with its elegant performance venue, daring use of color, and highly trained classical dancers—all helped to add an air of innovation and respectability. The fact that *Rêve d'Égypte* was adapted fifty years after the publication of the original text, and *Cléopâtre* more than seventy years after its text appeared in print, testifies to the enduring appeal of Gautier's Egyptian tales as a source of inspiration for all kinds of artists and artistic types, from choreographers, dancers, and pantomimes to writers, actresses, and cross-dressers. Indeed, 2011 marked the bicentennial of Gautier's birth, and a staged adaptation of *Le pied de momie* toured France—this time with marionettes—indicating the enduring appeal and inspiration of his tales.[47]

JULIANA STARR is associate professor of French and associate chair for foreign languages of the Department of English and Foreign Languages at the University of New Orleans. Her recent research involves feminism and interdisciplinarity in the novels of Judith Gautier and the operas of Louise Bertin. She is author of a number of articles on nineteenth-century depictions of women painters and artist models, and representations of voyeurism, in journals such as *French Studies Bulletin, Excavatio,* and *Women in French Studies.*

NOTES

1. See Lyu, "Unswathing the Mummy," 310. As she points out, Gautier witnessed the unsheathing of an Egyptian mummy at the 1867 Universal Exhibition in Paris.

2. See Showalter, *Sexual Anarchy*, 144.

3. Dobie, *Foreign Bodies*, 180.

4. Bentley, *Sisters of Salomé*, 134.

5. Francis and Gontier, *Creating Colette*, 222.

6. See Lottman, *Colette*, 64.

7. Francis and Gontier, *Creating Colette*, 224–226. See also Francis and Gontier, *Mathilde de Morny*.

8. See Thurman, *Secrets of the Flesh*, 171.

9. Ibid.

10. Ibid.

11. Quotations are taken from Gautier, *Récits fantastiques*. Clarimonde is compared to Cleopatra: "La grande courtisane Clarimonde est morte dernièrement, à la suite d'une orgie qui a duré huit jours et huit nuits.... On a renouvelé là les abominations des festins de Balthazar et de Cléopâtre" [The great courtesan Clarimonde died recently, after an bacchanal lasting eight days and eight nights.... She revived the abominations of the feasts of Balthazar and Cleopatra] (98), and "Clarimonde entendait la vie d'une grande manière, et elle avait un peu de Cléopâtre dans sa manière" [Clarimonde understood life on a grand scale and possessed something of Cleopatra in her manner] (105). And here is one of several evocations of a mummy: "Elle avait pour tout vêtement le suaire de lin qui la recouvrait sur son lit de parade" [Her sole article of clothing was the shroud of linen that covered her on her bier] (99).

12. Francis and Gontier, *Creating Colette*, 225.

13. Thurman, *Secrets of the Flesh*, 172.

14. Ibid.

15. Lottman, *Colette*, 77.

16. Quotations are taken from Gautier, *Le roman de la momie*. The exact quotation is, "Il portait partout avec lui ... une beauté dont on ne pouvait rien dire, sinon qu'elle était trop parfaite pour un homme" [He exuded everywhere he went ... an undeniable beauty, except that it was too perfect for a man] (152), and "le regard ferme de ses prunelles ... et le léger mouvement de *sneer* ... corrigeaient ce que cet ensemble aurait eu de trop efféminé" [the steady gaze of his pupils ... and his slight sneer ... corrected what would have been too effeminate in his features] (153). Interestingly, Méïamoun, the hero of Gautier's story *Une nuit de Cléopâtre*, is also described as androgynous, for he unites "la beauté de la femme à la force de l'homme" [the beauty of woman with the force of man] (17).

17. See Roberts, *Disruptive Acts*, 16.

18. Nyssia, too, in one of Candaule's erotic fantasies, is described as a mummy slowly removing her wrappings in a sort of striptease: "Lentement, une à une, elle laissa tomber sur ce fauteuil d'ivoire les draperies et les tuniques qui l'enveloppent tout le jour, comme les bandelettes d'une momie" [Slowly, one by one, she let fall on the ivory chair the swaths and tunics that envelope her all day, like the wrappings of a mummy]. Gautier, *Le roman de la momie*, 80.

19. The seventeenth-century works *La princesse de Clèves* and *L'astrée* come to mind as other texts that share this perspective.

20. Bentley, *Sisters of Salomé*, 131.

21. See de Cossart, *Ida Rubinstein*, 17–18, and Depaulis, *Ida Rubinstein*, 16. And, as Vicki Woolf tells us, Auguste Rodin and Isadora Duncan were also present on opening night. See Woolf, *Dancing in the Vortex*, 29.

22. Bentley, *Sisters of Salomé*, 133; Depaulis, *Ida Rubinstein*, 18.

23. Indeed, in Gautier's tale, Cleopatra laments that she is not loved: "Encore, si, pour tempérer cette tristesse, j'avais quelque passion au cœur, un intérêt à la vie, si j'aimais quelqu'un ou quelque chose, si j'étais aimée! mais je ne le suis point" [Still, if to temper this sadness I had a passion in my heart, an interest in life, if I loved someone or something, if I were loved! But I am not]. Gautier, *Le roman de la momie*, 13.

24. Ibid., 43.

25. De Cossart, *Ida Rubinstein*, 16.

26. Depaulis, *Ida Rubinstein*, 18.

27. See Mayer, "Ida Rubinstein," 33.

28. Bentley, *Sisters of Salomé*, 141.

29. Depaulis, *Ida Rubinstein*, 18.

30. Bentley, *Sisters of Salomé*, 132; Mayer, "Ida Rubinstein," 33.

31. Bentley, *Sisters of Salomé*, 131.

32. Depaulis, *Ida Rubinstein*, 19; Mayer, "Ida Rubinstein," 33.

33. De Cossart, *Ida Rubinstein*, 18.

34. Depaulis, *Ida Rubinstein*, 21.

35. Cocteau, "Note sur les ballets," cited in Depaulis, *Ida Rubinstein*, 19–20.

36. Depaulis, *Ida Rubinstein*, 21–23.

37. De Cossart, *Ida Rubinstein*, 16.

38. For Melanie Hawthorne, the unwrapping of the mummy in *Le roman de la momie* does indeed read as a sort of striptease. See Hawthorne, "Dis-covering the Female."

39. Bentley, *Sisters of Salomé*, 133–135.

40. Ibid., 134.

41. De Cossart, *Ida Rubinstein*, 17.

42. Bentley, *Sisters of Salomé*, 135.

43. Ibid.

44. De Cossart, *Ida Rubinstein*, 15–16.

45. Mayer, "Ida Rubinstein," 35. It should be noted that two years after *Cléopâtre*, in 1911, Rubinstein would do some gender-bending of her own, dancing at the Théâtre du Châtelet in the title role of the male saint in Gabriel d'Annunzio's five-hour pseudo-religious epic *Le martyre de Saint Sebastien*.

46. Roberts, *Disruptive Acts*, 16–17.

47. The play was originally staged by the Théâtre Grizzli in 2010 and toured in 2011. See http://www.theatre-grizzli.fr.

ELEVEN

Translating the Self: Colette and the "Fatally Autobiographical" Text

JANET BEIZER

ONE OF THE TEASES OF COLETTE'S AUTOBIOGRAPHICAL NOV-els is the tricky commute between art and life that she imposes on readers, who must consequently question translations, in both directions, between the two spheres.[1] In what follows, my reflections on Colette's maternal resurrections in *La Naissance du jour* inevitably labor under this strain, which becomes an inextricable thread of my text. In this light I begin with an anecdote that came to my attention through Judith Thurman's biography of Colette. Thurman recounts a childhood memory Colette's daughter related to a journalist. The adult Bel-Gazou remembers a vacation with her parents when she was five. It was 1918; her father was arriving home on furlough. "She and her mother, she recalled, had been waiting anxiously for Henry to arrive, and she had been dressed up to greet her father. While running down a flight of stone steps, she tripped, took a bad fall, headfirst, and scraped her face. Colette rushed over, but not to offer comfort. Her irritation expressed itself with a pair of slaps and this sentence: 'I'll teach you to ruin what I've made!'"[2]

To open a literary essay on *La Naissance du jour* with this biographical anecdote is to flout my best critical sensibilities and intents, but I do so with a sense of necessary perversity. The illegitimacy of my appropriation is compounded by its triple embedding, four times removed from Colette and unrelated to her writing: operating as a literary critic, I borrow from a biographer a journalist's recounting of a childhood memory of maternal handling related by Colette's adult daughter. I mean in this way to emblematize the challenges and risks of reading (for) the mother in any of Colette's three mother-centered novels, which have traditionally been assimilated by critics and biographers to Colette's own life story. Fiction and autobiography, biography and correspondence, indiscriminately bundled for decades by Colette's biographers and critics, have become virtually indistinguishable in the secondary work. If the establishment of such a continuum between the books and the life was encouraged and arguably launched by the efforts of her first husband and most zealous publicist, Willy, producer of a large-scale Colette industry, this was due to his extraordinary talents as a reader of cultural mythology.[3] His gifts included an intuitive grasp of a convention that I call the feminomorphing of women's books (reading books by women as if they were themselves women),[4] a convention Colette herself would refer to as "les oeuvres, fatalement autobiographiques, de la femme" [the fatally autobiographical writings of woman].[5] This is a fraught phrase to which I will return.

Like Colette (like a certain Colette), I would like to resist this life/work stew. I prefer to remove from my reading of *La Naissance du jour* the insights that come from interviews, correspondences, and biographies, to exclude them as lateral information, beside the literary point, in order to read Colette as I do the work of other writers: as a fine and precious artifact, apart. I say Colette: I mean the writer, the writing, the text. But before I know it, I find myself caught up with the remains of the woman, the living, the life—particularly when reading *La Naissance du jour*, whose wily snares wind us in novelistic filaments that defy an untangling of fictional from autobiographical and biographical threads.[6] I catch myself on the other side of a Möbius strip, having slipped inadvertently out of fiction, into autobiographical narrative and on into letters and life. I do not believe that the legitimacy of such a continuum can be assumed, and I do not know which was the first false step, or even if I am responsible for taking it. Sido and Colette are just two of a number of commuting characters in Colette's works, figures who wind their way between fiction and autobiography. The case of *La Naissance du jour* is especially complicated: historical figures such as the artists André Dunoyer de Segonzac and Luc-Albert Moreau sit down to dinner with Colette and her creatures of fiction, Vial and Hélène, while her mother's ghost hovers nearby and her real-life letters—rewritten—collaborate with Colette's text.[7] So we follow a sinuous trail that leads to questions at every bend.

If we are reading Colette's memoirs and autobiographical novels for the mother's traces, can we legitimately seek supporting evidence in, for example, the Claudine novels, which are widely accepted as thinly disguised (if salaciously embroidered) autobiographical accounts of Colette's adolescence and young womanhood? If not, how about *La Maison de Claudine,* a series of autobiographical vignettes that significantly are not called *La Maison de Colette*? Does the name of Claudine in the title (strictly irrelevant to the content of the text and surely commercially motivated) serve to fictionalize the memoir-like character of the text? Or to remind us that life transferred to writing can at best lie within a genre fluctuating between biography and fiction?[8] What about the fictions? Can we reconstruct the mother using descriptive or anecdotal details from the novels—and if not, what about scenarios of desire and loss continuous with the memoirs and letters?[9]

Like all of Colette's critics, like Colette in her flirtation with them, I cannot always keep her life and art pure. That is why, perhaps again like Colette, I play with the conventions that confuse the two. And that is why I open with everything I would like to banish from my own reading of Colette. To open with this castoff material is, in other words, to put it *en exergue,* from the Greek, *ergon* "œuvre," through the Latin, *exergum,* "espace hors d'œuvre" [a space outside the work], as the *Petit Robert* tells us.

Mettre en exergue: to place outside my work, as if by ritual purging, by an abjection of what threatens to contaminate it. I put *en exergue* all that I prefer not to consider, all that I want to exorcise from my text. I concentrate it, encapsulate it, cordon it off in that space *hors d'oeuvre*. But that outlying region is also a primary space, a privileged place that comes ahead of the rest of the text. An *hors d'oeuvre* with all the attendant ambiguity of that phrase: a place of exile, an outer darkness—but also, an *amuse-gueule,* an appetizer, a seductive foretaste of what is to come. What is outside the work also precedes the work; what is rejected is potentially the most influential part, by virtue of its position of primacy. The *hors d'oeuvre* comes to coincide with the *chef-d'oeuvre:* etymologically, the work at the head of what follows, the leading work.

By the classic logic underlying hierarchical thinking, what I marginalize spatially in my approach to Colette cannot effectively be excluded from it, because it is symbolically central to my thinking about her.[10] A pattern of conflictual representation dominates contemporary literary critical and biographical accounts of Colette, following her own ambiguous self-presentation, and scars my own thinking as well. That is, her life is ostensibly subordinated to her work, distinct from it, suppressed by it, only to reemerge within it, in unexpected forms and spaces. We can pluck from the daughter's memory of her mother, Colette, some threads to lead into the text of *La Naissance du jour*—as we simultaneously call attention to the questions of legitimacy and authenticity posed by letting auto/biography intrude, in just such a way, into fiction's text.

But let us pause to acknowledge the shock value of the anecdote. It provokes a visceral reaction on the part of the reader, eliciting sympathy for the doubly wounded child and horror for the mother's aggression.[11] It may be helpful here to step back and think about just what cultural notions of the mother, the maternal, and mother-love are implicitly invoked as they are radically subverted to the point of engaging our emotions. What sort of mother would rush to her hurt child's side to offer reprimand and punishment instead of consolation and comfort? In the grown daughter's words, "une bonne tape fut le premier de mes pansements" [a good slap was my first bandage].[12] What mother would make of her child a means by which to woo her man rather than an end in its own fledgling self? What mother would treat a child's injury as a blow to her own narcissism and a threat to her own integrity? And for what kind of mother is a child's subjectivity reconfigured as an objet d'art? Cultural expectations would have the "good mother" steadily at her child's side, offering encouragement and succor.[13] A "good mother" keeps the erotic and the maternal distinct. A "good mother" is instinctively aware of a child's needs, and places them before her own. A "good mother" is not constantly away while her child is raised by a governess and by consignment to friends. A "good mother" is, of course, rarely also a "good writer," if we take that to mean a reputed author with a strong publication record.

Is Colette then the proverbial "bad mother"?[14] Should such a question be raised in the context of a literary discussion, and does it matter for our reading of her work? Author of texts taken as maternal odes and

author-to-be of a *Supplément au Traité de l'Education des filles, de Fénélon*
[Supplement to Fénélon's Treatise on Girls' Education] (it never materi-
alized),[15] Colette might be likened to Jean-Jacques Rousseau, author of a
treatise on education and far from a model father.[16] And yet I wonder if
Colette's maternal shortcomings are not somehow more consequential
to the reception of her work as a writer than the analogous paternal failings of Rousseau are to his.

I am not alone in the temptation to include in my reading of Colette
elements usually considered to be bad form in literary criticism: loss of
critical distance, interference of life in art, gossip, emotional investment,
and identification. Colette's writing elicits very personal, idiosyncratic,
dialogic, relational readings, especially (if not exclusively) from her female critics.[17] Nicole Ward Jouve begins an enlightening study with
some confessional remarks that constitute her personal manifesto for
reading Colette: "It was my own dialogue with Colette I wanted to re-
count.... Immersed for months in Colette studies, and in Colette's own
works, I had so wanted to yield, be taken over.... To have any chance of
saying anything relevant about Colette, I must face up to her as I am, for
what I am worth. Thus I start from what I can deduce from my experience
of Colette."[18] Ward Jouve's words are representative of many women's
responses to Colette, including my own. Colette's writing resists me
but won't let me go. Her sentences elude me and dare me to pursue. Her
poetics of self and other challenges me to participate in an analogous
poetics and politics of reading, to reexamine my critical voice and my
critical stance, and to take the measure of my distance from her text. The
aesthetic questions raised by reading Colette are entangled with ethical
questions. What is at stake for women reading Colette? What do women
want from Colette? How can women's reading desire legitimate Colette
and, in turn, be legitimated, without violating the integrity of her writing
and living self, or our own?

The problem of subjectivity and relation raised for me by the biographical anecdote recurs on the level of reader response to *La Naissance
du jour* as we seek Colette (the writer, the woman) among her constructs,
and ourselves among her embedded readers. Which Colette are we reading? Which reader are we? These questions are uncannily shadowed
within the novel, which is, among other things, a meditation on recog-

nition and identification. A host of related puzzles ricochet in the space between biography and literary text. Here is one example:

Bel-Gazou bedecked in her finery for Henry, torn and undone like a gift whose wrapping has been ripped before ever reaching its recipient, spoils the surprise, shames the giver, and shifts the reader's interpretation from a maternal to an erotic register. The scene has other biographical resonances, and also literary counterparts. It anticipates a scene in *Sido* in which the child Minet-Chéri is wrapped in blue and tied with a ribbon, then sent with an ornament of flowers to Sido's best friend, the seductive Adrienne, as emissary, though one might say also as offering, as gift: a message of love. Minet-Chéri, herself seduced by Adrienne's wild charms, lingers, arouses Sido's jealousy—extends the mother's message, rewrites her text. Minet-Chéri, like Bel-Gazou, dispatched as a love letter, becomes a text that overflows its borders, a Frankensteinian creation, Colette's monster, a Galatea that begins to breathe on her own. This scene evokes another from the life narrative. Colette's stepson Bertrand, who was also her young lover in the early 1920s, was originally sent as an emissary by his cunning mother, Claire de Boas, who sought to use her charming sixteen-year-old boy to convince her ex-husband, through Colette, to allow her to continue to carry his name. Bel-Gazou wrapped by Colette for Henry, Minet-Chéri adorned by Sido for Adrienne, Bertrand dispatched by his mother to Colette, who is charmed more than was perhaps intended: here are the same crossed threads of nurturance and seduction that structure *La Naissance du jour,* which juxtaposes mothers and lovers.[19]

Following attempts to purge biography from my critical text, I found the *hors-texte* already within. In parallel fashion, I discovered that *La Naissance du jour* is a work that endlessly recontains its own outer bounds in Borgesian or Escheresque fashion, evacuating and then reabsorbing its apparent other. Have I come full circle at the point of entry into the literary text? Does art always mirror life? Does life necessarily produce art's legend? No. I do not want to imply that Colette's fiction is autobiographical. On the contrary, I propose that all her life's a book, and that life is her most extravagant work.

According to most accounts, Colette was less than a devoted mother. Her intense absorption in her work and life seemed to preclude the assimilation of a child's world into her own, and she quickly consigned her daughter to a governess. Colette, who spoke lucidly of the incompatibility of maternity and authorhood, regarded herself as essentially an author and accidentally a mother.[20] Late in life she would acknowledge her bias in a letter to her daughter: "Y eut-il jamais mère si peu maternelle? Je suis ton vieux gratte-papier, qui fut trop souvent obsédé de soucis matériels" [Was there ever such an unmaternal mother? I am your old scribbler, who was too often preoccupied with material concerns].[21] The words play on a material split, the *mater*nel ceding to the *mater*iality of writing. The adult Bel-Gazou spoke often and plaintively of her mother's dual loyalties: "Non, on ne pose pas de questions à une mère qui travaille. Je me retenais. Et c'était le plus dur. . . . Ce que je ne devinais pas, c'est que la plupart des réponses à toutes mes questions informulées, elle était occupée à les écrire. Non pour mon seul profit, pour le profit de beaucoup de gens [No, one doesn't interrupt a mother who is working, with questions. I held back. And this was the hardest part. . . . What I couldn't have guessed is that she was in fact busy writing the answers to all my unformulated questions. Not for my own benefit, for the benefit of many people].[22] The daughter's jealousy of the mother's books culminates in her sense of their mutual exclusivity: "Elle qui chaque jour enfantait, pouvait-on demander qu'elle mît au monde chaque matin des jumeaux: son travail et son enfant ?" [Could one ask this woman who went into labor every day, to give birth every morning to twins: her work and her child?].[23] This rivalry is the counterpart of the conflict Colette later referred to as "la compétition, livre contre enfantement" [the contest between book and childbirth].[24] Colette, whose favorite work of fiction was Balzac's *Le Chef-d'œuvre inconnu*, surely knew—in art and life—the precarious equilibrium, if not to say the radical incompatibility, of art and life.[25]

Colette seems to have resolved the problem of incompatibility, rhetorically at least, by assimilating her daughter to her work: my daughter, my text, the work of art I have made, punished for aesthetic flaw. "I'll teach you to ruin what I've made!" The filial opus defiled reappears in illness as aggressively defective: "Je me tourmente quand tu perds ta bonne mine, et cela me rend . . . un peu méchante. Quand tu es malade, c'est comme si tu m'avais fait quelque chose de mal" [I always seem angry with you when you're sick. . . . I worry when you don't look well, and that makes me . . . a little grouchy. When you're sick, it's as if you'd hurt me].²⁶ Small wonder if Colette expresses her daughter's shortcomings in terms of wounding imperfection and failed art, for she consistently represented herself from Sido's perspective as opus or masterpiece. If Colette's daughter in turn presented herself to interviewers as a failed masterpiece, a lesser work, in her mother's eyes, the letters let us understand just why, for Colette often addresses her daughter there as a creation who did not live up to her creators' inspiration, an unfinished work unworthy of her makers.

Bel-Gazou becomes an *oeuvre manquée* for reasons that Colette charges to a lack of originality or uniqueness. "Bavarder, rire . . . ce sont des choses banales. Une élève dissipée est une élève qui ressemble à cent, mille autres élèves. Tu ne te singularises pas. . . . Au contraire, tu deviens ce que j'ai toujours dédaigné: quelqu'un d'*ordinaire*" [Chattering, laughing . . . these are banal activities. An undisciplined student is a student who is like a hundred—no, a thousand—other students. You don't stand out. . . . On the contrary, you become what I have always despised: an *ordinary* person].²⁷ Elsewhere she chides: "Nous ne t'avons pas mise au monde pour cela. Ton père et moi nous sommes en droit d'exiger que notre fille . . . soit *quelqu'un*" [We didn't bring you forth for this. Your father and I have the right to require that our daughter . . . be *a somebody*].²⁸ This daughter failing to bring glory to her creators is routinely labeled commonplace, ordinary, lacking in distinction ["quelconque"]. Yet in a letter to her friend Germaine Patat, Colette suggests at least a fleetingly more nuanced understanding of the ordinary as it operates in her family's rather extraordinary psychosocial universe: "Quelle fichue situation d'être la fille de deux quelqu'un. Elle a un sacré besoin de s'appeler Durand, ma fille" [What a lousy situation to be the daughter of two somebodies. My daughter would be a hell of a lot better off if her name were Durand (i.e., Jones)].²⁹ Striving, in response to her mother's criticism, to distinguish herself, to transcend her relegation to the ordinary, the child attempts to write pithy, remarkable letters worthy of Colette, only to feel herself inevitably backsliding into banality: "C'est aujourd'hui ton anniversaire n'est-ce pas, maman? Je te souhaite un très heureux anniversaire. . . . J'aurais voulu t'écrire une lettre sensationnelle pour ce jour, mais il suffit que je veuille pour immédiatement pondre une banalité qui . . . ne traduit pas mes sentiments" [It's your birthday today, right, *Maman*? I wish you a very happy birthday. . . . I would have liked to write you a spectacular letter for today, but wanting to do that is enough to make me come up with a banality that doesn't translate my feelings].[30]

Might we connect childhood associations with creative ineptitude to the adult Bel-Gazou's abandonment of a career in journalism to open an antiques store, located on the Impasse de l'Ecritoire—roughly translatable as "Writer's Dead End Street"? Could we speculate on Colette's preoccupation, in *Naissance,* with being the daughter of her mother, leaving her own maternal subjectivity largely unvoiced? It is tempting to wonder whether she would have been able to articulate her identifications and dissociations with her own mother without having first acceded to maternal subjecthood. Colette's avowed disinclination to speak of her daughter in *La Naissance du jour,* and the silence in which she shrouds her there, similarly invite interpretation.

Yet I hesitate to proceed. At risk is my literary critical voice. With Colette, reductiveness looms in each sentence I write. I question my critical ethics, the critical ethos in which I was formed, and more specifically, the place and position of criticism in relation to a literary text and its author: its *orientation,* in the full etymological sense of relation to the Orient, the rising sun, the privileged source. If literature is that sun, am I not Icarus, if not Prometheus, flying too high, presuming too much, raiding the gods' own light? What is criticism's appropriate stance, its place, its route, in relation to the literary text? What is its geographical metaphor? How near to, how far from a literary text should a critic stand; how closely embrace, how distantly examine the writer?

The dialectic of distance and relation intrinsic to any epistemological undertaking in which a subject speaks of or for an object (a dialectic especially prominent in a narrative text) is exacerbated in Colette because of the whirling dynamic of self and other that she sets in play. As her would-be critic (her commentator or interpreter), I am sensitive to the danger of becoming her effective critic (her evaluator or judge), and I worry about a potential "critical imperative" model. Must literary criticism work under a latent doctrine of "manifest destiny"? Does it share with other modern intellectual disciplines a colonizing birthright from which it borrows its textual authority?[31] Reading Colette makes me increasingly reluctant to follow these critical conventions—the conventions of patriarchal criticism. I recognize in my work on Colette, with some uneasiness, a reactive (some might say feminist) intimacy with Colette. It is like Jouve's desire "to yield, to be taken over" (by Colette's text), or an extreme form of Ruth Behar's "vulnerable observer" version of anthropology's "participant observer" model.[32] Even as I applaud the concept of vulnerable observer as antidote to cold or distracted observation, I recognize the potential for vulnerable observer to slide into something like an "observant wound"—a subjectivity that registers little but its own emotivity or affective complicity, and risks a rude slap in the face: "I'll teach you to ruin what I've made."

I want to speak of Colette with neither authority nor complicity. Gilles Deleuze articulated a similar dilemma: "My ideal, when I write about an author, would be to write nothing that could cause her sadness, or if she is dead, that might make her weep in her grave. Think of the author you are writing about. Think of her so hard that she can no longer be an object, and equally so that you cannot identify with her. Avoid the double shame of the scholar and the familiar."[33] I'm taking a few liberties in my translation of Deleuze. I have feminized his author pronouns, and I would like to propose collapsing the "double shame" of which he speaks—that of the scholar and of the familiar—into a shame that, though double, is not partitioned in two, a shame that may well be the scholar's double burden. For the dual temptations of distance and identification (attributes of the scholar and the familiar, respectively, for Deleuze) describe the double specter haunting my own approach to Colette.

I would like to stand safely between authority and intimacy, less concerned with a critical approach or method than with a critical stance or ethos. I seek a criticism that is a return to reading: reading that is at once an interrogation of the text *and of the self,* an engagement of the self in a dynamic bilateral process, a process of critical relationship. Such a reading would involve a different kind of writing, one that would let a reader speak about a writer's work without needing to feel shame, without risking the violation of knowing the author's work or her person too well. A writing that would let a reader love a writer's work and yet speak words that would not eclipse the work and could not eclipse themselves.

A writing that would not attempt to fill in ellipses more articulately left as blanks, that would not "see" where the author was prophetically blind, but that might instead register a process of change, *of being oneself changed* by the reading process. A writing that would neither make a dead author "weep in her grave" nor, in the more likely Colettian scenario, let her have the last underground laugh.

Reading for the mother in Colette risks either engaging the reader in a dialectic of fusion and separation with the (literary) mother, or engaging Colette in a typically masculine "fatally autobiographical" reading. "Homme, mon ami," warns Colette, "tu plaisantes volontiers les oeuvres, fatalement autobiographiques, de la femme" (*Naissance*, 316) ["Man, my friend, you willingly mock the fatally autobiographical writing of women"] (*Break of Day*, 63). Addressing herself here to a male reader, she plays with conventions that assume any writing by a woman to be transparent, true, and autobiographically correct. Colette's phrase, "les oeuvres, fatalement autobiographiques, de la femme"—only half-rendered in the McLeod translation as "women's writings [which] can't help being autobiographical" (*Break of Day*, 63)—owes its force to its compounded ambiguity. To call women's works "fatally autobiographical" means, on the one hand, that they are doomed to be autobiographical—but does "autobiographical" refer to writing or to reading? It means, on the other hand, that they are fatal *because* autobiographical. Lethal writing. Who, or what, is the victim? As in the expression *la femme fatale*, which lends its force along with its potential reversibility to the notion of fatal feminine autobiography, the ostensible purveyor of death (the woman writer, her text) may well be the victim instead.

Certainly Colette felt misread, attacked in her status of author, when the journal *Femina* changed the title of her essay "Maternité" to "Impressions de maman: Les premières heures" [A Mother's Impressions: The First Hours] in order to represent it as a woman's autobiographical text.[34] Here is an excerpt from the letter she wrote to the editor in angry dismay: "Que je sois mère, cela ne regarde pas le lecteur. Je lui donne une œuvre que je souhaite littéraire, c'est *l'auteur* qui paraît devant lui, ce n'est pas la femme, et s'il a le droit de me juger comme écrivain, son droit s'arrête là" [That I am a mother is not the reader's business. I give the reader a work that I hope is literary; it's *the author* who appears before him, and not the

woman, and if it is his right to judge me as a writer, his right stops there].
Colette's rage at being misrepresented and misunderstood—*méconnue:*
taken for someone else, which is to say, confused with herself—is clear.
What is murkier is Colette's role in obscuring the distinction between
fiction and autobiography in the text of "Maternité," which begins with
a confirmation of pregnancy given by "un médecin que je connais à une
de ses clients que je connais mieux encore" [a doctor whom I know, to
a woman who is a patient of his, and whom I know even better].[35] We're
familiar with this kind of double entendre from the pages of *La Naissance
du jour:* as an artificer of autobiography, Colette presents a "me" who is
not quite me.[36]

Colette elaborates on the autobiographical conundrum by describing her writing as a kind of *constructed* autobiography: "Ce que je sais de
moi, ce que j'essaie d'en cacher, ce que j'en invente et ce que j'en devine"
(315) ["What I know about myself, what I've tried to hide, what I've invented and what I've guessed"] (62). Women's writing, she suggests, is
false autobiography (we might say today "autofiction"), a cunning prof-
fering of amorous confidences and half-truths that serve to hide deeper,
less "sexy" truths:

> En les divulguant, elle sauve de la publicité des secrets confus et considérables,
> qu'elle-même ne connaît pas très bien. Le gros projecteur, l'œil sans vergogne
> qu'elle manœuvre avec complaisance, fouille toujours le même secteur féminin,
> ravagé de félicité et de discorde, autour duquel l'ombre s'épaissit. Ce n'est pas
> dans la zone illuminée que se trame le pire. (315–316)

> By divulging these, she manages to hide other important and obscure secrets
> which she herself does not understand very well. The spotlight, the shameless
> eye which she obligingly operates, always explores the same sector of a woman's
> life, that sector tortured by bliss and discord round which the shades are thick-
> est. But it is not in the illuminated zone that the darkest plots are woven. (62–63)

Colette is suggesting that there's an entire (novelistic) world to explore
outside of the love plot.

By suggesting that sexual and romantic revelations in her writing are
not coextensive with truth, and in fact divulge no real secrets at all, Colette is combating not only cultural assumptions about women and writing but also a philosophical tradition that equates sex and truth (a truth
generally taken to be more accessible through women). Janet Malcolm

points to the triviality of sexual "truths" in her essay on Chekhov: "As if the documentary proof of sexual escapades or of incidents of impotence disclosed anything. . . . The letters and journals we leave behind and the impressions we have made on our contemporaries are the mere husk of the kernel of our essential life. When we die, the kernel is buried with us. This is the horror and pity of death and the reason for the inescapable triviality of biography."[37]

But the triviality of sex-based biography is amplified for Colette by the gender factor at the crux of her autobiographical protest. What's at stake in Colette's text is *women's art,* or the right to the artfulness of art when its maker happens to be a woman.

Colette's narrator/character, Colette, complains bitterly, as she distances herself from the attentions of Vial, of his attempts to know her through her books: "Nous n'avons que faire de mes livres ici, Vial" (341) ["We're not concerned with my books here, Vial"] (100). I certainly do not want to be another Vial, confusing Colette with Colette. I am reminded of Proust's insistence that when we think of an author, it is the books, and not the life, that matter, that "a book is the product of an other self."[38] This is perhaps what Colette had in mind as well when she wrote the initial epigraph (later discarded) for *La Naissance,* which she adapted from Proust: "Ce 'je' qui est moi et qui n'est peut-être pas moi" [this "I" who is me and who is perhaps not me].[39]

Yet the narrative of *Naissance* thickens even as the plot thins. Speaking of her renunciation of love, Colette (the narrator/character) mentions her earlier works, and how she has moved away from their focus on love: "Je m'y nommais Renée Néré, ou bien, prémonitoire, j'agençais une Léa. Voilà que, légalement, littérairement et familièrement, je n'ai plus qu'un nom, qui est le mien" (286) ["In them I called myself Renée Néré or else, prophetically, I introduced a Léa. So it came about that both legally and familiarly, as well as in my books, I now have only one name, which is my own"] (19). Since my impulse is to read *La Naissance* as Colette calls it—as a text to be dissociated from her life—I wonder how to read Colette's newly found writing identity: "Je n'ai plus qu'un nom, qui est le mien" (286) ["I now have only one name, which is my own"] (19)? It is hard to avoid hearing an invitation to an autobiographical pact.[40] This is the other side of Colette's fatally autobiographical writing: a writing that might be considered autobiographically *entrapping*, from the perspective of readers caught in a house of mirrors.

Colette had a tortuous relationship to mirroring and mimesis that can be traced through her fictions, letters, and essays.[41] One might see her writing as a history of attempts to escape the mirror structure and aesthetic, and of subsequent slides back in. As Michel del Castillo has suggested, Colette's struggle for autonomy had incessantly to confront the expectation that she be her mother's reflection, a constraint succinctly articulated in Sido's correspondence with her daughter as "Moi, c'est toi" [I am you].[42] In the dynamics of her relationship with her own daughter, Colette would alternate between a similar mirroring expectation and a recognition of her otherness. So, for example, she would write to Bel-Gazou words that echo her mother's claim on her: "J'aimerais te voir te classer devant moi comme un petit miroir de moi-même" [I would like to see you fall into place before me as a little mirror of myself].[43] Yet elsewhere she would deliberately recall her daughter's individuality:

> J'ai vu chez Lelong . . . de si jolis petits sweaters "jeunes" que je t'ouvre un crédit pour en choisir un. . . . Il y en a un bleu . . . en Shetland, tellement aimable que j'ai faille [*sic*] te le prendre, mais! . . . n'oublions pas que les parents ne doivent jamais construire pour les enfants—même en Shetland!

> When I was at Lelong's I saw such pretty, stylish sweaters that I left a credit so that you may choose one. . . . There was a blue Shetland one with a white collar and sleeves, so appealing that I almost bought it for you, but let's not forget that parents should never make plans for their children—even concerning Shetland![44]

In her public writing, Colette more routinely proclaimed a politics and an aesthetics of determined distance and nonreflectivity. To her character Vial as to the editor who published "Maternité," Colette, we have seen, adamantly made clear that her text was not to be read as a reflection of her life. In 1908, Colette had already constructed a parable of the dangers of literary mirroring, in a short text called "Le Miroir," in which the narrator arranges a meeting between herself and her character, Claudine, and protests: "Je ne suis pas votre Sosie" [I am not your double].[45] Meanwhile, Colette went about in the world dressed like Claudine, coiffed like Claudine, confused with Claudine; she would later borrow Claudine's name for her autobiographical house of fiction, and she would socialize, in her own name, with her character Vial in the pages of *Naissance.*

Like "Le Miroir," *La Naissance du jour* is a work concerned with the inaccessibility of life to art, but that nevertheless inextricably entangles life's tentacles in art, and so risks confusing and reordering—and symbolically dismantling—the mimetic hierarchy. The question of literature's responsibility to life is doubled by the problem I raised earlier, of criticism's responsibility to literature—a problem of reflection and identification that might be likened to a secondary mimesis, if criticism and literature are analogous in the sense of their impossible accountability to art and life. Phyllis Rose describes the dual dilemma: "A translation, a reduction, a condensation, an approximation, a metaphor is the best that can be achieved in art, no matter how inclusive, as an account of life, and the same is true for criticism as an account of art."[46] If we accept the analogy, it is clear that when literary mimesis is threatened, so too are traditional conceptions of criticism's fidelity to literature.

I conclude this essay by raising a few questions it leaves open. *La Naissance du jour:* a novel about mothers and lovers? Rather, a novel about the mother's ghost and the lover's shadow, mother and lover fading out to give center stage to a metaplot about finding another aesthetic, another ontology, another masterplot not reliant on reflection and mimesis. How might this aesthetic be defined? Colette's youngest stepson, Renaud de Jouvenel, noted that he couldn't recognize himself as he appeared in her letters: "Elle exagérait. . . . C'est qu'elle débordait de fantaisie, voyait les êtres au travers d'une loupe grossissante et déformante et . . . idéalisait, emportée par la chaleur de son tempérament, le besoin de tout transformer en matériau littéraire" [She exaggerated . . . because she was carried away by fantasy, saw people through a glass that magnified and deformed them, and . . . she idealized things, swept away by her own fervor, by her need to transform everything into literature].[47] Roughly summarized, this means that Colette needed literature so that she could transform everything. Writing, for Colette, was a *metamorphic* exercise, to use Julia Kristeva's term.[48] It proceeds, like metaphor, but more so, by holding two opposing entities together *in passing* in an ephemeral relationship based neither in resemblance nor antagonism, but in change. I cannot here develop my sense that Colette's writing is an extravagant experiment with an aesthetic based on change, but I point that way by adding the metaphor of "transposition" to that of "translation" with which I began to describe her travels between life and art. Life and art are two corresponding media for Colette, like painting and poetry; she transposes freely in both directions, challenging the reader to decipher and recode and make sense. In this she is not unlike Baudelaire's Dandy who, in Rosemary Lloyd's words, "gives him or herself to be read and seen as a work of art, constantly recreated. . . . This is performance art raised to the level of high culture."[49]

I close with the sense of being myself changed by reading Colette, recast as reader and critic. I now know that one does not read Colette to be held by the visions or embracing truths that warm us and fleetingly make us whole when reading Proust. Nor does one read her to pose as a reliable critical reflector. Reading Colette, anticipating resistance and resisting incoherence, one works to shape and hold meaning among the flickering nuances of her kaleidoscopic prose. I recognize the utter impossibility of resurrecting the mother in Colette, and Colette as mother. But still, I reread *La Naissance du jour* to be transformed by Colette's ungentle hand, as my own remakes her text.

JANET BEIZER is C. Douglas Dillon Professor of the Civilization of France at Harvard University. She is author of *Thinking through the Mothers: Reimagining Women's Biographies, Ventriloquized Bodies: Narratives of Hysteria in Nineteenth-Century France,* and *Family Plots: Balzac's Narrative Generations,* as well as numerous articles on French literature. She is currently working on discourses of food in French culture, and writing a book on the aesthetics of the harlequin.

NOTES

1. A more comprehensive version of this essay appears in Beizer, *Thinking through the Mothers,* 143–222.

2. Thurman, *Secrets of the Flesh,* 274. Thurman gives as an archival source BN 18718, Archives of the Bibliothèque Nationale, Paris.

3. Colette acted the character who dominated her early work, Claudine, on stage and in town; she was (often by design) confused with her character, which led to the marketing of a panoply of signature objects: Claudine dresses and hats, *glace* Claudine, *gâteau* Claudine, *cigarettes* Claudine, etc. See Marks, *Colette,* 73.

4. Lynne Huffer rightly applies to Colette Mary Ellman's observation that "books by women are treated as though they themselves were women." Huffer, *Another Colette,* 4.

5. Colette, *La Naissance du jour* in Colette, *Oeuvres,* 3:316. All references to this novel are to this edition and are provided in the text. Translations, which I have modified when necessary, are from Colette, *Break of Day*. In this case, McLeod's translation— "women's writings (which) can't help being autobiographical" (63)—does not do justice to Colette. Translations of other texts are my own unless otherwise noted.

6. Colette herself referred to *La Naissance du jour* as a novel in her correspondence. See Flieger, *Colette and the Phantom Subject of Autobiography,* 24. Questions about how art and life relate to each other, which are intrinsic to all literature, are intensified in Colette's text by her self-conscious play with them.

7. I have more to say later about these letters, written first by Sido but rewritten by Colette.

8. Eight decades later, the questions Colette's text evokes about how to classify works that fall between the lines of fiction and nonfiction, (auto)biography and novel, are familiar ones frequently raised by the books we read—though we are no more ready to supply easy answers. For a summary that expertly maps the rise of relevant inter-genres (auto/biography, autogynography, autobifictionalography, autographics, autofiction, biomythography, and so on) and discusses the web of concepts that have come with them (truthiness, emotional truth, autobiographical as opposed to confessional narrative, biologized versus anti-identitarian histories, relational narrative), see Miller, "The Entangled Self." See, too, an issue of *Magazine littéraire* entitled "Les Ecritures du moi: De l'autobiographie à l'autofiction."

9. Flieger calls such continuities "a phantasmal network," something like "an obsessional myth in Mauron's sense of the term." *Colette and the Phantom Subject of Autobiography,* 20.

10. See Peter Stallybrass and Allon White's analysis, via Hegel's *Phenomenology,* of symbolic extremities of high and low in European cultures, in *The Politics and Poetics of Transgression,* especially 5–6.

11. I should make clear that since we are always situated as readers, I am speaking first of—and as—the contemporary American reader, operating within a child-centered culture, and with all the cultural assumptions that position entails, and which no doubt intensify the perturbing effect of the story. See Carroll, *Cultural Misunderstandings.* As Anne de Jouvenel also reminds us in her preface to *Colette: Lettres à sa fille,* "a cette époque l'éducation des enfants était différente. . . . Les enfants n'avaient aucun droit, sauf celui de se taire et d'obéir . . . faire honneur à la famille" [children's education was different at the time—children had no rights—except those of being quiet, obeying, and honoring the family] (8).

12. Colette de Jouvenel, *Colette de Jouvenel,* 25

13. In interviews, a grownup Bel-Gazou reflected variously on the ways in which her mother did not correspond to the cultural norms of the maternal. For example, as Anne de Jouvenel relates, "On lui demandait souvent quelle sorte de mère était Colette, elle répondait: 'Si je devais dire que Colette était une mère maternelle, au sens où on entend cela ordinairement, ce ne serait pas exact. Une mère *maternelle* est censée vivre penchée sur son enfant. L'enfant étant le centre de tout, et parfois peut-être jusqu'à l'excès. Non, ma mère n'était pas cela'" [She (Colette de Jouvenel) was often asked what kind of mother Colette was. She answered, "If I were to say that Colette was a maternal

mother, in the ordinary sense of the term, that wouldn't be correct. A *maternal* mother is supposed to spend her life huddled over her child, the child being the center of everything, sometimes to excess. No my mother wasn't like that"]. *Colette: Lettres à sa fille*, 18. Likewise, Colette was intensely aware of the tension she would call, in *L'étoile vesper*, "la compétition, livre contre enfantement" [the contest between book and childbirth]. See Colette, *Oeuvres*, 4:876; all subsequent references in the text are to this edition. Translations, with my modifications, are from Colette, *The Evening Star*, in *Recollections*, trans. David Le Vay. Her daughter in turn reflected on the contest from her own perspective: "Un enfant accepte mal de partager sa mère. . . . Il me fallait apprendre à partager avec une 'oeuvre.' Une oeuvre. . . . Pouvait-on, pouvais-je lui demander d'avoir toutes les vertus? Celles d'un écrivain qui composera soixante volumes et celles de la mère poule qui m'aurait dédié le plus clair et le plus chaud de son temps?" [A child doesn't easily agree to share her mother. . . . I had to learn to share her with a "work." A work. . . . Could she be expected—could I expect her—to possess every virtue? Those of a writer who wrote sixty volumes, and those of a mother hen devoting to me her clearest and most enthusiastic hours?]. Quoted in Pichois and Brunet, *Colette*, 346–347.

14. Speculations about Colette's failings as a mother are legion in the biographies and literary criticism. Some commentators link her maternal shortcomings directly to her success as a writer, as if one were a consequence of the other. Michel del Castillo distinguishes himself from most critics by separating the woman from the opus. Del Castillo, *Colette*.

15. Announced by the Editions du Trianon in 1927. See Pichois and Brunet, *Colette*, 349.

16. For the narrative about Rousseau's abandonment of his five children, see, for example, the editors' notes in Rousseau, *Oeuvres complètes*, or Leo Damrosch's in his *Jean-Jacques Rousseau*. At the risk of generalizing I suggest that commentary on Rousseau's abandonment of his children and what we might call Colette's emotional abandonment of her daughter differ in nature. For Rousseau, critics and biographers tend to place the abandonment in historical-psychological context and to make psychoanalytic-formal links with his development as a writer. For Colette the mode tends to be rather uncomplicated reproach.

17. See Del Castillo's *Colette* for a personally invested account on the part of a man who was a friend of Colette de Jouvenel. An unexamined world exists in the interstices between Colette's texts and her readers. There is a reading of readings of Colette (and especially of *La Naissance du jour*, with its embedded reader, Vial) to be done that would help enormously to elucidate her work.

18. Ward Jouve, *Colette*, 4–6.

19. More than one commentator, however, has suggested that Claire de Boas knew exactly what she was doing when she asked Bertrand to intercede on her behalf, and that the Colette-Bertrand affair was engineered to take revenge on her ex-husband, Bertrand's father and Colette's current husband. See Kristeva, *Le Génie féminin*, 77; Thurman, *Secrets of the Flesh*, 291; and Pichois and Brunet, *Colette*, 330n55.

20. "Quand j'étais jeune, si je m'occupais, par exception, à un ouvrage d'aiguille, Sido hochait son front divinateur: 'Tu n'auras jamais l'air que d'un garçon qui coud.' Ne m'eût-elle pas dit: 'Tu ne seras jamais qu'un écrivain qui a fait un enfant.' Elle n'aurait pas ignoré, elle, le caractère accidentel de ma maternité" (Colette, *L'Étoile vesper*, 876) ["If, exceptionally, when I was young I busied myself with some needlework, Sido would

shake her divinatory brow: 'You'll never look like anything but a boy sewing.' Had she not said to me: 'You'll never be more than a writer who has produced a child'? She, at any rate, would not have been unaware of the fortuitous nature of my maternity"] (Colette, *Evening Star*, 282).

21. Colette to Colette de Jouvenel, October 27, 1952, in Colette, *Colette: Lettres à sa fille*, 514.

22. Ibid., 18–19.

23. Ibid., 19.

24. Colette, *L'Étoile vesper*, 876; *Evening Star*, 281. In the extended citation it becomes clear that one must choose between mediocre writing and mediocre mothering: "Mon brin de virilité me sauva du danger qui expose l'écrivain, promu parent heureux et tendre, à tourner auteur médiocre, à préférer désormais ce que récompense une visible et matérielle croissance: le culte de enfants, des plantes, des élevages sous leurs formes diverses" (876) ["My strain of virility saved me from the danger which threatens the writer, elevated to a happy and tender parent, of becoming a mediocre author, of preferring henceforward the advantages conferred by a visible and material growth: the worship of children, of plants, of breeding in its various forms"] (281–282).

25. During the time Colette and her stepson/lover Bertrand de Jouvenel revisited her childhood haunts, which led to the writing of her first mother book, *La maison de Claudine,* they read and reread Balzac's *Le Chef-d'oeuvre inconnu.* See Kristeva, *Le Génie féminin,* 481, and Jouvenel, *Un Voyageur dans le siècle,* 57.

26. Colette to Colette de Jouvenel, March 1922, in Colette, *Colette: Lettres à sa fille,* 44.

27. Colette to Colette de Jouvenel, 1923, in ibid., 59.

28. Ibid.

29. Colette to Germaine Patat, cited by Anne de Jouvenel in Colette, *Colette: Lettres à sa fille,*17.

30. Colette to Colette de Jouvenel, January 26, 1928, in ibid., 140–141. See Michael del Castillo's commentary, *passim,* on the fate of Colette de Jouvenel's writing, "suffocated" by her mother. Anne de Jouvenel notes in her preface to Colette, *Colette: Lettres à sa fille,* that when Colette de Jouvenel (her aunt) abandoned journalism and became an antiques dealer, her address was "Writing Case Dead End" ["Impasse de l'écritoire"]. Jouvenel, *Colette,* 17.

31. See Behar, *The Vulnerable Observer,* 4.

32. Ward Jouve, *Colette,* 4; Behar, *The Vulnerable Observer,* 4.

33. Deleuze and Parnet, *Dialogues,* 119. I am grateful to Claire Lyu for the reference and the conversation.

34. The title given on the cover, as in Colette's letter, was "Impressions d'une jeune maman" [Impressions of a Young Mother]. *Femina* also added this introductory caption to Colette's text: "*Femina* est heureuse de signaler à ses lectrices le début de la collaboration de Colette, l'éminent écrivain dont les romans et les articles, profondément humains et qui révèlent une sensibilité si aiguë jointe aux plus précieux dons du style, sont unanimement admirés. La belle page que nous publions est un véritable poème de la maternité; seule une plume féminine était capable d'une description et d'une analyse aussi justes, relatant avec autant de délicatesse le réveil émouvant de la jeune mère qui, au sortir du lourd sommeil artificiel, va contempler enfin le cher petit visage inconnu de l'enfant nouveau-né; nous sommes certains que nos lectrices comprendront toute la pure beauté de ces lignes remarquables. N.D.L.R" [*Femina* is happy to notify its readers

of the beginning of its collaboration with Colette, the eminent author whose profoundly human novels and articles, marked by a highly sensitive nature coupled with supreme gifts of style, are unanimously admired. The fine page we are publishing is a true ode to maternity; only a woman's pen would be capable of such an accurate description and analysis, relating with such delicacy the moving awakening of a young mother, who, leaving a heavy induced sleep, comes at last to contemplate the dear little unknown face of the newborn child; we are sure that our female readers will understand the pure beauty of these remarkable lines. N.D.L.R.]. My source for this information, as well as for Colette's letter quoted below, is Pichois and Brunet, *Colette*, 260–261.

35. Colette, "Maternité," in *Paysages et portraits*, in Colette, *Œuvres complètes*, 5:316.

36. Philippe Lejeune in fact excludes Colette from the French autobiographical canon because she doesn't adhere to conventions of authorial sincerity. Lejeune, *L'autobiographie en France*, 72–73. And Valérie Lastinger observes that the play of real and textual identities in the text is "une autre façon de morceler, de désintégrer le moi du je-narrateur" [another way to disintegrate, to put into pieces, the identity of the narrating self]. Lastinger, *"La Naissance du jour,"* 550–551.

37. Malcolm, *Reading Chekhov*, 35.

38. "Un livre est le produit d'un autre moi que celui que nous manifestons dans nos habitudes, dans la société, dans nos vices. Ce moi-là, si nous voulons essayer de le comprendre, c'est au fond de nous-même, en essayant de le recréer en nous que nous pouvons y parvenir" [A book is the product of another self than the one we display in our habits, our social life, and our vices. If we want to try to understand that self, it is deep within us, by trying to recreate it there, that we may be able to]. Proust, *Contre Sainte-Beuve*, 221–222.

39. Her source was a note preceding the publication of *Du côté de chez Swann*. See Pichois's commentary in Colette, *Œuvres*, 3:275n1.

40. See Lejeune, *Le Pacte autobiographique*. However, as I noted earlier, Lejeune specifically excludes Colette from the autobiographical canon because he finds her deficient in sincerity.

41. On mirrors in Colette, see Corbin, *The Mother Mirror*.

42. Cited from Sido, *Lettres à sa fille*, by Michel del Castillo, in *Colette*, 97.

43. Colette to Colette de Jouvenel, November 1926, in *Colette: Lettres à sa fille*, 113.

44. Colette to Colette de Jouvenel, March 1932, in ibid., 235.

45. Colette, "Le miroir," in *Les vrilles de la vigne*, in Colette, *Œuvres*, 1:1030.

46. Rose, *The Year of Reading Proust*, 30.

47. Jouvenel, "Mon enfance à l'ombre de Colette," 5.

48. Kristeva, *Le Génie feminin*, especially 132–139.

49. Lloyd, *Baudelaire's World*, 188.

PART FOUR
TRANSLATION IN PROCESS
AND PRACTICE

TWELVE

René Char: Translating a Mountain

MARY ANN CAWS

IT WAS PROBABLY THE TASK OF A LIFETIME, TRANSLATING René Char. He certainly would have found that right and fitting and just. Arrogant as that may sound, it was quite simply in his case that a poem—and so, poetry—was the equal of living. Had one not been convinced of that, why would one spend any time at all doing such an all-consuming task? And that very task was, of course, what I had taken upon myself, once I had encountered this poet, whom his friend the American poet William Carlos Williams compared to a mountain, no doubt for his moral as well as physical stature.

I want to start by quoting from one of the many letters sent me by my friend Jacqueline Lamba, the penultimate wife of André Breton, whose *Mad Love* was written for her, and which I translated.[1] That translation was its own task but vastly different in its extent and its kind of difficulties from any other task I had undertaken. Her letter dates from August 23, 1976, and the part I am referring to concerns translation:

A propos de traduction, quand la parole est plus que belle, sans doute se passé-t-il la même chose que pour les tableaux de grande qualité. Les voir reproduits d'abord dans une autre couleur (ce qui peut aussi changer par surcroît les valeurs de ton [comme tu sais]) ne change rien au choc initial. C'est toujours le même ni moins ni plus beau pour moi, que l'on retrouve ensuite dans l'original—ou bien transporte-t'on toujours le choc initial aveuglément?

[About translation, when the language is far more than beautiful, it probably happens just in the same way as for great paintings. Seeing them reproduced first in another color (which can also change the tonal values [as you know]) changes nothing in relation to the initial shock. I find that it's always the same, neither more beautiful nor less so, that you find afterward in the original—or then does one always, as if blindly, transport exactly the initial shock?][2]

In translating someone like Char, I would always hope to transport the "choc initial" whenever I can. Jacqueline had known Char far before I had met either of them, and finally went to visit him again. Going to see Char was always a terror for any of us, including Jacqueline, who left there by mistake her own paintings, rolled up. Were they ever recovered? I am uncertain, but the very question led to a further wonder: did any of us who loved him ever recover anything or ourselves from being with him?

When I began to write on René Char, in 1972, we were living in Paris on a sabbatical leave. I sent him my initial attempt at discussing his poetry, to his house, Les Busclats, in L'Isle-sur-Sorgue, with understandable trepidation. He wrote to ask me to phone him in Paris the next week, which I did, with increased trepidation. Following his invitation then, I did indeed go to encounter him in his apartment on the rue Chenelailles.

The door cracked open to let me perceive one eye, far, far above my own, and the welcome was itself far, far above what I might have expected. Captivated, I instantly decided to continue my work on his work—that seems to be the most appropriate way to describe our meeting, after which he said, "Vous ne me détestez pas, n'est-ce pas?" [You don't hate me, do you?]. No, I did not exactly detest him.

My husband came over in the summer to meet my poet in the Vaucluse. I could not help thinking of what André Breton had once written about living in that part of the country: "habiter un cabanon dans le Vaucluse. . ." And subsequently, we moved our children into the ruin of a Provençal *cabanon* we purchased near Carpentras, not so very far from him, as a family, in the space of poetry he had created, or that is the way I see it. He gave us stones to build upon—you will build your house on poetry, he said to me—and we became *pays,* as he said. His country was ours. His mountain, the Mont Ventoux, became our own.

From our hill, down which I would take my slow, if trusty, motorbike, or *vélomoteur,* we would predict his temper by the weather on the mountain—cloudy or bright. I would take a *boule* of freshly baked bread from the neighboring village, Mazan, on the back of my bike, with a pot of local honey, over some hills and roads large and small, to work with him, with such intensity as I had not known before, and have not known since. When I would leave, he would fill my arms with lavender from his garden.

That is the way work went, year after year, in summer and in the January vacation I had from teaching, when I would go over to discuss my ongoing work with him. He kept photographs of my children in his glass-fronted bookcase and would come to see us in our small old *cabanon* in a field near his mountain. We would consult him about our dried-up spring. To this spring, he would say, "Mon amie, coule pour nous" [My friend spring, run for us]. Our children would draw him pictures, and he would give them poems and books and painted stones. When we would go over as a family, he would take them to pick potatoes and melons behind his house, and would give them marshmallows from the pharmacy. In short, we loved him, and believed he returned the love: I take that still now as a given.

How to say it? I became one of his translators. He would reassure me that any meaning lost from the original would be righted later in its true balance. Often, he would insist upon the act of transference, poem to poem: "The true knowledge, the one that lasts for the reader of a book of poems, would be that you, a poet, should tell us about what you do, step by step, when you carry into your language a foreign poet." This was written by Jonathan Griffin, for our cotranslation of his poems, and I shared completely in his thought.[3] Char did, and we did, what we could, encouraged by the poet.

I felt encouraged doubly by working with Char in my interpretation—thinking then, as I have never ceased to do, that translating is the deepest reading possible. I cherished his belief (here I am quoting one of his letters to me, from February 1984) that the ways I was struggling with, translating and writing around that immensity of a mountain he was, like his poems, would lead to other ways of dealing with texts and things beyond them: "Vos chemins mettent au monde des chemins. Bons croisements en perspective. Oui, certes; l'exigence morale. Vers la poésie. . . . Juste vue que la vôtre" [Your paths give birth to other paths. Good crossings, in perspective. Yes, of course, moral exigency. Toward poetry. Your viewpoint is right].[4] But the paths were mountainous, with every mountain different; the journey was arduous, and my sense of inadequacy never failed, even as I thought I might have many times. They resembled the mountain roads on which I rode my slow-going motorbike to reach Les Busclats. Then I think of how that road looked, so very local and how he reminded me it was the only way to the universal. Char thought, believed, knew—in the poetic sense, knew—himself to be Orion, sometimes Orion the giant blinded, as in the Poussin painting in New York's Metropolitan Museum. My family and I would look up at the late night sky from outside the *cabanon* and see him there, as Orion, over the many years we lived there, near him, and, in a sense, through his poetry.

So, over time, the translations evolved. I quote a few examples of that evolution, between my first publication of them in the Princeton volume of 1976, and the follow-up by New Directions, with all its changes, in 1992, resulting from our work together until his death in 1988.[5]

I should say this first, about his face, which I fell in love with, as so many others had done. Before this, I had only loved the face of André Breton, which had been, originally, the reason for which I had taken the leap or the dive into Surrealism. Char's face was itself a mountain, like his person and his poems as I began to see them. You have chosen, he said, to live in and by a mountain. That mountain was, of course, his: le Mont Ventoux, the Windy Mountain. We knew, or rather I knew, and had no choice ultimately, that I would be living with it always. I would write on him and he would say—in a perfect poetic line, of course—the others are absence and you alone are presence. I cannot forget that day of work, or living, or any of the others. It wasn't that I believed it exactly, but all the same I stayed, writing text after text, book after book, on René Char, three in all.[6] But none of the writing ever had the feeling of that exact intensity of translating what and whom I loved.

Let me start with the poem "Allégeance," a title that I could have translated as "Faithfulness." But I had cast my allegiance and meant it that way: translation was never not personal for me. In the beginning, the voice I heard was—since I loved him—mine, I suppose, about him. This is my first, unpublished (of course) translation:

Dans les rues de la ville il y a mon amour. Peu importe où il va dans le temps divisé. Il n'est plus mon amour, chacun peut lui parler. Il ne se souvient plus: qui au juste l'aima?

[In the streets of the town goes my love. Small matter where he moves in divided time. He is no longer my love, anyone may speak with him. He remembers no longer; who exactly loved him?]

I do not see how that could have been different. So, in the beginning, the translation came out as "he." No, I did not publish that one, because Char said to me, *"mon amour"* is of course the Elizabethan term for "my beloved"—ah, so I retranslated it as "it," to avoid the specific person. That was in 1976:

Dans les rues de la ville il y a mon amour. Peu importe où il va dans le temps divisé. Il n'est plus mon amour, chacun peut lui parler. Il ne se souvient plus: qui au juste l'aima?

[In the streets of the town goes my love. Small matter where it moves in divided time. It is no longer my love, anyone may speak with it. It remembers no longer; who exactly loved it?]

Dreadful. Really dreadful, and I published it on page 95 in my book of Princeton translations. Clearly, I could not live with that, and that translation I finally changed, as I point out in a moment. Now that pronoun "it" comes up again as a problem in the translation of "Le Martinet," the Marten or the Swift, and there was not the issue. Here is the unpublished first try at a translation:

Martinet aux ailes trop larges, qui vire et crie sa joie autour de la maison. Tel est le coeur....
    Il n'est pas d'yeux pour le tenir. Il crie, c'est toute sa présence. Un mince fusil va l'abattre. Tel est le coeur.

[Swift with wings too wide, wheeling and shrieking its joy around the house. Such is the heart....
    No eyes can hold it. It shrieks for its only presence. A slight gun is about to fell it. Such is the heart.]

Pretty awful, this beginning, in which I had kept the impersonal "it" for the bird, because it was an animal. Big mistake, after deciding to call it a swift, for metaphoric and sonoric reasons, instead of a marten.... But then, of course, it was so deeply, tragically personal, that I changed, rightly I think, to the personal "he":

Martinet aux ailes trop larges, qui vire et crie sa joie autour de la maison. Tel est le coeur....

Il n'est pas d'yeux pour le tenir. Il crie, c'est toute sa présence. Un mince fusil
va l'abattre. Tel est le coeur.

[Swift with wings too wide, wheeling and shrieking his joy around the house.
Such is the heart....
     No eyes can hold him. He shrieks for his only presence. A slight gun is about
to fell him. Such is the heart.]

Since Char was again speaking, it had to be the masculine pronoun.
In that case, I had no regrets: the person of the poem demanded that
choice.[7]

Then, one day, rather late in the afternoon, the poet and I arrived at
the poem entitled "Grège," meaning "le feu grégeois" or bonfire.... But
I hesitated, and asked what actually it meant to him here. "Ah," he said,
"if we had had a child together, it might have been called 'Grège.'"[8] So
things veered and were constantly veering between the impersonal and,
more often, the personal, or poetically personal. The footnote I gave for
this translation does not note that part of his remark.

For the cover of the New Directions volume, on which we worked
as more or less a threesome—Char and his companion, Tina Jolas, and
myself—we chose a moving portrait by Gisèle Freund, removing the
part of the portrait in which he is holding a cigarette. That was already
a translation of a photograph and has its own moral complication.[9] In
this volume, there once more arose the Allegiance problem, as I think
of it, and this time, I bit my translator's tongue and put "she," as perhaps
I should have done in the beginning. "Mon amour," after all, was "son
amour"—his love and not mine. Enough said, perhaps, about that fidelity
and its consequences.

I conclude with a translation that took a great deal of time and seems
to me to be located at the height of difficulty in both languages. This
poem, "Le visage nuptial," begins with a farewell to everyone outside
the just coupled couple, and makes its and their way up a slope, as if
up a mountain. As if up the Mont Ventoux, so remarkable a rise in the
Vaucluse, rising from nothingness on either side—a superb image with
which to work.

It is of course a poem of love and lovemaking. So I want to concentrate, first, on the central word that gives the whole thing away, so glori-
ously is it the hinge of the affair:

Vitre inextinguible: mon soufflé affleurait déjà l'amitié de ta blessure
Armait ta royauté inapparente.
Et des lèvres du brouillard descendit notre plaisir au seuil de dune, au toit d'acier.
La conscience augmentait l'appareil frémissant de ta permanence;
La simplicité fidèle s'étendit partout.

[Unquenchable pane: my breath was already grazing the friendship of your wound,
Arming your hidden royalty.
And from the lips of the fog descended our joy with its threshold of dune, its roof
    of steel.
Awareness increased the quivering array of your permanence;
faithful simplicity spread everywhere.]

It is the word in the passage quoted here—"plaisir"—about which Char exclaimed, how puritanical is the Anglo-Saxon language! How to express the climax of the sexual act? I could not possibly put anything about an orgasm, which would, in any case, destroy the subtlety of the poem. I found only "joy," knowing it had to be read over-joyously to work alongside the original. Ah, said René Char, I shall simply rewrite the poem.[10] Nice, but of course, impossible.

So there it is, the poem stands, footnoteless, knowing that any textual expression will be, ineluctably, less faithful than my final allegiance to "Allégeance..." and yet, and yet.

The majestic poem, majestic above all else, erotic in its very majesty, ends with an invocation as if in a religious ritual:

Voici le sable mort, voici le corps sauvé:
La femme respire, L'Homme se tient debout.

[This is the sand dead, this the body saved:
Woman breathes, Man stands upright.]

The capitalized Man felt very René Char to me, and of course the woman just sort of lies there and gets to breathe and HE stands upright. I am a feminist, and do not love that idea; however, that's the way he wrote it, and the doubled "voici ... voici" conveys the bread and wine of ritual salvation. A strong ending for an incredibly massive and mountainous poem.

Let me sum it up this way: we have to read that "plaisir" and that poem in full voice, if I may put it like that—reading in a full voice, in the full voice that fidelity can be, to a tone, a mountain, and a beloved face.

MARY ANN CAWS is Distinguished Professor of English, French, and Comparative Literature at the Graduate Center of the City University of New York. She is an *officier* of the Palmes Académiques and fellow of the American Academy of Arts and Sciences. Among her many publications are, most recently, the *Modern Art Cookbook, Salvador Dalí, Glorious Eccentrics: Modernist Women Painting and Writing, Pablo Picasso, Surprised in Translation,* and *To the Boathouse: A Memoir.*

NOTES

1. Breton, *Mad Love.*
2. This and other letters mentioned below are in my personal collection.
3. Char, *Poems of René Char,* xxvii.
4. I am translating in every case as literally as possible, this not being the place for poetic translation.
5. Char, *René Char: Selected Poetry.* The poems "Allegiance" and "The Swift" are found on pages 58 and 64 respectively. "The Nuptial Countenance" is found on pages 29–33. In the massive publication of René Char, *Furor and Mystery and Other Poems,* there is a double translation of "Allegiance" by Mary Ann Caws and one by Patricia Terry, whose translation of "The Swift" is also given (313, 305).
6. *René Char; The Presence of René Char; L'oeuvre filante de René Char.*
7. See more on this in my essay "René Char: Resistance and Grandeur," 550–551.
8. Ibid., 552.
9. Char, *Selected Poems.* See http://www.ndbooks.com/book/selected-poems26/.
10. "Just put a footnote that I have changed my poem so that you could translate it." Caws, "René Char: Resistance and Grandeur," 553.

THIRTEEN

Translation and the Re-Conception of Voice in Modern Verse

CLIVE SCOTT

TWO CRUCIAL PROPOSITIONS UNDERPIN MY OWN THINKING about translation, and it is important to reiterate these at the outset. First, we are wrong to allow literary translation—and I emphasize *literary* translation—to be governed by a translation designed for readers who are ignorant of the source language (SL). My objections to this are fivefold:

1. It endows the translator with too much unquestioned authority.
2. It expressly designs a text to be read by someone in no position to judge it, to judge either its reliability or its quality.
3. It produces a translated text without one's really knowing what constitutes a proper use of the reader's intelligence and imagination.
4. It can afford to have few literary ambitions of its own and therefore makes little contribution to the establishment of translation as a literature in its own right, developing new forms and new expressive languages.
5. From an eco-ethnic point of view, it is up to the target text (TT) to preserve the language of the source text (ST). Translation should set itself steadfastly against linguistic hegemonization. Translation cannot be the servant of an attitude which supposes that learning foreign languages is unnecessary, that intercultural dialogue can be dispensed with. On the contrary, translation should seek to make the knowledge of other languages indispensable to its own enjoyment.

My second argument is that translation studies has invested too heavily in a theory and analytical method based on the objective of a *single-version* translation. If the normal expectation were that a translator would or should produce at least four versions of the ST, what theoretical framework would translation then entail? Would not that theoretical framework naturally gravitate toward a careful review of genetic and textual models? Surprisingly, perhaps, translation would no longer be an exercise in the solution of linguistic difficulties, nor would it primarily be about "correct" interpretation. It would be the translator's task to question our perception of the text, to diversify the text's perceptibility. And immediately the reader would have a significant role not just in consuming a single text but in negotiating among several texts, in making judgments about textual status and linguistic effect.

Stemming from these propositions is the view that the proper judgement of a TT should be based not on its degree of faithfulness to the ST (whatever that might be), but on the degree of the fruitfulness of the relationship between the TT(s) and the ST, on what that relationship provides in the way of literary insights into both texts. Judgments by degree of faithfulness assume that the ST is not itself a changing text, in a constant state of becoming something else, of no longer comprehending itself. But if we adopt a Bergsonian view of literary history, that is, history seen as progressively cumulative and always present to itself at all its points, then we must correct our own preferred formulation thus: the quality of a translation depends on the fruitfulness of the relationship between the TT(s) and the ST, *both considered as texts in motion.*

The Bergsonian view of literary history inevitably means that all texts are expanding with the uses to which they are put, not only by virtue of the ways they are written about and cited, but in the diversity of their alternative manifestations. Marcel Proust's *A la recherche du temps perdu,* for example, has begotten theater, radio, film, and comic-strip adaptations, as well as becoming the source of cookbooks, literary tours, and axioms for the proper conduct of life. Translation often imagines that it can and should recover a pristine text; even if such a thing were possible, it is doubtful whether modern textual studies would agree that it was the right policy. Translation encounters the ST as an expanded and expanding text, a text in a constant process of cultural reassimilation, and the TT must correspondingly seek to be something expanding and ramifying. On its journey in time, the ST loses comprehension of itself, constantly outreaches its origins; it comes to self-consciousness in the TT. And the page of the tabular text, the kind of text that this essay wishes to promote, is the guarantor, the evidence, of that self-consciousness.

Another quarrel that I have with translation as it is generally perceived is its implication that the translator works with the known. Two languages, already consecrated, already set in their differential systems, are juxtaposed in two corresponding textual manifestations and negotiate their differences through procedures of equivalence and compensation. The repositories of that knowledge are the bilingual dictionary and the thesaurus. Translation is thus haunted by a suspicion that (1) all translators armed with the same knowledge of source and target languages and cultures would make the same choice, the best choice, give or take a few personal variations, and (2) that anyone with sufficient knowledge could make that choice. The possibility that, through the process of translation, the target language might enlarge itself is confined to what might be achieved through foreignization, or through imports from the ST.

What I aspire to are two things: first, a translation that carries the ST on its ongoing journey into the future, a translation that moves into the unknown, and by that I mean the unknown of its own language, the target language, and not necessarily by the device of importation; and second, a translational practice that has nothing to do with objectives of critical consensus but rather in which choices are so existentially and psychologically driven that no other translator would make them.

My own translational practice has for the moment attached itself to the translation of the linear into the tabular, which I perceive as being the most direct route to my desiderata. The translation of the linear into the tabular, which I also regard as the equivalent of the translation of the Barthesian *lisible* into the *scriptible,* obviously has a literal application explored in my translations of Rimbaud's *Illuminations* and of Apollinaire.[1] But I am just as anxious to propose that the linear and tabular are important to the translator as mindsets, as writerly and readerly postures toward text. In pursuit of this proposition, I have produced a table of twenty transformations that are involved in the shift from a linear to a tabular mode of perception (see appendix). This is not an exhaustive list, but the transformation numbered 17 is important for my arguments here. What I want to underline is that the tabular version does not ask its linear ST, "What do you mean?" but rather, "What is it that you cannot tell me?" and "What is it that I do not know?"

How does one write tabular? This question is significant in two respects. First, one says that writing tabular cannot be taught—it is not a system like linear writing, even if it draws on the same alphabet. The translator is not drawing on a linguistic knowledge so much as learning an appropriate knowledge, a knowledge appropriate to the ST, by a process of trial and error. Tabular writing is ineluctability experimental—just as the reading of the tabular is. We cannot be taught how to read tabular either—reading remains innocent, endlessly inventive, improvised. The TT unwrites the ST, turns it into the unwritable, the unwritten.

As I have already implied, I have further quarrels with what I am perhaps too conveniently thinking of as standard translation studies. Translation studies has no theory of reader response (what is the proper way in which to read a translation *bearing in mind that it is a translation*?). Translation studies has no theory of text, therefore the difficulties presented by text are mechanical ones: How much of the ST can I transfer to the TT? How can I prevent form and content parting company in the TT? And most pertinently for our present purposes, translation studies has no apparent interest in translation as an act that may involve a revoicing of the text. Let me take a small example. When we speak of foreignizing strategies, we generally have in mind importations of a lexical or syntactic kind; metaphor and idiom are other channels of foreignness. But voice apparently is not. That is quite simply to say that translation's preoccupation with the linguistic blinds it to the paralinguistic; while it worries about style and register, it does not allow that translation is equally about the translation of the linguistic into a paralinguistic wholeness, into a text that positively begins to imagine a readerly input through the conduit of paralanguage, which positively wishes the reader to dramatize the ST's intrusions and the TT's responses, through paralinguistic realization. As a start, we can employ devices of orthography to begin to suggest accent. We are already accustomed to adjusting our sense of accent when we encounter "splendor" spelled with a "u." If I meet "photography" spelled with f rather than ph, then I might think of a German voice, or an Italian one. In my own translation of Apollinaire's "La porte" (see below), I have maintained the circumflex in "hôtel." When we bend our language toward the languages of other nations, we meet all the prejudices and shortcomings of our own alphabet. If only for a start, we could draw on a wider range of diacritical marks, as Vietnamese does, to explore not just pronunciation and accent but vocal coloration, tone, stress quality, and so on.

The development of the voice over the past century has occurred on two principal fronts: (1) in the properties of the voice itself, and (2) in the voice's extension beyond its own known boundaries. The development of the properties of the voice itself partly relates to what our ears are now sensitive to. If, in the late nineteenth century, verse acousticity was associated with the poet's *chant profond*, with the personalization and psychologization of text, with verbal impressionism, in the twentieth century, it has perhaps been treated more as the eruption of the psycho-physiological, as in glossolalia, echolalia, and Tourette's syndrome, that is, as an incipient vocal pathology. And as this has happened, so a cleavage has occurred between the psycho-physiological voice and the expressive voice, between the pronunciatory and the discursive, between timbre and rhythm. This cleavage, traced in the contrary pulls of the tabular and the linear, defines the life of the twentieth-century text. At the same time, the rhetorical value of sound, embodied in the tired pursuit of alliteration and assonance and overfamiliar intonation patterns, has been pushed aside—we remember Filippo Tommaso Marinetti pronouncing the death of free verse in 1913 and complaining about its preoccupation with facile sound effects, monotonous cadences, foolish chiming, and so on.[2] We must now respond to sound with a voice and ear attuned to psychophonetic values, to articulatory modulations, to the willful autonomies of phonemes and morphemes. Let us also remember Apollinaire's call for a new body-functional acoustic language in "La victoire" (first published in *Nord-Sud*, March 15, 1917):

> On veut de nouveaux sons de nouveaux sons de nouveaux sons
> On veut des consonnes sans voyelles
> Des consonnes qui pètent sourdement
>   Imitez le son de la toupie
> Laissez pétiller un son nasal et continu
> Faites claquer votre langue
> Servez-vous du bruit sourd de celui qui mange sans civilité
> Le raclement aspiré du crachement ferait aussi une belle consonne

[We want new sounds new sounds new sounds
We want consonants without vowels
Consonants that go off voicelessly
     Copy the sound of the spinning top
Let crackle a continuous nasal sound
Make your tongue click
Use the muffled noise of someone eating without manners
The aspirated hack of spitting would make a fine-sounding consonant][3]

The development of the properties of voice relate also to technological advances, and in particular to the tape-recorder and its poets of the 1950s and 1960s (François Dufrêne, Bernard Heidsieck, Henri Chopin, Franz Mon, Ferdinand Kriwet, Pierre and Ilse Garnier). For these poets, the tape made possible a mining of vocal resources which up to that point had been beyond the reach of exploitation. The tape restored to the voice its multidimensionality, its true acoustic range. Pierre Garnier expresses it thus:

> Mais ce qui aujourd'hui favorise son [la poésie phonétique] développement c'est l'apparition d'un instrument remarquable: la magnétophone; l'impossible d'hier devient le possible d'aujourd'hui: la connaissance exacte et approfondie de sa langue par le poète lui-même, l'étude directe aux différentes vitesses, aux différents tons, les montages, les superpositions, les perspectives soniques, donc la création de paysages linguistiques, la possibilité pour le poète d'enregistrer son émotion, enfin les multiples attraits soudain découverts d'une œuvre poétique créée exclusivement pour l'oreille.
>
> [But what today favors the development of phonetic poetry is the advent of a remarkable instrument: the tape-recorder. The impossible of yesterday becomes the possible of today: an exact and detailed knowledge of his mother-tongue by the poet himself, direct study at different speeds, in different tones, montages, superimpositions, acoustic perspectives, and thus the creation of linguistic landscapes, the possibility for the poet to record his emotions, and, finally, the suddenly discovered, multiple attractions of a poetic work created exclusively for the ear].[4]

Suddenly the voice found itself polarized, in a wonderfully dynamic tension, between the sounds of its primitive origins and the possibilities of its science-fictional futures. But these possibilities had already been foreseen by Apollinaire, from 1914, in his canvassing of cinema and the phonograph as the future vehicles of poetry's reproduction and transmission. And from the outset, Apollinaire had imagined the further implications of phonographic recording, to be able to compose directly on to disc with all the ambient noises: "Comme si le poète ne pouvait pas faire enregistrer directement un poème par le phonographe et faire enregistrer en même temps des rumeurs naturelles ou d'autres voix dans une foule ou parmi ses amis?" [As if the poet could not record a poem directly onto the gramophone and at the same time record natural noises or other voices in a crowd or among his friends?].[5]

The reference here to ambient noises takes us to our second concern: the extension of the voice beyond its own known boundaries. By this I mean two things: first, the intrusion into the text of Futurist *bruitismo,* noises that might be recorded into the text or that the voice might be asked to perform. Second, I mean different degrees of dehumanization or devocalization of the voice under pressure from a language without syntactic or rhythmic discursiveness, or without vocal origins (in what voice does one read dictionary entries, or shopping lists, or shop signs?). In his instructions to the modern declaimer, entitled "Dynamic and Synoptic Declamation" of March 11, 1916, Marinetti, aside from advising his subject to make use of a certain number of elementary instruments like hammers, little wooden tables, automobile horns, and so on, to produce simple or abstract onomatopoeias, also decreed that the Futurist declaimer must "completely dehumanize his voice, systematically doing away with every modulation and nuance," and "metallize, liquefy, vegetalize, petrify, and electrify his voice, grounding it in the vibrations of matter itself as expressed by words-in-freedom."[6]

Looking back to Garnier's words about the effects of poetry's adoption of the tape-recorder, we can see the new principles of structure entailed by the voice's new enunciatory landscapes and by the tabular text—montage, superimposition, a cinematic sequence made from cutting between different speeds, tones, voices. Rhythm then lies not in syntagmatic continuities, but in the enchained discontinuities of shot, in what is put together with what. Reading, whatever form it takes, is not now about sense-making but about the pace of the arrival of materials and their structural tempo. This rhythm of adjustment, this preparedness to reorient structural and emotional drives, is the essence of the reading of this poetry beyond free verse. Cutting and collage are tireless processes of vocal adaptation.

Metricity favors quantitative accounts of language (number of syllables, number of measures, number of lines) in which units are reckoned to be separable and equal to each other; it is principally concerned with what measures add up to, the syllabic aggregate of the line, rather than with what they create as an unfolding dynamic. In other words, the measures of a line are treated as a sequence of juxtaposed, self-immobilizing, recuperable units rather than as a continuous metamorphosis of evanescent spans of voice. What would we need to do in order to recover the qualitative and heterogeneous in our experience of accent and syllable, to make these things a vehicle of intuitive connection? What do we need to do in order to open channels between the text and the reader's inner duration? One solution is simply performance, which has the effect of making rhythm a force of becoming, of cumulative change, and of making the linguistic susceptible to all manner of paralinguistic coloration. Another solution is the tabularization of text, whereby a new temporality is fed into the experience of reading: not a time that is teleological, directional, made up of isochronous intervals, but a time whose very continuity is made up of its heterogeneity, elasticity, digressiveness. The linear page is the page we pass through; the tabular page is the page we spend time in. A final solution is to read the text as if paralinguistic features were part of the process of composition, an informing impulse of the writing, setting out to transform images, concepts, words into energies and acoustic events. We need a scansional system that captures not numbers of syllables and positions of accents but those features that the ear is even more responsive to in performance: loudness, speed, varying degree and quality of accentuation, pausing, interruption.

In conclusion, I would like to make a few observations about my version of Apollinaire's "La porte," hoping that its general intention will already be apparent from the foregoing. Apollinaire's text runs as follows:

> La porte de l'hôtel sourit terriblement
> Qu'est-ce que cela peut me faire ô ma maman
> D'être cet employé pour qui seul rien n'existe
> Pi-mus couples allant dans la profonde eau triste
> Anges frais débarqués à Marseille hier matin
> J'entends mourir et remourir un chant lointain
> Humble comme je suis qui ne suis rien qui vaille
>
> Enfant je t'ai donné ce que j'avais travaille[7]

The first draft of my version is set out in Figure 13.1.

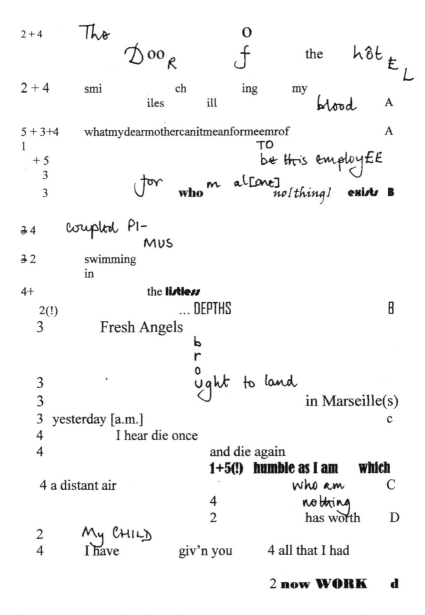

2 + 4   The

D oo R   O   f   the   hôt E L

2 + 4   smi   ch   ing   my

iles   ill   blood   A

5 + 3+4   whatmydearmothercanitmeanformeemrof   A

1
+ 5   TO
3   be this employEE
3   for who m al[one] no[thing] exists B

3 4   coupled PI-
        MUS

3 2   swimming
      in

4+   the listless

2(!)   ... DEPTHS   B
3   Fresh Angels
       b
       r
       o
3   ught to land
3   in Marseille(s)
3 yesterday [a.m.]   c
4   I hear die once
4   and die again
     1+5(!) humble as I am which
4 a distant air   who am   C
      4   nothing
      2   has worth   D
2   My CHILD
4   I have   giv'n you   4 all that I had

      2 now WORK   d

Figure 13.1. Representation of vocality in tabular text translation, incorporating handwritten forms.

1. I have used some handwritten elements in this translation, in the attempt to run the whole gamut of voice, supposing that handwriting guarantees a unique vocality in the writing. Handwriting is the anachronistic survival of identity in the age of typeface, an identity waiting to be uncovered by graphologists. But handwriting peculiarly serves tabularity perhaps, in that it insists that the work is to be read in a here and now as it was written in a here and now, rather than reproduced and consumed at some future date. Handwriting thus contributes significantly to the urgency with which the tabular text inserts itself into time.

2. There are fonts that imitate the hand, as here Viner Hand ITC. But fonts, too, suggest sculptural or architectural styles (Bauhaus 93); spatial pressures, like the compression in Bernard MT Conder; or amplifications, not necessarily in decibels, like Elephant or Bodoni MT Black. The buccal cavity and the mechanisms of articulation produce actualizations of the voice in shapes, volumes, intensities, structures. Times New Roman is the default font, the default voice, a point of departure and return. In the end, we may dream of the whole family of fonts as an intricate system of diacritics, conveying voice quality and phonetic values.

3. In the left-hand margin and with encroachments deeper into the page as the poem progresses, I have retained versificatory information from the ST, so that it can become the instrument of its own undoing, in two senses: First, and most obviously, English cannot sustain the patterns of the French, or, rather, can only do so by discreet changes or by stretching and deforming the available language. Put another way, metrical considerations become the agents of the destruction of that discourse which they are supposed to maintain. Second and relatedly, a way of describing the acousticity of verse that is based on the linguistic—syllabic number, accentuation—tries, inappropriately and ineffectually, to describe a verse made entirely of the paralinguistic, of changing patterns of pitch, loudness, pausing, tempo, timbre, tone.

4. The rhyme-scheme in the right-hand margin reminds one of the journey the translation has taken and dramatizes the noncoincidence of ST and TT—translation is designed to measure distances and differences. It reminds one, too, of the acoustic destructiveness of rhyme, of the way in which rhyme-schemes turn contingent and unassimilated sound, turn raw acousticity, into a "higher-order" sound-structure that

is justified only by its capacity to chime and, in French verse, to signal metrical accent.

My case, then, is simply this: that it is translation's business, in translating the linear into the tabular, (1) to translate text into voice, written language into language paralinguistically charged, vocal and acoustic anachronism into the vocal and acoustic revolution our voices and ears are heirs to; (2) to translate an "unproblematic" language into a problematic one, one that we do not know how to speak, a possible language, a language of possibilities, a language made speculative by the very process of translation; and (3) to make reading as experimental and expressive as it is investigative, and thus to make translation a value, not by virtue of its ability to communicate a text in another language but by virtue of its capacity to foster an autobiography of reading and, correspondingly, an ongoing meditation about writing the activity of another text.

APPENDIX

From Linearity to Tabularity: Twenty Transformations

1. Tabularity turns linear text into experimental writing and experimental reading, and, in doing so, implicitly offers a critique of linear thinking.
2. The tabular text turns text into event; tabular layout is not so much a disposition as a field of energies released. In other words, the tabular text is not so much interested in meaning as a product as in meaning as an activity, or to use Barthesian terms, not so much interested in *signification* as in *signifiance.*
3. The very act of choosing a support for the text in tabular writing figures the intervening consciousness of the translator. To create the screen of the page is an act of appropriation, expressly *advertised* as an act of appropriation, the removal of something from the world in order to make an autonomous object, in order to emphasize the self-sufficient materiality of the text. And every typographic deviation or variation within that screen becomes, as it were, a point of renewed (self-) consciousness. Tabular typography is forever pushing toward

the condition of metatypography.[8] Translation more frequently concerns itself with the translation of texts without a perceived support or screen, for which any support will do, since linearity constantly accommodates itself to the support or annexes the support to itself.

4. The tabular text reintroduces the alphabet—which in linear writing is predominantly pared down to phonogrammatic being—to the presence within itself of potential ideograms and pictograms, and indeed to a different way of being phonogrammatic. We know what the shortcomings of our alphabetic writing are:

   a. it derives principally from a structural analysis of language rather than from any direct transcription of language physically experienced—hence the appropriateness of Ferdinand de Saussure's insisting that the sounds of the written language are "images acoustiques";[9]

   b. it has no interest in the suprasegmental features of the spoken language (e.g., tone, phrasing, pattern of sense stress, intonation, etc.). Yet these are an integral part of language's communicative efficacy.

   We might say that the tabular text dealphabetizes the alphabet, introduces it to another order of being and acting. What do we mean by that? In the early ideographic systems of Mesopotamia, Egypt, and China, the ideogram is "un signe que l'on interroge, un signe susceptible d'assumer des fonctions verbales très différentes selon le contexte où il apparaît" [a sign to be interrogated, a sign susceptible of assuming a range of very different functions according to the context in which it appears].[10] Tabularity destabilizes the alphabetic character in multiplying its functions and applications.

5. Tabularity multiplies margins and in so doing destroys the single enunciatory position. Translation shifts the ST toward the heteroglossic and multivocal.

6. A tabular text cannot be quoted—it can only perform itself or be performed—or shifted to a support with a different format. AND YET...

7. The tabular text is the text that invites infinite reconstruction, making room for redispositions and additions, alerting the reader to the play of potentialities. The tabular text is perpetually unique and perpetually a draft-text. Thus the tabular text makes possible both supreme choice and chance.

8. In the tabular text, time is located in the page rather than in the text. Another way of putting this: a linear text is like a train passing through an empty landscape. The train is set in motion by the reading eye; the text's lines are the lines. This is regulated travel, with destinations and timetables and the injunction to move on. In tabular text, the text itself is the country through which the train passes—but it does not pass, because this is the landscape of a marshalling yard, of sidings and shuntings and endless formations and deformations of trains.

9. The tabular text is the text without beginning or end. No correct reading shape is achieved, no reading pathway is predicted or privileged. The one-after-the-other is not that of discursive sequence but of shopping lists. This increases the vulnerability of the reader.

10. The tabular text fully activates blank space as an expressive constituent of the page. Henri Meschonnic is no doubt right to differentiate between the qualities of blank space that different poets cultivate (Mallarmé, Claudel, Apollinaire, Reverdy).[11] But readerly subjectivity finds countless options open to it. We might speak of space as a new polysyntax. We might refer to a "sémantisme spatial." Words generate spaces, traversals, durations, rhythms of scale, the meanings of space (desert, precipice, galaxy, room, city, solitude). Once space becomes standardized—between words, for example— consciousness departs from it and it assumes a uniform visibility/intelligibility in the text; it acts as a border, a point of disjunction rather than of articulation. Space is infinitely a metaphor of spaces that consciousness can create.

11. The tabular text replaces perspectival space with planar space.

12. This shift from the perspectival to the planar has a vocal equivalent: vocalization pure and simple gives way to a

sliding scale from vocalization through devocalization to various kinds of oralization (noises) (= speech mode listening becomes non–speech mode listening, a differentiation complicated by the differentiation between acoustic sound and articulated sound, this is a form of foreignization).[12]

13. This shift from the perspectival to the planar has a temporal equivalent: that is to say, a time that is teleological, directional, homogeneous, made up of isochronous intervals, is replaced by a time whose very continuity is made up of its heterogeneity, elasticity, digressiveness. The linear page is the page we pass through; the tabular page is the page in which we spend time.

14. Tabularity creates a space in which each text can generate its own semiotic. By virtue of what does a particular poem have four rather than twelve margins? Why are lines spaced in such and such a manner?

15. The shift from linear to tabular text produces a cinematization of discourse. Verse sacrifices the articulation of discursive syntax to the splicing together of cuts, to "editing" by "shot." The tabular introduces the ethos of montage: anything can enter, can be montaged into its self-adapting structure (expanding text). This rhythm of adjustment, this preparedness to reorientate structural and emotional drives, is the essence of this kind of reading. Rhythm lies not in syntagmatic continuities but in the enchained discontinuities of shot, in what is put together with what. Stéphane Mallarmé, in his preface to *Un coup de dés* (1897), already adopted this language of image-sequence, in which space itself is the instrument of the cut: "Le papier intervient chaque fois qu'une image, d'elle-même, cesse ou rentre, acceptant la succession d'autres" [The paper intervenes each time an image, of its own accord, ceases or withdraws, accepting the succession of others].[13] Reading, whatever form it takes, is not now about sense-making but about the pace of the arrival of materials and their structural tempo.

16. The tabular text entails the destruction of the mediating subject in favor of a dispersed subjectivity. The choice facing the linear translator, crudely put, is "Shall I sacrifice my own presence to the continuing subjecthood of the ST's author, or should I intervene and interpose my own subjecthood between that of the ST's author and the reader?" In tabularity, subjecthood is dispersed, transformed into an availability of subject positions. There is neither subjecthood of the author nor that of the translator, but an inhabitable space of subjective consciousness (nonperspectival): "The writer must displace the individual ego to allow the larger language, the full relevance of the human voice, to emerge."[14]

17. Perhaps we should also suggest that the tabular text is informed by textual futurity in a way that the linear text is not. The linear text is a text that repeats itself. It may indeed repeat itself with differences, but these are differences of readerly perception and reception rather than differences of textual being. We are always in a position to endow a text with a future: we adapt, translate, reinterpret, and so on. But I am thinking of translation as a process that not so much bestows, by gracious gift as it were, a future on a text (for as long as the translation lasts), but that creates a text which demands futures, presupposes futures, has futures in its own instability, reconstructibility. One of the important manifestations of the future-orientatedness of the tabular text is its apparent refusal to bind words to their pasts. In reading linear texts, we are willy-nilly *recalling* words in previous manifestations. If translation requires, in many senses, the creation of a new language, recognizable but unfamiliar, then the tabular page is most likely to produce it.

18. It should also be noted that the shift from the linear to the tabular radically shifts one's understanding of linguistic rhythm. Linear text has traditionally encouraged an analysis of rhythmic properties based on syllabic values and accentuation, and has assumed that these characteristics

motivate performance, whatever other paralinguistic features
might be activated by performance. Much modern tabular
poetry deactivates syllabic numeracy (counting is no longer
reliable) and makes accent discursively insignificant (word-
fragmentation, monolexical lines). Besides, performance
makes the suprasegmental effects—tone, intonation,
loudness, tempo, sense-stressing, voice-timbre—perceptually
more conspicuous.

19. The difference between the linear and the tabular is also
covered by Johanna Drucker's distinction between the
unmarked (literary, the text speaks for itself) and the
marked (commercial, evidence of intervention) text.[15] Of the
unmarked text, Drucker writes, "All interference, resistance,
must be minimized in order to allow the reader a smooth
reading of the unfolding linear sequence." In the marked
text on the other hand, "different parts of it appear to 'speak'
differently, to address a reader whose presence [is] inscribed
at the outset by an author in complicity with the graphic
tools of a printer who recognized and utilized the capacity
of typographic representation to manipulate the semantic
value of the text through visual means." The marked text,
we might say, transforms the reader as third person into the
reader as second person, the accusative into the vocative.
But the addresser has not the integrated identity of a single
first-person voice, but is, instead, a strange mixture of a
disembodied, performative voice playing different roles, and a
non-voice of verbal presentation.

20. Perhaps the most important underlying distinction between
the linear text and the tabular text is the different ways in
which they emerge from the *management of the page*. An
empty page is the field of scriptural action for the person who
sits before it: "In front of his blank page, every child is already
put in the position of the industrialist, the urban planner."
But here, according to his own terms, Michel de Certeau
turns the writer into a strategist rather than a tactician (as
he himself admits): the page is a space into which a model
of structure can be introduced and which is then followed,

complied with, by the reader. In that the model embodied has a prior existence, the text is not so much produced as reproduced.[16] The linear text thus not only predicts the relationship between reader and writer, by making the "submissive or compliant" response of the reader predictable, but it predicts the relationship between the ST and the TT. The tactician or tabular writer, coming across the linear text, subverts it, trespasses on its territory, scattering the pieces of its game, rewriting its rules. The intruder has no real text of his own; he has wildly performed someone else's text, according to his own whims, which themselves demand a new order of decipherment, a new approach to reading unguided by a code. In Saussurean terms, the tabular text is the *parole* that displaces the *langue* of the linear text, which replaces the essential with the accidental (however premeditated), the social with the individual.

CLIVE SCOTT is professor emeritus of European literature at the University of East Anglia and a fellow of the British Academy. His principal research interests lie in French and comparative poetics, in literary translation, particularly the experimental translation of poetry, and in photography's relationship with writing. He is the author of *The Poetics of French Verse: Studies in Reading, Channel Crossings: French and English Poetry in Dialogue, 1550–2000,* (awarded the R. H. Gapper Book Prize, 2004), *Literary Translation and the Rediscovery of Reading, Translating the Perception of Text: Literary Translation and Phenomenology, The Spoken Image: Photography and Language,* and *Street Photography: From Atget to Cartier-Bresson.* His interests in translation and photography combine in his recently published *Translating Apollinaire.*

NOTES

1. Scott, *Translating Rimbaud's "Illuminations"*; Scott, *Translating Apollinaire.*
2. Filippo Tommaso Marinetti, "Destruction of Syntax—Imagination without Strings—Words in Freedom" (May 1913), in Rainey, ed., *Modernism,* 30.
3. Apollinaire, *Œuvres poétiques,* 310.
4. Garnier, *Spatialisme et poésie concrète,* 41.

5. Apollinaire, *Œuvres en prose complètes II*, 976–977.

6. Flint, ed., *Marinetti*, 144.

7. Apollinaire, *Œuvres poétiques*, 87.

8. Meschonnic, *Critique du rythme*, 321.

9. Saussure, *Cours de linguistique générale*, 98.

10. Christin, *L'image écrite*, blurb.

11. Meschonnic, *Critique du rythme*, 310–316.

12. See Tsur, *What Makes Sound Patterns Expressive?* 11–51.

13. Mallarmé, *Œuvres complètes I*, 391.

14. Worthen summarizing Charles Olson ("Projective Verse," 1950); see W. B. Worthen, *Print and the Poetics of Modern Drama*, 118.

15. Drucker, *The Visible World*, 94–97. The quotations that follow are from p. 95.

16. Certeau, *The Practice of Everyday Life*, 134, 135.

FOURTEEN

Rethinking Originality / Making Us See: Contemporary Art's Strategic Transpositions

CATHERINE BERNARD

ORIGINALITY AND APPROPRIATION

Confronting, reworking, appropriating the past has always been instrumental to the production of the new, as Robert Rosenblum insists in his introduction to the catalogue of *Encounters: New Art from Old,* an exhibition organized at the British National Gallery in 2000, for which the National Gallery had commissioned twenty five contemporary artists—from Lucian Freud to Cy Twombly, from Claes Oldenburg to Howard Hodgkin—to create original works in homage and reaction to works they had chosen in the gallery's collections.[1] One cannot deny, however, that art's relation to its own aesthetic memory has undergone a profound change under the pressure of the modern imperative. Without fully disowning its forefathers, modern art has insisted on the organic necessity for art to break with laws and norms perceived to be academic, constricting, and, for many modernist critics, unduly subservient to appearances and a shallow mimesis. For the modernists, art had to move beyond the fascination with surface detail in order to rediscover the essence of inner vision. In so doing, art had to look back—even beyond the Renaissance—to look to the present, and embrace the future, in the very movement that made it hark back to a logic predating illusionism. When expounding the curatorial logic behind the post-Impressionist exhibition he had organized at the Grafton Gallery in 1910, Roger Fry made it a point to insist on the conflicted relation to the past and the present the post-Impressionists entertained: "These artists have, as it were, stumbled upon the principles of primitive design out of a perception of the sheer necessities of the actual situation."[2] Repossessing the past, reclaiming it, thus offered renewed access to the present, the "actual," while intensifying art's self-reflexive historicity.

Not all modernist movements chose to acknowledge the residual presence of a distant aesthetic past at the heart of the very new. For the Futurists and the Vorticists, the past had to be exorcised, violently if need be, and Ezra Pound's 1934 exhortation to his fellow poets to "make it new" necessarily entailed an antagonistic confrontation with the past that left little room for the rejuvenating dialectics of transposition.[3] Although apparently indifferent to modern art's relation to the past, Marcel Duchamp's radical conceptualism also substantially altered modern art's relation to its filiation and historicity. Playful, as in his 1919 *L.H.O.O.Q.*— a transposition of Leonardo da Vinci's *Mona Lisa* into one of his ready-mades, complete with moustache and goatee—or more arcane, as in his 1912 *Nu descendant l'escalier*—a futuristic reworking of the tradition of the nude for our modern age of flux—Duchamp's critical appropriation of aesthetic traditions deprived any acknowledged reference to the past of its former innocence.[4]

In the wake of Duchamp's critical conceptualism, the heightened self-referentiality of much of modern and contemporary art has turned all appropriations or transpositions of past references into a purposeful gesture. Consequently, the art of transposition has recently taken on renewed relevance, albeit in a conflicted manner. The essence of art being shown to lie in art's capacity to speculate on its own aesthetic economy, the historicist logic of interpictoriality has been foregrounded and more forcefully harnessed to the overarching specular agenda of the contemporary. Sherrie Levine's and Mike Bidlo's appropriation art is a good case in point. Levine's 1979 *After Walker Evans* series and Bidlo's mock or *faux* Matisses and Picassos entail a conceptual reflection on aesthetic authority and the exhaustion of the new that does seem to condemn the artist to a form of solipcism and to spell "the end of art."[5] Yet theirs is also a deceitfully self-defeating posture, a lure that aims precisely at exposing the intricate relation of influence and creativeness. In that sense Levine's and Bidlo's specularity encapsulates some of the key issues asked by or of contemporary art: Is the former art of transposition gone awry? Is art trapped in a compulsion of repetition that spells its exhaustion? Is the triumph of aesthetic autonomy and autotelic self-referentiality incompatible with a form of critical *praxis* that would still grant art some sort of purchase outside its strict boundaries? Is art merely a kind of sophisticated game of Trivial Pursuit? Or is the doubling up inherent in quotation and transposition a way of demystifying authority, even as it seems to magnify the authority of art, as Benjamin Buchloh intuits when he describes how the authorial subject of much of contemporary art both negates and defines itself "simultaneously in the act of quotation"?[6]

Contemporary art's ongoing recourse to the practice of transposition is undoubtedly a paradoxical one. By harnessing the ancient logic of transposition to the more conceptual and autotelic one of appropriation, contemporary art seems to have brought the *praxis* of interpictoriality to an end, and to suggest that contemporary aesthetics are condemned to a form of melancholy "hauntology,"[7] that very same "hauntology" itself being perfectly in keeping with the erosion of emotion and of aesthetic experience, diagnosed by Fredric Jameson as being at the heart of postmodernism and what he perceives as a "waning of affect."[8]

Such diagnosis, however, misses the critical thrust of aesthetic mimicry. I would like to contend that transposition has acquired greater critical acumen in contemporary art by foregrounding our relation to aesthetic experience. Visual absorption thus dovetails with critical acknowledgment. By accessing the artistic past through its renewed presence, the work of art enacts our often-repressed relation to history itself. In modernist fashion, that relation is exposed over and over again as culturally inscribed and thus denaturalized. To quote James Clifford, such a critical double-take makes "the investigator's culture newly incomprehensible."[9] The smooth linearity of art history is revealed for what it is: a narrative informing our very relation to the beautiful, to visual pleasure, and to aesthetic meaning.

Needless to say, such a critical take on the past and on aesthetic practice has to do with the modernist and formalist logic of defamiliarization—*ostranie*—as defined by Viktor Shklovsky in his famous essay of 1917, "Art as Technique."[10] Familiar and yet strange, well known and yet new, the same and yet different, the past returns at the heart of those quotational or appropriated images, and allows the unsaid, the untold, to surface and shine under a renewed light. The past does return but under a different guise: that of the historical repressed. In many cases, it also returns under the guise of the phenomenological unconscious, an unconscious disclosed within the process of transposition. And if the present seems then to mimic the past all too faithfully, it is precisely to fully exploit the critical power of mimicry, defined elsewhere by Homi Bhabha as working "at the crossroads of what is known and permissible and that which though known must be concealed; a discourse uttered between the lines and as such both against the rules and within them."[11]

TRANSPOSITION AND DISPLACEMENT

By transposing the past into the present, art opens the past up to interpretation and, as suggested by Bhabha, achieves that most paradoxical and critical of all positionings, which consists in working both from within the established discourse and from without. Yet one should maybe distinguish between different modalities of transposition. Édouard Manet's *Déjeuner sur l'herbe,* for instance—itself closely inspired by Titian's *Pastoral Symphony*—has inspired a long series of modernist or more recent painters: from Paul Cézanne's (1876–1877) to Pablo Picasso's series painted in 1960–1961, to Alain Jacquet's pop reworking of the motif in 1964. For all their technical freedom, these transpositions seem to abide by the logic of the new already central to Manet's work exhibited at the Salon des Refusés of 1863. Even Jacquet's seemingly iconoclastic photographic enlargement combined with the typically pop use of serigraphy on paper does not radically displace Manet's agenda.

The effect is quite different with Jeff Wall's own version of Manet's masterpiece in *The Storyteller* (1986).[12] In that transparency in light box of vast dimensions (2290 × 4370 mm), four people are to be seen sitting on the left-hand side of a photograph of the underside of a concrete flyover. The scene is ominously bleak, its meaning obscure and suspended. Literally decentered, displaced to the margins of the vacant image, Manet's reference hardly shimmers on the periphery of our aesthetic memory. Crudely relocated to one of those no-man's lands our modern gaze deliberately ignores, as we translate ourselves from one destination to another, the modernist vocabulary of dissidence is exposed as the ineffectual other of a world that has little room for art, a world left to the ugliness of functionalism and brutalist urbanism.

Working in the wake of Wall's ruthless reappropriations of our global imaginary museum, English photographer Tom Hunter also works to displace, transfigure, and defamiliarize our imaginary museum. In his *Woman Reading a Possession Order,* he chooses to appropriate one of the best known images of Dutch Renaissance art: Vermeer's 1657 *Girl Reading a Letter at an Open Window.* In Hunter's photograph, which is part of a series of portraits of Hackney squatters, Hunter produces a short circuit of the peaceful image of feminine propriety.[13] The seemingly self-possessed girl standing in the full, frontal light of the window of a dingy room, a baby lying by her side, offers more than an ironically updated image of timeless femininity. Hunter's transposition is about dispossession, property, and the proper in more than one way. By borrowing his composition from Vermeer, he does not merely transpose Vermeer's vernacular vocabulary to our modern days; he achieves a double strategic relocation of the motif. The timelessness of Vermeer's scene is brutally reinscribed in an all too literal economic and historical context: that of poverty and deprivation. But Hunter's photograph plays with Vermeer's image, explicates it in another way still. It does not only unfold the covert Christian idiom of Vermeer's oil—and after all Vermeer's art is, among other things, very much about folding and unfolding. Vermeer's humble still-life ensconced in the folds of the table spread is transmogrified into what it can only be, interpictorially, that is, the fruit of the girl's womb. The secular transposition intends to be scandalous, to brutally literalize the humble discretion of Vermeer's motif, and to repossess itself of art's critical *praxis,* of its capacity to work allegorically, while—and this is what is possibly so scandalous about this work—remaining true to the aesthetic agenda of art, if only in its remarkable handling of *chiaroscuro.*

By daring to confront high art with its repressed other—here the dispossessed—and to update it violently so that its double returns with a vengeance, both Wall's and Hunter's works seem to echo with Michel Foucault's words about "the unthinkable" in *The Order of Things* when he insists that man's brotherly other stands side by side with him, in a form of irretrievable duality, and that it is precisely the task of modern thought to lie as close as possible to that other in order to think it through.[14]

LIFE TRANSPOSED AND EXPOSED

One may argue that still-life, as a genre, does not yield itself so readily to such a critical reading, that its programmatic purpose is not to make such an aesthetic, antagonistic *praxis* possible. And yet, one may also argue that the allegorical agenda of still-life from the start also seems to trump the critical move involved in the transposition and brutal updating which appropriation art, or quotational art, may want to engineer, and which is so programmatic to Hunter's and Wall's photographs. As Rosemary Lloyd so aptly insists in her essay devoted to the literary still life, *Shimmering in a Transformed Light,* still-life is always already a critical genre that somehow carries its own hermeneutic displacement or transposition in the very folds of its surface. It entails "an intensification of the act of looking" itself characteristic of the modern critical stance and of its *praxis*.[15] The permanence of the genre in contemporary photography entails a new twist of its hermeneutic code, which highlights still further its modernist thrust and leaves still more room precisely for the expression of this "unthinkable" Foucault encourages us to probe.

Modern transpositions of the genre have a long history that dates back undoubtedly to Cézanne's both monumental and sensuous still-lifes and to their paradoxical geometric tangibility. It is such palpability that D. H. Lawrence celebrated in his famous essay of 1929, in which he traces the process by which the "revolution" of Cézanne's vision consists in divesting the still-life of its allegorical function in order to return it— and reality at large, including the human figure—to the "appleyness" of apples on a table.[16]

The history of photographic still life is also a long one, going back, perhaps, to the early days of photography and William Henry Fox Talbot's *Photogenic Drawings,* and, in the early years of the twentieth century, to the visual experimentations of Man Ray, Paul Strand, Edward Weston, André Kertész, and Alfred Stieglitz.

Choosing to work within the well-registered vocabulary of still-life implies for today's artists making an aesthetic decision not so remote from that of conceptual artists working within the idiom of Duchamp's readymades. Still-life, with its preordained form and range of subjects, its allegorical depth and pragmatic agenda, is there to be reworked, translated, and reinvented. The formal and hermeneutic constraints are—if I may say so—too contractual not to be, from the start, strategic to the aesthetic move that inspires an artist to return to that precise genre. It is precisely the specularity that is so crucial to the allegorical program of the genre—as Baron Adolf de Meyer well understood, with his photographic still-lifes' play on the art of transparency—that is foregrounded and highlighted in the very transposition and updating of the genre, a self-reflexiveness that Rosemary Lloyd also deems central to the literary still-life which provides "an exercise for both writer and reader in how to read the world and the text."17

Choosing to translate the standard iconography of the genre into the photographic medium is yet another turn of the hermeneutic and aesthetic screw. With photographic still-life, the allegorical spectrality of the genre, its intimations of mortality, are displaced onto the medium itself. It is today but a critical cliché to insist, after Roland Barthes and Susan Sontag, on the ghostlike or spectral presence of the motif in photography. In *La chambre claire*, Barthes chooses for instance to speak not of the motif of a photograph, but of its "spectrum," so as to encapsulate both the idea of the visual spectacle entailed by the image and that of the return of the repressed presence of death at the heart of all photographs.18 Thus, one may suggest that with photographic still-life, the haunting anticipation of death returns once more but squared—*au carré*—in the very spectrality of the medium, in its brutal and transparent capacity to capture life as life on the wane, as life as it will never be experienced again. Photographic still-life thus produces a perfect fit between the meta-aesthetic program of the art of quotation and the allegorical purport of the genre itself. The past returns over and over again in these images, which are—to quote Lucy Lippard on the critical impact of contemporary art—"both new and ancient," and that "elbo[w] [their] way into the future while remaining conscious and caring of [their] past."19 One may even argue further that such a perfect fit lies also in these images' fetishist quality, in their pressing although uncanny capacity to capture our modern fascination with death, a fascination that Rosemary Lloyd also sees to be central, for instance, to Pierre Loti's 1890 *Le roman d'un enfant*, where the fascination with objects captures the "sadness that comes from the realization that objects, bearers of fossils and totems though they may be, can never bring back the past, which seems dead and beyond recall."[20]

With photography, death imprints itself on the surface of the image, if only because photography displaces the issue of mimesis onto the crude, raw terrain of reality, of facts. The hydrangea of Adolf de Meyer's 1907 pared-down photograph was really picked by somebody and was eventually thrown away. The water did eventually go stale and was thrown away. Even in the most mannerist and de-realized of still-lifes—such as American artist Zachary Zavislak's—the beholder knows, even subliminally, that the tomatoes did eventually rot away, and that part of the poignancy of the image lies in the all too naked reality of the thingness of the things here exposed in their concrete vulnerability. These still-lifes are, after all, still life—"de la vie malgré tout," to adapt the title of one of Georges Didi-Huberman's essays on photography.[21] They still capture life and death.

Thus the still-life does indeed "shimmer in a transformed light." As Rosemary Lloyd insists with respect to the literary still-life, it is its heuristic and hermeneutic function itself that shimmers, caught as this mixed genre is between its traditional abstract implications and the pressing tangibility of things. This tangibility both reinforces the allegorical import of the *vanitas* and trumps it, since death is precisely the one experience of the real that cannot be sublated and can only return as trauma.

This is the paradox that English photographer and video-artist Sam Taylor-Johnson has relentlessly tried to capture in her videos and the stills taken from them—for instance in her 2002 *A Little Death* (a four-minute sped-up film/DVD of a decaying hare) or in her acclaimed 2001 film/DVD *Still Life*: a 3.44-minute sped-up video of a bowl of rotting fruit. Taylor-Johnson's *Still Life* combines the raw nakedness of photography with the narrativity of video. The basic premise of all still-lifes is thus literalized. We actually witness the decay of the bowl of fruit

in these three minutes and forty-four seconds, which makes the teleological principle all too real, without any hope of allegorical or spiritual
redemption sublating the narrative.[22] Life is no longer suspended, and
its entropic movement stilled and framed. The ontological terror of time
returns in accelerated form.

Like Hunter's *Woman Reading a Possession Order,* Taylor-Johnson's
literal still-life also unfolds the hidden agenda of the genre it refers back
to, resorting to caravagesque effects and a sophisticated handling of
chiaroscuro, in order to activate our visual and cultural memory, while
bringing it into violent clash with the physicality of death. Like Hunter,
Taylor-Johnson engages directly with the history of art in ways that both
lay bare its iconographic mechanisms and literalize its hermeneutic message. A bowl of fruit is a bowl of fruit is a bowl of fruit. . . . Gertrude
Stein's enigmatic modernist motto—which here I have adapted to serve
my purpose—has never seemed more apt to capture the dizzying intertwining of modernist self-referentiality and raw referentiality. As Taylor-
Johnson's avowed reference to Caravaggio and the long history of the
still-life shows, *Still Life* flaunts its sophisticated pictoriality. It turns that
pictoriality and the modernist emphasis on visual effect into a motif.[23]
Its intense physicality also reminds us of the circuitous way by which art
takes us back to life even as it puts it at a distance and transforms it. In a
darkly humorous and allegorical way, *Still Life* does indeed give us food
for thought, but it is bitter and unsavory food, as all still-lifes do, that are
true both to their allegorical formula and to the "appleyness" or "peachi-
ness" of their material, in all its splendid and fragile transience. In so
doing, it also heals the breach of referentiality that Michel Foucault explored in *Ceci n'est pas une pipe.*[24] Or rather, it both keeps open and closes
the gap between icon and signified. Taylor-Johnson's still-life is a still
life, which, like all *vanitas,* should be read allegorically. It also functions
like an extended metonymy in which visual representation lies in direct
contact with the skin of reality. With Fredric Jameson, when analyzing
contemporary video, one may thus suggest that in this transposition,
video allows the various implications of the genre and its favorite motif
to come "in play simultaneously."[25]

Next to the plate of fruit lies a pen. The object is striking, and telling
in more than one way via this simultaneous play of effects. As a metaphor

of the artist's signature, it functions like an embedded sign, a small allegorical effect in which the entire allegorical regime of the work comes to
rest. The pen is also a signature effect in another way. Its modern, stream-
lined, standard shape stands in sharp and telling contrast with the timelessness of the fruit motif. While the fruit rots away, and its rot produces
myriad flies, which in their turn disappear, the pen remains unchanged,
its head pointing stubbornly to the plate of fruit and the life-and-death
drama taking place on it. The pen is a marker both of modernity and
intangibility; it is eventually its dead rigidity and inorganicity that strike
us as slightly threatening, for these are uncanny in their minerality. And
yet, in its stubborn deadness, the pen does also encapsulate the entire
postmodernist agenda of Taylor-Johnson's work, in its capacity to crys-
tallize the very discursiveness of the work, its allegorical shimmering,
and powerful phenomenological effect, so that the work "appears to gaze
directly back at us, to reflect back on us," as well as on our modernity and
timeless anxiety in front of change and transience.[26]

What is taking place in this transposition? Both a work of homage
and a work of mourning, both a dispossession—art relinquishing its
modernist hope of "making it new"—and a repossession of our capacity
to be affected and to think that affect through. In 3.44 minutes, *Still Life*
both unfolds and crystallizes the programmatic meaning of the genre
while forcing us to an experience whose temporality is too disturbing
not to be profoundly *unheimlich*. Maybe in such affective contemplation
lies the very essence of art as aesthetic *praxis*? We thought we had fully
come to terms with the lessons of the genre, but maybe this is where the
haunting hermeneutic power of aesthetic experience lies: in its capacity
to keep us standing in the "shimmering light" of meaning, meaning that
is too close to the bone not to affect us, but also too infinitely complex
not to lock us into a no-less-infinite and defamiliarizing contemplation.

CATHERINE BERNARD is professor of English literature and history
of art at the University Paris Diderot—Paris 7. She has published
extensively on contemporary art—David Hockney, Rachel Whiteread,
and Gillian Wearing—as well as on recent English fiction—Martin
Amis, Peter Ackroyd, Pat Barker, and Graham Swift. Her research
has also focused on Virginia Woolf and modernism more widely. She

has coedited several volumes of articles on Woolf and has contributed to the edition of Woolf's fiction for the Gallimard-Pléiade series. She has also edited and translated a selection of Woolf's essays for Gallimard. She is currently working on a monograph devoted to the poetics of body politics in recent British literature and visual arts.

NOTES

1. Rosenblum, *Encounters*, 8.
2. Fry, "The Grafton Gallery—1," 86.
3. Pound, *Make It New.*
4. On Marcel Duchamp's conflicted relation with the past in relation to the modernity and ahistoricity of art, see de Duve, *Nominalisme pictural.*
5. On this anxiety about the end of art and the apparent triumph of "aesthetic entropy," see Danto, "Introduction: Modern, Postmodern, and Contemporary," especially 12.
6. Buchloh, "Allegorical Procedures," 52.
7. I am of course referring to Jacques Derrida's coinage in *Spectres de Marx,* 31.
8. See Jameson, *Postmodernism,* 15.
9. Clifford, *The Predicament of Culture,* 147.
10. Shklovsky, "Art as Technique."
11. Bhabha, *The Location of Culture,* 89.
12. http://www.tate.org.uk/whats-on/tate-modern/exhibition/jeff-wall/room-guide /jeff-wall-room-4.
13. http://www.saatchi-gallery.co.uk/artists/artpages/tom_hunter_woman.htm.
14. See Foucault, *Les mots et les choses,* 337–338.
15. Lloyd, *Shimmering in a Transformed Light,* 49.
16. See Lawrence, "Introduction to These Paintings," 339.
17. Lloyd, *Shimmering in a Transformed Light,* 3.
18. Barthes, *La chambre claire,* 22–23.
19. Lippard, "Mapping," 166.
20. Lloyd, *Shimmering in a Transformed Light,* 39.
21. I am referring to Didi-Huberman, *Images malgré tout.*
22. On the treatment of time in video, see Belting, "The Temporality of Video Art."
23. On the importance of effect, see also Lloyd, *Shimmering in a Transformed Light,* 75–90.
24. Foucault, *Ceci n'est pas une pipe.*
25. Fredric Jameson, "Surrealism without the Unconscious," in Jameson, *Postmodernism,* 85.
26. Lloyd, *Shimmering in a Transformed Light,* 118.

BIBLIOGRAPHY

Ager, Dennis. *Identity, Insecurity and Image: France and Language.* Clevedon, Eng.: Multilingual Matters, 1999.

Aldéguier, Jean-Baptiste-Auguste d'. *Le flâneur; ou, Mon voyage à Paris.* Paris: N.p., 1825.

Apollinaire, Guillaume. *Œuvres en prose complètes II.* Edited by Pierre Caizergues and Michel Décaudin. Paris: Gallimard, 1991.

——. *Œuvres poétiques.* Edited by Marcel Adéma and Michel Décaudin. Paris: Gallimard, 1965.

Audin, Jean-Marie-Vincent. *Le véritable conducteur parisien de Richard.* Paris: Terry, 1828.

Auguste Rodin: Images of Desire. 1995; Munich: Schirmer/Mosel, 2005.

Bachelard, Gaston. *L'eau et les rêves.* New edition. 1942; Paris: Corti, 1947.

Bal, Mieke. *Quoting Caravaggio: Contemporary Art, Preposterous History.* Chicago: University of Chicago Press, 1999.

Balcou, Jean, and Yves Le Gallo, eds. *Histoire littéraire et culturelle de la Bretagne.* 3 vols. Paris: Champion-Slatkine, 1987.

Balibar, R., and D. Laporte. *Le français national: Politique et pratique de la langue nationale sous la Révolution.* Paris: Broché, 1974.

Balzac, Honoré de. *Les Chouans.* Edited by Pierre Gascar. Paris: Gallimard, 1972.

——. *La Comédie humaine.* Edited by Pierre-Georges Castex et al. 12 vols. Paris: Gallimard, 1976–1981.

——. *Ferragus: La fille aux yeux d'or.* Edited by Michel Lichtlé. Paris: Garnier-Flammarion, 1988.

——. *Histoire des Treize.* Paris: Librairie Générale Française, 1983.

——. *L'Œuvre de Balzac.* Edited by Albert Béguin and Jean A. Ducourneau. 16 vols. Paris: Club Français du Livre, 1966.

——. *Le Père Goriot.* Edited by Pierre-Georges Castex. Revised edition. 1960; Paris, Garnier, 1981.

Bandy, W. T., and Claude Pichois. "Un inédit: 'Hiawatha. Légende indienne,' adaptation de Charles Baudelaire." *Études baudelairiennes* 2 (1971): 7–68.

Bann, Stephen. *The True Vine: On Visual Representation and the Western Tradition.* Cambridge: Cambridge University Press, 1989.

Barthes, Roland. *La Chambre claire.* Paris: Gallimard/Le Seuil, 1980.

Bassnett, Susan. *Translation Studies.* Revised edition. 1980; London: Routledge, 1991.

Bassnett, Susan, and André Lefevere, eds. *Constructing Cultures: Essays on Literary Translation.* Clevedon, Eng.: Multilingual Matters, 1998.

———. *Translation, History, and Culture.* London: Pinter, 1990.

Bassnett, Susan, and Harish Trivedi, eds. *Postcolonial Translation: Theory and Practice.* London: Routledge, 1999.

Baudelaire, Charles. *Correspondance.* Edited by Claude Pichois. 2 vols. Paris: Gallimard, 1973.

———. *Œuvres complètes.* Edited by Claude Pichois. 2 vols. Paris: Gallimard, 1975–1976.

———. *The Prose Poems and La Fanfarlo.* Translated by Rosemary Lloyd. Oxford: Oxford University Press, 1991.

Baudille, Yves. "Du vécu dans le roman: Esquisse d'une poétique de la transposition." *Revue des sciences humaines* 263 (2001): 75–101.

Behar, Ruth. *The Vulnerable Observer: Anthropology That Breaks Your Heart.* Boston: Beacon Press, 1996.

Beizer, Janet. *Thinking through the Mothers: Reimagining Women's Biographies.* Ithaca, N.Y.: Cornell University Press, 2009.

———. "Uncovering *Nana*: The Courtesan's New Clothes." *L'Esprit créateur* 25 (1985): 45–56.

Bellos, David. *Is That a Fish in Your Ear: Translation and the Meaning of Everything.* New York: Faber and Faber, 2011.

Belting, Hans. "The Temporality of Video Art." In *Art History after Modernism,* 85–95. Chicago: University of Chicago Press, 2003.

Benda, Mihály. "Sur les 'expressions macaroniques' de la critique d'art de Théophile Gautier (dialogue entre peinture et littérature)." *Verbum Analecta Neolatina* 11, no. 1 (2009): 63–86.

Benjamin, Roger. *Orientalist Aesthetics: Art, Colonialism and French North Africa, 1880–1930.* Berkeley: University of California Press, 2003.

Benjamin, Walter. *Charles Baudelaire: Un poète lyrique à l'apogée du capitalisme.* Translated and edited by Jean Lacoste. Paris: Payot, 1982.

Bentley, Toni. *Sisters of Salomé.* New Haven, Conn.: Yale University Press, 2002.

Berg, William J. *The Visual Novel: Emile Zola and the Art of His Times.* University Park: Pennsylvania State University Press, 1992.

Bertho, Catherine. "L'invention de la Bretagne: Genèse sociale d'un stéréotype." *Actes de la recherche en sciences sociales* 35 (1980): 45–62.

Best, Janice. "Portraits d'une 'vraie fille': *Nana,* tableau, roman et mise-en-scène." *Les cahiers naturalistes* 66 (1992): 157–166.

Bhabha, Homi K. *The Location of Culture.* London: Routledge, 1994.

Bordas, Éric. "L'orient balzacien; ou, L'impossible narratif d'un possible romanesque—L'exemple de *La fille aux yeux d'or.*" *Studi francesi* 122 (1997): 322–330.

Bouverot, Danielle. "La métaphore dans le langage de la critique d'art." *Travaux de linguistique et de littérature* 21, no. 1 (1983): 187–196.

Boym, Svetlana. *The Future of Nostalgia.* New York: Basic Books, 2001.

Brady, Patrick. *"L'œuvre" d'Émile Zola: Roman sur les arts; manifeste, autobiographie, roman à clefs.* Geneva: Droz, 1968.

Breton, André. *Mad Love.* Translated by Mary Ann Caws. Lincoln: University of Nebraska Press, 1987.

Breton, Jules. *Nos peintres du siècle: L'art et les artistes.* Paris: Société d'édition artistique, 1899.

Briggs-Lynch, Elizabeth. "Manet's *Nana:* The Connection with Zola's *L'Assommoir* and *Nana.*" In *Emile Zola and the Arts,* edited by Jean-Max Guieu and Alison Hilton, 9–14. Washington, D.C.: Georgetown University Press, 1988.

Brizeux, Auguste. *Marie: Roman.* 1831; Paris: Auguste Auffray et Urbain Canel, 1832.

——. *Œuvres de Auguste Brizeux.* Edited by Auguste Dorchain. 4 vols. Paris: Garnier Frères, 1910.

Brooks, Peter. *Body Work: Objects of Desire in Modern Narrative.* Cambridge, Mass.: Harvard University Press, 1993.

Broudic, Fañch. *Qui parle Breton aujourd'hui? Qui le parlera demain?* Brest: Brud Nevez, 1999.

Bruce, Robert. *"Orbis pictus redivivus." Word and Image* 1 (1985): 109–129.

Bruller, Jean. "Évolution du livre collectionneur de 1919 à nos jours." *Arts et métiers graphiques* 59 (1937): 31–36.

Bryson, Norman. "Intertextuality and Visual Poetics." *Style* 22, no. 2 (Summer 1988): 183–193.

Buchloh, Benjamin. "Allegorical Procedures: Appropriation and Montage in Contemporary Art." *Artforum,* September 1982, 43–56.

Burke, Peter. *Language and Communities in Early Modern Europe.* Cambridge: Cambridge University Press, 2004.

Calvino, Italo. "La città-romanzo in Balzac." In *Perché leggere i classici,* 173–179. Milan: Mondadori, 1991.

Cambry, Jacques. *Voyage dans le Finistère.* Facsimile edition. 1836; Geneva: Slatkine Reprints, 1979.

Cargo, Robert T. "Baudelaire, Longfellow, and 'A Psalm of Night'." *Littérature comparée* 54, no. 2 (April–June 1980): 196–201.

Carroll, Raymonde. *Cultural Misunderstandings: The French-American Experience.* Translated by Carol Volk. Chicago: University of Chicago Press, 1988.

Castillo, Michel Del. *Colette: Une certaine France.* Paris: Stock, 1999.

Caws, Mary Ann. *L'oeuvre filante de René Char.* Paris: Nizet, 1981.

——. *The Presence of René Char.* Princeton, N.J.: Princeton University Press, 1976.

——. *René Char.* Boston: Twayne, 1977.

——. "René Char: Resistance and Grandeur." In René Char, *Furor and Mystery and Other Writings,* trans. and ed. Mary Ann Caws and Nancy Kline, 531–558. Boston: Black Widow Press, 2010.

Certeau, Michel de. *The Practice of Everyday Life.* Translated by Steven Rendall. Berkeley: University of California Press, 1984.

Certeau, Michel de, Julia Dominique, and Jacques Revel. Une politique de la langue: La révolution française et les patois. Paris: Gallimard, 1975.

Chabrier, Christina Ferree. "Aesthetic Perversion: Octave Mirbeau's *Le jardin des supplices." Nineteenth-Century French Studies* 34, nos. 3–4 (Spring–Summer 2006): 355–370.

Char, René. *Furor and Mystery and Other Poems.* Translated by Mary Ann Caws and Nancy Kline, introduction by Sandra Bermann, preface by Marie-Claude Char. Boston: Black Widow Press, 2011.

——. *The Poems of René Char.* Translated by Mary Ann Caws and Jonathan Griffin. Princeton, N.J.: Princeton University Press, 1976.

——. *Selected Poems.* Edited by Mary Ann Caws and Tina Jolas. New York: New Directions, 1992.

Chateaubriand, François-René. *Œuvres romanesques et voyages.* Edited by M. Regard. Vol. 1. Paris: Gallimard, 1969.

Choisy, Francois-Timoléon de. *Aventures de l'abbé de Choisy habillé en femme.* Edited by Marc de Montifaud. Brussels: C. Gilliet, 1884.

Christin, Anne-Marie. *L'image écrite; ou, La déraison graphique.* Paris: Flammarion, 1995.

Citron, Pierre. *La poésie de Paris dans la littérature française de Rousseau à Baudelaire.* 2 vols. Paris: Minuit, 1961.

Clark, Roger. *Zola: "Nana."* London: Grant and Cutler, 2004.

Clayson, Hollis. *Painted Love: Prostitution in French Art of the Impressionist Period.* New Haven, Conn.: Yale University Press, 1991.

Clifford, James. *The Predicament of Culture: Twentieth Century Ethnography, Literature and Art.* Cambridge, Mass.: Harvard University Press, 1988.

Cocteau, Jean. "Note sur les ballets." In Arsène Alexandre and Jean Cocteau, *L'art décoratif de Léon Bakst: Essai critique,* 17–49. Paris: Maurice de Brunoff, 1913.

Colette. *Break of Day.* Translated by Enid McLeod. New York: Farrar, Straus and Giroux, 1961.

———. *Colette: Lettres à sa fille, 1916–1953.* Edited by Anne de Jouvenel. Paris: Gallimard, 2003.

———. *The Evening Star.* In *Recollections.* Translated by David Le Vay. New York: Macmillan, 1972.

———. *Œuvres.* Edited by Claude Pichois and Alain Brunet. 4 vols. Paris: Gallimard, 1984–2001.

———. *Œuvres complètes.* Edited by Claude Pichois. 16 vols. Paris: Club de l'Honnête Homme, 1973–1976.

Collier, Peter, and Robert Lethbridge, eds. *Artistic Relations: Literature and the Visual Arts in Nineteenth-Century France.* New Haven, Conn.: Yale University Press, 1994.

Constant, Benjamin. *Œuvres.* Paris: Gallimard, 1957.

Constantine, Mary-Ann. "Ballads Crossing Borders: La Villemarqué and the 'Breton Lenore'." *Translation and Literature* 89, no. 2 (1999): 197–216.

———. *Breton Ballads.* Aberystwyth: Cambrian Medieval Celtic Studies, 1996.

Cooke, Peter. *Gustave Moreau et les arts jumeaux: Peinture et littérature au dix-neuvième siècle.* Bern: Peter Lang, 2003.

Corbin, Laurie. *The Mother Mirror: Self-Representation and the Mother-Daughter Relation in Colette, Simone de Beauvoir,* and Marguerite Duras. New York: Peter Lang, 1996.

Cousins, Russell. *Zola: "Thérèse Raquin."* London: Grant and Cutler, 1992.

Crépet, Eugène, and Jacques Crépet. *Ch. Baudelaire: Étude biographique . . . suivi par Baudelairiana d'Asselineau.* Paris: Albert Messein, 1919.

Cronin, Michael. *Translating Ireland.* Cork: Cork University Press, 1996.

Curtius, E. R. *European Literature and the Latin Middle Ages.* Princeton, N.J.: Princeton University Press, 1953.

Dampmartin, Vicomte de. *Un provincial à Paris pendant une partie de l'année 1789.* Strasbourg: La Société Typographique, 1790.

Damrosch, Leo. *Jean-Jacques Rousseau: Restless Genius.* New York: Houghton Mifflin, 2005.

Danto, Arthur. "Introduction: Modern, Postmodern, and Contemporary." In *After the End of Art:. Contemporary Art and the Pale of History,* 3–19. Princeton, N.J.: Princeton University Press, 1997.

Dawkins, Heather. *The Nude in French Art and Culture, 1870–1910.* Cambridge: Cambridge University Press, 2002.

Dayan, Peter. *Art as Music, Music as Poetry, Poetry as Art, from Whistler to Stravinsky, and Beyond.* Burlington, Vt.: Ashgate, 2011.

———. *Music Writing Literature, from Sand via Debussy to Derrida.* Burlington, Vt.: Ashgate, 2006.

Deaucourt, Jean-Louis. *Premières loges: Paris et ses concierges au XIXe siècle.* Paris: Aubier, 1992.

De Cossart, Michael. *Ida Rubinstein, 1885–1960: A Theatrical Life.* Liverpool: Liverpool University Press, 1987.

de Duve, Thierry. *Nominalisme pictural: Marcel Duchamp. La peinture et la modernité.* Paris: Editions de Minuit, 1984.

Deleuze, Gilles, and Claire Parnet. *Dialogues.* Translated by Hugh Tomlinson and Barbara Habberjam. New York: Columbia University Press, 1987.

Delon, Michel. "Le boudoir balzacien." *L'année balzacienne* 19 (1998): 227–245.

Denis, Maurice. *Du symbolisme au classicisme: Théories.* Edited by Olivier Revault d'Allonnes. Paris: Hermann Mesnil, 1964.

Depaulis, Jacques. *Ida Rubinstein: Une inconnue jadis célèbre.* Paris: Honoré Champion, 1995.

Derrida, Jacques. *Spectres de Marx.* Paris: Galilée, 1993.

Didi-Huberman, Georges. *Images malgré tout.* Paris: Editions de Minuit, 2003.

Dietler, Michael. "'Our Ancestors the Gauls': Archaeology, Ethnic Nationalism and the Manipulation of Celtic Identity in Modern Europe." *American Anthropologist* 96 (1994): 584–605.

Dobie, Madeleine. *Foreign Bodies: Gender, Language, and Culture in French Orientalism.* Stanford, Cal.: Stanford University Press, 2001.

Drost, Wolfgang. "Pour une réévaluation de la critique d'art de Gautier." *Cahiers de l'Association Internationale des Études Françaises* 55 (2003): 401–421.

Drucker, Johanna. *The Visible World: Experimental Typography and Modern Art, 1909–1923.* Chicago: University of Chicago Press, 1996.

Duras, Claire-Louisa-Rose-Bonne Lechal Kersaint, Duchesse de. *Ourika.* 1823; Paris: Ladvocat, 1824.

Ehrard, Jean, and Paul Viallaneix, eds. *Nos ancêtres les Gaulois.* Clermont-Ferrand: Association des Publications de la Faculté des Lettres et Sciences Humaines, 1982.

Engstrom, Alfred. "Baudelaire and Longfellow's *Hymn to the Night.*" *Modern Language Notes* 74 (December 1959): 695–698.

Evenepoel, Henri. *Lettres à mon père.* 2 vols. Brussels: Musées Royaux des Beaux-Arts de Belgique, 1994.

Ferguson, Priscilla Parkhurst. *Paris as Revolution: Writing the Nineteenth-Century City.* Berkeley: University of California Press, 1994.

"Le flâneur parisien." *Le Figaro,* November 13, 1831, 2.

Flieger, Jerry Aline. *Colette and the Phantom Subject of Autobiography.* Ithaca, N.Y.: Cornell University Press, 1992.

Forsdick, Charles. "Between 'French' and 'Francophone': French Studies and the Postcolonial Turn." *French Studies* 59, no. 4 (2005): 523–530.

Forsdick, Charles, and David Murphy. "Introduction: The Case for Francophone Postcolonial Studies." In *Francophone Postcolonial Studies: A Critical Introduction,* edited by Charles Forsdick and David Murphy, 1–14. London: Arnold, 2003.

Foucault, Michel. *Ceci n'est pas une pipe.* Paris: Fata Morgana, 1973.

——. *Les mots et les choses.* Paris: Gallimard, 1966.

Fowler, Alastair. "Periodization and Interart Analogies." In *Literatur und Bildende Kunst: Ein Handbuch zur Theorie und Praxis eines komparatistischen Grezgebietes,* edited by Ulrich Weisstein, 86–101. 1972; Berlin: E. Schmidt, 1992.

Francis, Claude, and Fernande Gontier. *Creating Colette,* vol. 1, *From Ingenue to Libertine, 1873–1913.* South Royalton, Vt.: Steerford Press, 1998.

——. *Mathilde de Morny: La scandaleuse marquise et son temps.* Paris: Librairie Académique Perrin, 2000.

Fried, Michael. *Manet's Modernism; or, The Face of Painting in the 1860s.* Chicago: Chicago University Press, 1996.

Froment, M. *Histoire de Vidocq, chef de la police de la sûreté, écrite d'après lui-même.* 2 vols. Paris: Lerosey, 1829.

——. *La police dévoilée depuis la Restauration.* 3 vols. Paris: Lemonnier, 1829.

Fromentin, Eugène. *Correspondance*. Edited by Barbara Wright. 2 vols. Paris: CNRS-Éditions/Universitas, 1995.

———. *Œuvres complètes*. Edited by Guy Sagnes. Paris: Gallimard, 1986.

Fry, Roger. "The Grafton Gallery—1." In *A Roger Fry Reader*, edited by Christopher Reed, 86–89. Chicago: University of Chicago Press, 1996. Originally published in *The Nation*, November 19, 1910.

Garb, Tamar. *Bodies of Modernity: Figure and Flesh in Fin-de-Siècle France*. London: Thames and Hudson, 1998.

Garnier, Pierre. *Spatialisme et poésie concrète*. Paris: Gallimard, 1968.

Gartner, Matthew. "New Study Examines the *Song of Hiawatha* as Controversial Bestseller." *Longfellow House Bulletin* 5, no. 1 (June 2001): 1–2.

Gautier, Théophile. "De l'application de l'art à la vie usuelle." *La Presse*, December 13, 1836.

———. *Récits fantastiques*. Paris: Classiques Français, 1993.

———. *Le roman de la momie précédé de trois contes antiques*. Paris: Garnier Frères, 1963.

Genlis, Stéphanie-Félicité du Crest, Comtesse de. *Les chevaliers du cygne; ou, La cour de Charlemagne*. Paris: Lemierre, 1795.

———. *La femme auteur*. Edited by Martine Reid. Paris: Gallimard, 2007.

Gillespie, Stuart, and David Hopkins. *The Oxford History of Literary Translation in English*, vol. 3, *1670–1790*. Oxford: Oxford University Press, 2005.

Goldscheider, Cécile. "Assemblages et métamorphoses dans l'œuvre d'Auguste Rodin." *Gazette des Beaux Arts* 111 (January–February 1988): 137–140.

Gontard, Marc. "Pour une littérature bretonne de langue française." In *Écrire la Bretagne: 1960–1995*, edited by Bernard Hue and Marc Gontard, 17–31. Rennes: Presses Universitaires de Rennes, 1995.

Goulet, Andrea. *Optiques: The Science of the Eye and the Birth of Modern French Fiction*. Philadelphia, University of Pennsylvania Press, 2006.

Green, Anna. *French Paintings of Childhood and Adolescence, 1848–1886*. Aldershot, Eng.: Ashgate, 2007.

Greenblatt, Stephen. "The Interart Moment." In *Interart Poetics: Essays on the Interrelations of the Arts and Media*, edited by Ulla Britta Lagerroth, Hans Lund, and Erik Hedling, 13–16. Amsterdam: Rodopi, 1997.

Grégoire, Henri. *De la littérature des nègres; ou, Recherches sur leurs facultés intellectuelles, leurs qualités morales et leur littérature*. Paris: Chez Maradan, 1808.

Gsell, Paul. *Auguste Rodin, l' art, entretiens réunis par Paul Gsell*. Paris: Grasset, 1911.

Guentner, Wendelin, ed. *Women Art Critics in Nineteenth-Century France: Vanishing Acts*. Newark: University of Delaware Press, 2013.

Guichardet, Jeanine. *Balzac, archéologue de Paris*. Paris: SEDES, 1986.

Guiomar, Jean-Yves. *Le bretonisme: Les historiens bretons au XIXe siècle*. Mayenne, France: Imprimerie de la Manutention, 1987.

Hacking, Ian. *The Taming of Chance*. Cambridge: Cambridge University Press, 1990.

Hamrick, Lois Cassandra. "The Role of Gautier in the Art Criticism of Baudelaire." Ph.D. dissertation, Vanderbilt University, 1975.

Harvey, David. *Paris, Capital of Modernity*. New York: Routledge, 2003.

Haskell, Eric T. "Illustrations for Baudelaire's *Les Fleurs du Mal*: Symbolist Dreams and Decadent Nightmares." *Symposium* 38, no. 3 (1984): 179–195.

Hawthorne, Melanie. "Dis-covering the Female: Gautier's *Roman de la momie*." *French Review* 5 (April 1993): 718–729.

Heffernan, James A. W. *Museum of Words: The Poetics of Ekphrasis from Homer to*

Ashberry. Chicago: University of Chicago Press, 1993.

Hélias, Per-Jakez. *Le cheval d'orgueil*. Paris: Plon, 1975.

Heppenstall, Rayner. *French Crime in the Romantic Age*. London, Hamish Hamilton, 1970.

Hertz, Henri. "Émile Zola, témoin de la vérité." *Europe* 83–84 (1952): 27–34.

House, John. *Impressionism: Paint and Politics*. New Haven, Conn.: Yale University Press, 2004.

Huffer, Lynne. *Another Colette*. Ann Arbor: University of Michigan Press, 1992.

Hugo, Victor. *La légende des siècles*. Paris: Gallimard, 2002.

Huxley, Aldous. *The Cicadas and Other Poems*. New York: Harper and Brothers, 1929.

Huysmans, J.-K. *A rebours*. Paris: Garnier-Flammarion, 1978.

Irmscher, Christoph, *Longfellow Redux*. Urbana-Champaign: University of Illinois Press, 2006.

Jacob, Le Bibliophile. "Les noms des rues." *Nouveau tableau de Paris au XIXe siècle* 3 (1834): 75–109.

James, Ian. *The Fragmentary Demand*. Stanford, Cal.: Stanford University Press, 2006.

Jameson, Fredric. *Postmodernism, or, The Cultural Logic of Late Capitalism*. London: Verso, 1991.

Jenson, Deborah. *Trauma and Its Representations: The Social Life of Mimesis in Post-Revolutionary France*. Baltimore: Johns Hopkins University Press, 2001.

Jouvenel, Bertrand de. *Un voyageur dans le siècle*. Paris: Laffont, 1979.

Jouvenel, Colette de. *Colette de Jouvenel*. Paris: Société des Amis de Colette, 1982.

Jouvenel, Renaud de. "Mon enfance à l'ombre de Colette: Lettres de Colette à Renaud de Jouvenel." *La revue de Paris*, December 1966, 5, 56.

Kadish, Doris Y. *Politicizing Gender: Narrative Strategies in the Aftermath of the French Revolution*. New Brunswick, N.J.: Rutgers University Press, 1991.

——, ed. *Slavery in the Caribbean Francophone World*. Athens: University of Georgia Press, 2000.

Kadish, Doris Y., and Françoise Massardier-Kenney, eds. *Translating Slavery: Gender and Race in French Women's Writing, 1783–1823*. Kent, Ohio: Kent State University Press, 1994.

Kaplan, Julius. *Catalogue of Gustave Moreau Exhibition*. Los Angeles and New York: Los Angeles County Museum of Art and New York Graphic Society, 1974.

Käsper, Marge. "Sur des propos à propos des impressionnistes—traduire la critique d'art." *Romansk Forum* 16 (2002): 577–585.

Katz, Maya Balakirsky. "Photography versus Caricature: 'Footnotes' on Manet's *Zola* and Zola's *Manet*." *Nineteenth-Century French Studies* 34 (2006): 323–335.

Kelley, David. "Transpositions." In *Artistic Relations. Literature and the Visual Arts in Nineteenth-Century France*, edited by Peter Collier and Robert Lethbridge, 178–191. New Haven, Conn.: Yale University Press, 1994.

Kerbrat-Orecchioni, Catherine. *Les actes de langage dans le discours*. Paris: Nathan, 2001.

Kern, Stephen. *Eyes of Love: The Gaze in English and French Paintings and Novels, 1840–1900*. London: Reaktion Books, 1996.

Kervarker (La Villemarqué). *Barzhaz Breizh*. Lesneven, France: Hor Yezh, 1998.

Kiberd, Declan. *Inventing Ireland: The Literature of the Modern Nation*. London: Vintage, 1996.

Krieger, Murray. *Ekphrasis: The Illusion of the Natural Sign*. Baltimore: Johns Hopkins University Press, 1992.

Kristeva, Julia. *Le génie féminin: Colette*. Paris: Fayard, 2002.

Lacambre, Geneviève. *Gustave Moreau: Between Epic and Dream*. Paris: Réunion des Musées Nationaux and Art Institute of Chicago, 1999.

Lastinger, Valérie. "*La Naissance du jour*: La désintégration du 'moi' dans un roman de Colette." *French Review* 61, no. 4 (March 1988): 542–551.

La Villemarqué, Hersart de. *Le Barzhaz Breizh: Trésor de la littérature orale de la Bretagne*. 1839; Spézet, France: Coop Breizh, 1997.

———. "Préambule de la première et de la seconde édition." In *Barzaz Breiz: Chants populaires de la Bretagne*. 4th edition. Paris: A. Franck, 1846.

———. "La renaissance bretonne." In *La Bretagne contemporaine: Sites pittoresques, monuments, costumes, scènes de mœurs, histoire, légendes, traditions et usages des cinq départements de cette province*, 1–26. Paris: Charpentier, 1865; Grenoble: 4 Seigneurs, 1977–1979.

Lawrence, D. H. "Introduction to These Paintings." In *Selected Essays*, 307–346. Harmondsworth, Eng.: Penguin, 1950.

Lebesque, Morvan. *Comment peut-on être breton? Essai sur la démocratie française*. Paris: Seuil, 1970.

Le Braz, Anatole. *La légende de la mort chez les Bretons Armoricains*. 2 vols. 1893; Rennes: Terre de Brume, 1994.

Lefrançois, Thierry, ed. *Eugène Fromentin au Musée des Beaux-Arts de La Rochelle, suivi d'une évocation sommaire des œuvres de son père*. La Rochelle, France: Imprimerie Rochelaise, 1988.

Lejeune, Philippe. *L'autobiographie en France*. Paris: Armand Colin, 1971.

———. *Le pacte autobiographique*. Paris: Seuil, 1975.

Lemaître, Jules. *Les contemporains: Etudes et portraits littéraires*. 3rd series. Paris: H. Lecène et H. Oudin, "Nouvelle bibliothèque littéraire," 1887.

———. *Les contemporains: Etudes et portraits littéraires*. 4th series. Paris: H. Lecène et

H. Oudin, "Nouvelle bibliothèque littéraire," 1889.

Le Menn, Gwennolé. "Langue et culture bretonnes." In *Histoire générale de la Bretagne et des Bretons*, edited by Yannick Pelletier, 2:463–577. Paris: Nouvelle Librairie de France, 1990.

Le Mercier d'Erm, Camille. *Les bardes et poètes nationaux de la Bretagne armoricaine*. Rennes: Plihon and Hommay, 1918.

Lethbridge, Robert. "Le jeu des formes: Autour de *La balançoire* de Renoir." In *Le dialogue des arts: littérature et peinture aux XIXe et XXe siècles*, edited by Laurence Richer, 127–136. Lyon: Centre d'Etudes des Interactions Culturelles, 2002.

———. "Manet's Textual Frames." In *Artistic Relations: Literature and the Visual Arts in Nineteenth-Century France*, edited by Peter Collier and Robert Lethbridge, 144–158. New Haven, Conn.: Yale University Press, 1994.

———. "Le miroir et ses textes," *Les cahiers naturalists* 67 (1993): 157–167.

———. "Zola and Contemporary Painting." In *The Cambridge Companion to Emile Zola*, edited by Brian Nelson, 67–85. Cambridge: Cambridge University Press, 2007.

Lexandre, A. *Un pélerinage*. Paris: Dentu, 1879.

Lippard, Lucy. "Mapping." In *Art in Modern Culture: An Anthology of Critical Texts*, edited by Francis Frascina and Jonathan Harris, 160–169. London: Phaidon, 1992.

Little, Roger. "World Literature in French; or, Is Francophonie Frankly Phoney?" *European Review* 9, no. 4 (2001): 421–436.

Lloyd, Rosemary. *Baudelaire's Literary Criticism*. Cambridge: Cambridge University Press, 1981.

———. *Baudelaire's World*. Ithaca, N.Y.: Cornell University Press, 2002.

———. *Shimmering in a Transformed Light: Writing the Still Life*. Ithaca, N.Y.: Cornell University Press, 2005.

Longfellow, Henry Wadsworth. *Song of Hiawatha*. 1855; Boston: Tickernor and Fields, 1856.

Lottman, Herbert. *Colette: A Life*. Boston: Little, Brown, 1991.

Lotz, Hans-Joachim. "L'image irréelle, bizarre et mythique de Paris chez Balzac et Baudelaire." In *Paris au XIXe siècle: Aspects d'un mythe littéraire*, edited by Roger Bellet, 93–106. Lyon: Presses Universitaires de Lyon, 1984.

Louth, Charlie. *Hölderlin and the Dynamics of Translation*. Oxford: Legenda, 1998.

Lucbert, Françoise. *Entre le voir et le dire: La critique d'art des écrivains dans la presse symboliste en France de 1822 à 1906*. Rennes: Presses Universitaires de Rennes, 2005.

Ludovici, Anthony M. *Personal Reminiscences of Auguste Rodin*. London: John Murray, 1926.

Luzel, François-Marie. *Bepred Breizad toujours Breton: Poésies bretonnes, avec traduction française en regard*. Morlaix, France: Haslé, 1865.

———. *Gwerziou Breiz-Izel*. 2 vols. Lorient: Corfmat, 1868.

Lyon-Caen, Boris. "Configurations identitaires et poétique de la singularité dans *La comédie humaine*." In *Balzac et la crise des identités*, edited by Emmanuelle Cullmann, José-Luis Diaz, and Boris Lyon-Caen, 87–107. Saint-Cyr-sur-Loire: Christian Pirot, 2005.

Lyu, Claire. "Unswathing the Mummy: Body, Knowledge, and Writing in Gautier's *Le roman de la momie*." *Nineteenth-Century French Studies* 33–34 (2005): 308–319.

Macdonald, Christie, and Susan R. Suleiman, eds. *French Global: A New Approach to Literary History*. New York: Columbia University Press, 2010.

Macpherson, James. *Fragments of Ancient Poetry Collected in the Highlands of Scotland and Translated from the Gaelic or Erse Language*. Edinburgh: G. Hamilton and J. Balfour, 1760.

———. *The Works of Ossian, the Son of Fingal in Two Volumes. Translated from the Gaelic Language by James Macpherson*. 3rd edition. 2 vols. London: T. Becket and P. A. Dehondt, 1765.

Magazine littéraire. Special issue: "Les Écritures du moi: De l'autobiographie à l'autofiction." 409 (May 2002).

Mahuzier, Brigitte. "Rodin's Sapphic Designs." *GLQ: A Journal of Lesbian and Gay Studies* 7, no. 3 (2001): 401–415.

Majewski, Henry. *Transposing Art into Texts in French Romantic Literature*. Chapel Hill: North Carolina Studies in the Romance Languages and Literatures, 2002.

Malcolm, Janet. *Reading Chekhov: A Critical Journey*. New York: Random House, 2001.

Maleuvre, Didier. *Museum Memories: History, Technology, Art*. Stanford, Cal.: Stanford University Press, 1999.

Mallarmé, Stéphane. *Correspondance, 1862–1871*. Edited by Henri Mondor. Paris: Gallimard, 1959.

———. *Écrits sur l'art*. Edited by Michel Draguet. Paris: GF Flammarion, 1998.

———. *Œuvres complètes I*. Edited by Bertrand Marchal. Paris: Gallimard, 1998.

Marinetti, Filippo Tommaso. *Marinetti: Selected Writings*. Translated by R. W. Flint and Arthur A. Coppotelli. London: Secker and Warburg, 1972.

Marks, Elaine. *Colette*. New Brunswick, N.J.: Rutgers University Press, 1960.

Marks, Laura U. *The Skin of the Film: Intercultural Cinema, Embodiment, and the Senses*. Durham, N.C.: Duke University Press, 2000.

Massol, Chantal. *Une poétique de l'énigme: Le récit herméneutique balzacien*. Geneva: Droz, 2006.

Massol-Bedoin, Chantal. "La charade et la chimère: Du récit énigmatique dans *La fille aux yeux d'or.*" *Poétique* 89 (February 1992): 31–45.

———. "L'énigme de *Ferragus:* Du roman noir au roman réaliste." *L'année balzacienne* 8 (1987): 59–77.

Mayer, Charles S. "Ida Rubinstein: A Twentieth-Century Cleopatra." *Dance Research Journal* 20, no. 2 (1989): 33–51.

McLeod, John. *A Voyage to Africa, with Some Account of the Manners and Customs of the Dahomian People.* London: John Murray, 1820.

Meschonnic, Henri. *Critique du rythme: Anthropologie historique du langage.* Lagrasse, France: Verdier, 1982.

Michel, Arlette. "*La duchesse de Langeais* et le romanesque balzacien." In *Figures féminines et roman,* edited by Jean Bessière, 89–108. Paris: Presses Universitaires de France, 1982.

Miller, Nancy K. "The Entangled Self: Genre Bondage in the Age of the Memoir." *Proceedings of the Modern Language Association* 122, no. 2 (March 2007): 537–548.

Mirbeau, Octave. *Les écrivains.* 2 vols. Paris: Flammarion, 1925–1926.

Mitchell, W. J. T. *Iconology: Image, Text, Ideology.* Chicago: University of Chicago Press, 1986

———. *Picture Theory: Essays on Verbal and Visual Representation.* Chicago: University of Chicago Press, 1994.

Mitterand, Henri. "Le musée dans le texte." *Les cahiers naturalistes* 66 (1992): 13–22.

Moffett, Charles S., ed. *The New Painting: Impressionism, 1874–1886.* Geneva: Richard Burton, 1986.

Montandon, Alain. "Écritures de l'image chez Théophile Gautier." In *Icons, Texts, Iconotexts,* edited by Peter Wagner, 105–120. New York: Walter de Gruyter, 1996.

———. "La séduction de l'œuvre d'art chez Théophile Gautier." In *Théophile Gautier, L'Art et l'Artiste,* 2:349–368. Montpellier, France: Université Paul Valéry, 1983.

Montifaud, Marc de. *Marc de Montifaud devant l'opinion publique, sa justification: Lettre à M. Félix Delhasse.* London: N.p., 1882.

———. "Michel-Ange: *Le jugement dernier.*" *L'Artiste,* March 15, 1865, 136–137.

———. "Salon de 1865." *L'Artiste,* May 1, 1865, 193–200.

———. "Salon de 1866, II." *L'Artiste,* June 15, 1866, 196–205.

———. "Salon de 1867," *L'Artiste,* June 1, 1867, 448–456.

———. "Salon de 1867." *L'Artiste,* July 1, 1867, 95–113.

———. "Salon de 1868." *L'Artiste,* June 1, 1868, 395–418.

———. "Salon de 1872." *L'Artiste,* June 1, 1872, 238–246.

———. "Salon de 1873." *L'Artiste,* June 1, 1873, 265–287.

———. "Salon de 1877, I." *L'Artiste,* May 1, 1877, 334–343.

Moreau, Gustave. *L'assembleur de rêves.* Edited by Pierre-Louis Mathieu. Fontfroide, France: Fata Morgana, 1984.

———. *Correspondance d'Italie.* Edited by Luisa Capodieci. Paris: Somogy, 2002.

———. *Écrits sur l'art.* Edited by Peter Cooke. 2 vols. Fontfroide, France: Fata Morgana, 2002.

Moretti, Franco. *Atlas of the European Novel, 1800–1900.* New York: Verso, 1998.

Naficy, Hamid. *An Accented Cinema: Exilic and Diasporic Filmmaking.* Princeton, N.J.: Princeton University Press, 2001.

Nancy, Jean-Luc. "La blessure—la cicatrice." In Elisabeth Perceval, *La Blessure,* 115–126. Paris: Les Petits Matins/ARTE Éditions, 2005.

———. *L'intrus.* Paris: Galilée, 2000.

Newton, Joy. "Cézanne's Literary Incarnations." *French Studies* 61 (2007): 36–41.

——. "Émile Zola impressionniste (II)." *Les cahiers naturalistes* 34 (1967): 124–138.

Oliver, Andrew. "'Scènes de la vie parisienne': Opacité et transparence: *La fille aux yeux d'or*." In *Lettres en seconde: Balzac et la nouvelle (3): L'École des lettres* 13 (July 2003): 63–81.

Paban, Gabrielle de. *Le nègre et la créole; ou, Mémoires d'Eulalie D****. Edited by Marshall C. Olds. 1825; Paris: L'Harmattan, 2008.

Pagès, Alain, and Owen Morgan. *Guide Émile Zola*. Paris: Ellipses, 2002.

Pelletier, Yannick, ed. *Histoire générale de la Bretagne et des Bretons*. 2 vols. Paris: Nouvelle Librairie de France, 1990.

Petitier, Paule. "La mélancolie de *Ferragus*." *Romantisme* 117 (2002–2003): 45–58.

Peyré, Yves. *Peinture et poésie: Le dialogue par le livre, 1874–2000*. Paris: Gallimard, 2001.

Pichois, Claude. *Le romantisme II, 1843–1869*. Paris, Arthaud, 1979.

Pichois, Claude, and Alain Brunet. *Colette*. Paris: Editions de Fallois, 1999.

Pichois, Claude, and Jacques Dupont. *L'atelier de Baudelaire: "Les Fleurs du Mal."* Édition diplomatique. 4 vols. Paris: Champion, 2005.

Piles, Roger de. *Cours de peinture par principes*. Edited by Jacques Thuillier. 1708; Paris: Gallimard, 1989.

Pisani, Michael V. *Imagining Native America in Music*. New Haven, Conn.: Yale University Press, 2005.

Poe, Edgar Allan. *Histoires grotesques et sérieuses*. Translated by Charles Baudelaire. Paris: Gallimard/Folio, 1978.

Pointon, Marcia. "Biography and the Body in Late Renoir." In *Naked Authority: The Body in Western Painting, 1830–1908*, 83–97. Cambridge: Cambridge University Press, 1990.

Pound, Ezra. *Make It New*. London: Faber and Faber, 1934.

Press, Ian J. "Breton Speakers in Brittany, France and Europe: Constraints on the Search for an Identity." In *The Changing Voices of Europe: Social and Political Changes and Their Linguistic Repercussions, Past, Present and Future*, edited by M. M. Parry, W. V. Davies, and R. A. M. Temple, 213–226. Cardiff: University of Wales Press, 1994.

Proust, Marcel. *Contre Sainte-Beuve*. Edited by Pierre Clarac. Paris: Gallimard, 1971.

Quellien, Narcisse. *Chansons et danses des Bretons*. Paris: Maisonneuve et Leclerc, 1889.

Rabinow, Rebecca, ed. *Cézanne to Picasso: Ambroise Vollard, Patron of the Avant-Garde*. New York and New Haven, Conn.: Metropolitan Museum of Art and Yale University Press, 2006.

Rainey, Lawrence, ed. *Modernism: An Anthology*. Oxford: Oxford University Press, 2005.

Rannou, Pascal. "Approche du concept de littérature bretonne de langue française." In *Métissage du texte: Bretagne, Maghreb, Québec*, edited by Bernard Hue, 75–86. Rennes: Presses Universitaires de Rennes, 1994.

——. *Inventaire d'un héritage: Essai sur l'œuvre littéraire de Pierre-Jakez Hélias*. Relecq-Kerhuon, France: An Here, 1997.

——, ed. *Visages de Tristan Corbière*. Morlaix/Montroulez, France: Skol Vreizh, 1995.

Raynal, Guillaume-Thomas. *Histoire philosophique et politique des établissements et du commerce des Européens dans les deux Indes*. 8 vols. 1770; Geneva: Chez Jean-Léonard Pellet, 1780.

Reff, Theodore. "Degas and the Literature of His Time." In *French Nineteenth-Century Painting and Literature*, edited by Ulrich Finke, 182–231. Manchester: Manchester University Press, 1972.

Richard [Jean-Marie-Vincent Audin]. *Le véritable conducteur parisien*. Paris: Terry, 1828.

Rilke, Rainer Maria. *Auguste Rodin*. Translated by Catherine Caron. Rennes: La Part Commune, 2004.

Roberts, Mary Louise. *Disruptive Acts: The New Woman in Fin-de-Siècle France*. Chicago: University of Chicago Press, 2002.

Robinson-Valéry, Judith. "'The Rough' and the 'Polished'." *Drafts* 89 (1996): 59–66.

Rodin, Auguste. *Art. Conversations with Paul Gsell*. Translated by Jacques de Caso and Patricia B. Sanders. Berkeley: University of California Press, 1984.

———. *Images of Desire*. 1995; Munich: Schirmer/Mosel, 2005.

Rose, Phyllis. *The Year of Reading Proust: A Memoir in Real Time*. Washington, D.C.: Counterpoint, 1997.

Rosenblum, Robert. *Encounters: New Art from Old*. London: National Gallery, 2000.

Rothwell, Andrew. "Introduction." In Émile Zola, *Thérèse Raquin*, translated by Andrew Rothwell, vii–xxxv. Oxford: Oxford World's Classics, 1992.

Rouault, Georges. *Souvenirs intimes*. Paris: E. Frapier, 1926.

Rousseau, Jean-Jacques. *Œuvres complètes*. Edited by Bertrand Gagnebin and Marcel Raymond. Paris: Gallimard, 1959.

Sabatier, Pierre. *L'esthétique des Goncourt*. Paris: Librairie Hachette, 1920.

Sainte-Beuve, Charles Augustin. *Correspondance générale*. Edited by Jean Bonnerot. 19 vols. Paris: Stock, 1935–1983.

Sarda, Marie-Anne, ed. *Paysages de rêve de Gustave Moreau*. Brou and Reims: Monastère Royal and Musée des Beaux-Arts, 2004.

Saussure, Ferdinand de. *Cours de linguistique générale*. Edited by Charles Bally and Albert Sechehaye. Paris: Payot, 1972.

Schiff, Richard. *Cézanne and the End of Impressionism*. Chicago: University of Chicago Press, 1984.

Scott, Clive. *Translating Apollinaire*. Exeter: Exeter University Press, 2014.

———. *Translating Rimbaud's "Illuminations."* Exeter: University of Exeter Press, 2006.

Scott, David. *Pictorialist Poetics: Poetry and The Visual Arts in Nineteenth-Century France*. Cambridge: Cambridge University Press, 1988.

———. "Writing the Arts: Aesthetics, Art Criticism and Literary Practice." In *Artistic Relations: Literature and the Visual Arts in Nineteenth-Century France*, edited by Peter Collier and Robert Lethbridge, 61–75. New Haven, Conn.: Yale University Press, 1994.

Self, Geoffrey. *The Hiawatha Man: The Life and Work of Samuel Coleridge-Taylor*. Aldershot, Eng.: Scolar Press, 1995.

Sheringham, Michael. *Everyday Life: Theories and Practices from Surrealism to the Present*. Oxford: Oxford University Press, 2006.

———. *French Autobiography: Devices and Desires*. Oxford: Oxford University Press, 1993.

Shklovsky, Viktor. "Art as Technique." In *Russian Formalist Criticism: Four Essays*, edited by Lee T. Lemon and Marion J. Reis, 3–24. Lincoln: University of Nebraska Press, 1965.

Showalter, Elaine. *Sexual Anarchy: Gender and Culture at the Fin de Siècle*. New York: Penguin, 1990.

Souvestre, Émile. *Les derniers Bretons*. Edited by Dominique Besançon. 2 vols. Rennes: Terre de Brume, 1997.

Staël, Anne-Louise Germaine de. *Corinne; ou, L' Italie*. Edited by Simone Balayé. Paris: Gallimard/Folio, 1985.

Stallybrass, Peter, and Allon White. *The Politics and Poetics of Transgression*. Ithaca, N.Y.: Cornell University Press, 1986.

Starr, S. Frederick. *Bamboula! The Life and Times of Louis Moreau Gottschalk*. New York: Oxford University Press, 1995.

Stedman, Laura, and George M. Gould. *Life and Letters of Edmund Clarence Stedman*. New York: Moffat, Yard, 1910.

Stendhal. *Œuvres romanesques complètes*. Edited by Y. Ansel. Vol. 3. Paris: Gallimard, 2014.

St.-Pierre, Paul. "Translation and Writing." *Texte* 4 (1985): 223–234.

Symington, Miceala. "Poétique de la critique picturale symboliste." *Modern Language Notes* 114 (December 1999): 1110–1118.

Tanguy, Bernard. *Aux origines du nationalisme breton*. 2 vols. Paris: Union Générale d'Éditions, 1977.

Thibaut, Jean-François. "Renoir illustrateur de *L'Assommoir*." *Les Cahiers naturalistes* 66 (1992): 147–156.

Thomas, M. Wynn. *Corresponding Cultures: The Two Literatures of Wales*. Cardiff: University of Wales Press, 1999.

Thomas, M. Wynn, and Rhian S. Reylonds. *A Bibliography of Welsh Literature in English Translation*. Cardiff: University of Wales Press, 2005.

Thompson, James, and Barbara Wright. *Eugène Fromentin: Visions d'Algérie et d'Égypte*. Paris: Art Creation Realisation, 2008.

Thompson, Victoria E. "Telling 'Spatial Stories': Urban Space and Bourgeois Identity in Early Nineteenth-Century Paris." *Journal of Modern History* 75 (September 2003): 523–556.

Thurman, Judith. *Secrets of the Flesh: A Life of Colette*. New York: Knopf, 1999.

Tilby, Michael. "Balzac et le jeu parodique dans *Gambara*." *L'année balzacienne* 7 (2006): 83–117.

Tintner, Adeline. "What Zola's *Nana* Owes to Manet's *Nana*." *Iris: Notes in the History of Art* 8 (1983): 15–16.

Toury, Gideon. "Translation, Literary Translation, and Pseudotranslation." *Comparative Criticism* 6 (1995): 73–85.

Tsur, Reuven. *What Makes Sound Patterns Expressive? The Poetic Mode of Speech Perception*. Durham, N.C.: Duke University Press, 1992.

Ullman, Stephen. *Style in the French Novel*. Cambridge: Cambridge University Press, 1957.

Valazza, Nicolas. *Crise de plume et souveraineté du pinceau: Écrire la peinture de Diderot à Proust*. Paris: Classiques Garnier, 2013.

Valenciennes, Pierre-Henri de. *Élémens de perspective*. Reprint edition. 1799; Geneva: Minkoff, 1973.

Vanoncini, André. "La disparition des espaces urbains dans *La comédie humaine*." In *Paris et le phénomène des capitales littéraires*, 1:125–137. Paris: Université-Sorbonne, n.d.

——. "Les 'trompettes de 1789' et 'l'abattement de 1814': Moments du tableau parisien dans *La fille aux yeux d'or*." *L'année balzacienne* 11 (1990): 221–232.

Venuti, Lawrence. *Translation Changes Everything: Theory and Practice*. London: Routledge, 2013.

Verlaine, Paul. *Les poètes maudits*. Edited by Michel Décaudin. Paris: SEDES, 1982.

Wagner, Peter, ed. *Icons-Texts-Iconotexts: Essays on Ekphrasis and Intermediality*. New York: Walter de Gruyter, 1996.

Ward Jouve, Nicole. *Colette*. Bloomington: Indiana University Press, 1987.

Weber, Eugen. *Peasants into Frenchmen*. Stanford, Cal.: Stanford University Press, 1976.

Williams, Heather. "Between French and Breton: The Politics of Translation." *Romance Studies* 27, no. 4 (2009): 223–233.

——. *Postcolonial Brittany: Literature between Languages*. Oxford: Peter Lang, 2007.

———. "Writing to Paris: Poets, Nobles and Savages in Nineteenth-Century Brittany." *French Studies* 57, no. 4 (2003): 475–490.

Woolf, Vicki. *Dancing in the Vortex: The Story of Ida Rubinstein.* Amsterdam: Harwood, 2000.

Worthen, W. B. *Print and the Poetics of Modern Drama.* Cambridge: Cambridge University Press, 2005.

Wright, Barbara. *Eugène Fromentin: A Life in Art and Letters.* Bern: Peter Lang, 2000.

Zola, Émile. *Correspondance.* Edited by B. H. Bakker et al. 10 vols. Montreal: Presses Universitaires de Montréal, 1978–1995.

———. *Écrits sur l'art.* Edited by Jean-Pierre Leduc-Adine. Paris: Gallimard, 1991.

———. *The Masterpiece.* Edited by Roger Pearson. Oxford: Oxford World's Classics, 2006.

———. *Nana.* Translated by Douglas Parmée. Oxford: Oxford World's Classics, 1992.

———. *Les Rougon-Macquart.* Edited by Henri Mitterand. 5 vols. Paris: Gallimard, 1960–1966.

———. *Thérèse Raquin.* Edited by Henri Mitterand. Paris: Garnier-Flammarion, 1970.

INDEX

Page numbers in italics refer to figures and tables.

CPSIA information can be obtained
at www.ICGtesting.com
Printed in the USA
BVOW07s1225080917
494373BV00007B/16/P